No Jurisdiction

THE SUNY SERIES

HORIZONS OF CINEMA

MURRAY POMERANCE | EDITOR

RECENT TITLES

A complete listing of books in this series can be found online at www.sunypress.edu

No Jurisdiction

Legal, Political, and Aesthetic Disorder in Post-9/11 Genre Cinema

Fareed Ben-Youssef

SUNY
PRESS

Cover Image: The post-9/11 superhero mourns: Batman (Christian Bale) stands on the edge of ruins in *The Dark Knight* (Christopher Nolan, Warner Bros., 2008). Courtesy PhotoFest New York.

Published by State University of New York Press, Albany

© 2022 State University of New York

All rights reserved

Printed in the United States of America

No part of this book may be used or reproduced in any manner whatsoever without written permission. No part of this book may be stored in a retrieval system or transmitted in any form or by any means including electronic, electrostatic, magnetic tape, mechanical, photocopying, recording, or otherwise without the prior permission in writing of the publisher.

For information, contact State University of New York Press, Albany, NY
www.sunypress.edu

Library of Congress Cataloging-in-Publication Data

Name: Ben-Youssef, Fareed, 1987– author.
Title: No jurisdiction : legal, political, and aesthetic disorder in post-9/11 genre cinema / Fareed Ben-Youssef.
Description: Albany : State University of New York Press, [2022] | Series: SUNY series, horizons of cinema | Includes bibliographical references and index.
Identifiers: LCCN 2021051933 | ISBN 9781438489278 (hardcover : alk. paper) | ISBN 9781438489261 (pbk. : alk. paper) | ISBN 9781438489285 (ebook)
Subjects: LCSH: September 11 Terrorist Attacks, 2001, in motion pictures. | Motion pictures and the September 11 Terrorist Attacks. | Motion pictures and the War on Terrorism, 2001–2009. | Film genres—United States. | Motion pictures—Political aspects—United States—History—21st century.
Classification: LCC PN1995.9.T46 B46 2022 | DDC 791.43/6552—dc23/eng/20220203
LC record available at https://lccn.loc.gov/2021051933

10 9 8 7 6 5 4 3 2 1

Contents

Illustrations

Acknowledgments

It all started with *Batman* #399.

When I was a very young child, standing in an arts and crafts store in Sidney, Montana, I came across a packet of shrink-wrapped comic books. *Batman* #399 sat at the front of the packet.

The comic book cover featured a shrunken head, an ax, and a cityscape illuminated by lightning, promising a new, violent world. From the moment I stared at that comic, I felt pulled into Batman's Gotham City. Tim Burton's 1989 *Batman* came out around this time, which only further reinforced my status as an honorary citizen of the superhero's home.

This book interrogates my support of often-brutal vigilantes such as Batman, even during a time when the U.S. government adopted a kind of vigilante logic in its fight against terrorism after 9/11. Although they inspire oppressors, I still eagerly devour the comics and watch the movies featuring such heroes.

Such an interrogation of my shock and awe for these tainted objects demands supporters and confidants willing to plunge with me into the muck of these contradictory films. Many have conversed with me and mulled over my words. They deserve my warmest acknowledgment.

When the project started life as a dissertation, my chair, Miryam Sas, shaped my thinking. My mind always raced during our conversations, but she helped slow me down to navigate through the minefield of academic debates. She stayed by my side throughout the preparation of this book, from the initial proposal to the final touches on my marketing questionnaire. Her compassionate mentorship has propelled me through the foggy world of academia, shining a bright light (or is it a Bat Signal?) for me to follow.

Many of my interpretations in this book were crystallized while drinking the smoothest of cappuccinos at the Fertile Grounds Café in

Berkeley, California, with David Cohen. The legal scholar understands the importance of cinema as a tool for public education about the law and its human costs. He pushed me to think historically about laws made in our moment of crisis and reminded me that we are not living in an exceptional time. Rather, the label of exceptional can obscure the precedents to the unlawful actions that so shock us today.

Anton Kaes helped me to take a similarly long view of contemporary films. Many of our conversations on the war film, going back to World War I, lingered on the way such films show how traumas suffered on the front lines insidiously pervade the home front. Kaes cultivated in me a more careful eye toward cinema, one attentive enough to see how the medium visualizes individuals' and the broader culture's invisible pains.

Finally, D. A. Miller often discussed with me the films featured in this book during delicious meals in San Francisco. At Pizzeria Delfina, we would tear into films as incisively as I tore into my chicken alla diavola. While he pushed me to bring my eye ever closer to each work, to be more sensitive to the contradictions of their forms, his own implicated writing style—shifting attention between the art he examines and his own life experience—became a model that I continue to emulate. Miller has shown me how to be a more honest and self-aware critic, and how such honesty could deepen my scholarship.

When developing my dissertation into this book, these stalwart advisers were joined by a wonderful team. At SUNY Press, editor-in-chief James Peltz first saw potential in a project that took as a source of inspiration a line by the supervillain the Joker, "Batman has no juris-diction." Hearing the line, he repeated it under his breath and smiled. Series editor Murray Pomerance ended our first meeting by asking me about my personal investment in the project—he recognized that these films speak to the intersections of my identity and has helped me make sense of my selves. My opening chapter detailing my walk through the 9/11 Memorial Museum, which influenced the autobiographical turn the manuscript would later take, would not have been written if he had not pushed me to consider films dealing directly with 9/11. At every stage of the writing process, both Peltz and Pomerance have been nothing but supportive.

Anonymous readers at the press also showed fine-grained attention to an earlier draft of the manuscript, providing me with actionable ways to promote the value of my voice. It has been a joy to work with a press so committed to adding further diversity to film studies.

Many of those featured in my autobiographical vignettes have helped ensure that the book can reach all audiences. These include Deena Varner, along with my sisters Leïla Ben-Youssef and Nadia Ben-Youssef. Their incisive commentary encompassed everything from my argumentation at the broadest level to the most minute particularities of my sentences. With a winning candor, they identified whenever an interpretative leap was taken or when my words became a touch opaque or jargon laden. This work is more crystalline and taut because of their rigorous efforts.

Lastly, the language of the piece has continually been refined by my personal editors—Kate Chouta and Leslie Kriesel. Chouta assisted me through the dissertation, while Kriesel helped me with the preparation of this book. Writing can sometimes feel like you are on a tightrope—one false step and the show might be over. Both of my editors have offered me a safety net, allowing me to push forward with more confidence.

No Jurisdiction has benefited from the support of these individuals and so many others (Maman et Baba, merci pour tout!). I am happy to have wandered with them through the Gotham City that I have never really left since catching my first glimpse of *Batman* #399. Now, arriving at the end of this project, I am left wondering: Where will our spirited conversations take us next?

I, for one, cannot wait to find out!

Portions of the reading of *Adieu Gary* in chapter 5 appeared in my article "Disrupted Genre, Disrupted Lives: *Adieu Gary* and the Post-9/11 Banlieue as Ghost Town," *Studia Filmoznawcze* (Film Studies), Special Issue on the Transnational Western, 38 (June 2017): 75–89.

Portions of the reading of *The Counselor* in chapter 2 appeared in my article "Where Our Hungers Trump Morality: The Border in Ridley Scott and Cormac McCarthy's *The Counselor*," *Southwestern American Literature* 42, no. 2 (2017): 7–27.

Introduction

Hollywood at Ground Zero:
Confessions of a Conflicted Fan

A 9/11 Film Study without Films About 9/11?

Hollywood haunts Ground Zero at the 9/11 Memorial Museum in New York City, which features a constantly expanding collection of artistic responses to the attack.[1] Chief curator Jan Ramirez notes that "[t]here was such a phenomenal . . . response to 9/11. So many people felt prompted to do something—quilting or painting or collaborative music-making. We certainly couldn't accommodate it all, but we could design and have a very kind of democratic site where people can self-identify as artists" (qtd. in Finn 2014). Although the memorial acts as a monument to how a trauma is represented in art, Ramirez bristles at the idea that such initiatives can bring closure. "History doesn't work that tidily" (qtd. in ibid.). The 9/11 Memorial Museum testifies to history's untidy nature: the ruins of the towers exist alongside both arts and crafts submitted by individuals and Hollywood movie posters. Visitors encounter homemade quilts and Spider-Man, amateur paintings and Godzilla.

No Jurisdiction is an untidy post-9/11 film study. It often elides direct confrontation with 9/11, looking instead for how the attacks haunt Hollywood. We see them mostly in glimpses—briefly on television or in the background of shots. In this vision of Hollywood, the attacks and their legal consequences occupy a mythic realm. We will spend much more time in the streets of the fictional Gotham City with Batman and a San Francisco of the 1970s terrorized by the Zodiac Killer, a vision of an American city as a shadow-filled nightmare, than in the New York City of September 2001. But beyond analyzing superhero films' visual allusions to the imploding towers and gun-wielding FBI agents' spongy War on Terror legal logic, I also want to understand my own untidy sympathy with these violent heroes who leave me both exhilarated and repulsed.

Initially, this book featured only films about such heroes and contained no discussion on works directly about 9/11 and its aftermath. Such movies always struck me as nationalistic propaganda, with none of the ethical muddiness that draws me to superhero movies such as Christopher Nolan's *The Dark Knight* (2008). Growing up in eastern Montana as the son of immigrant cinephiles, I often encountered Hollywood co-opted as a propaganda tool by the U.S. government following 9/11. For years, my local movie theater would screen Chuck Workman's montage film *The Spirit of America* (2001) prior to all feature presentations. Workman's three-minute film, produced immediately following the attacks, presents iconic sequences from across Hollywood history. With its glamorizing shots of Matt Damon as a grizzled soldier and Mel Gibson as a Revolutionary patriot, it would make my skeptical father roll his eyes. He was tired of the jingoism on display, and I sympathized with his frustration. In the time when the country marched into war against Near Eastern populations, it was disheartening to see the cinematic entertainments that we both loved reduced to or nakedly exposed as mere ideological weapons. Reenactments of 9/11, in line with the ostensible wide-eyed tone of Workman's short film about Hollywood, seemed to be uncritical celebrations of America and its undiminished (and uncritical) spirit in times of crisis.

Although Workman's film was synonymous with the attacks in my mind, the 9/11 Memorial Museum does not include it. While featuring many Hollywood movies, the museum also curiously shares my book's blind spot. Its exhibit privileges posters of superheroes flying next to the towers while ignoring films directly about the events. References to reenactments such as Paul Greengrass's *United 93* (2006) and Oliver Stone's *World Trade Center* (2006), both of which portray the towers before the attacks, are nowhere to be found. It is striking that the 9/11 Memorial Museum so completely elides Hollywood's own portrayal of 9/11. The absence of these reenactments in a museum designed to remember the day suggested the possibility that these films might challenge the very idea of memorialization, framing the limits of direct confrontation with trauma. The shared omission invited a second look at Hollywood's portrayal of 9/11.

When contemplating a review of these productions, I remembered how my understanding of *The Spirit of America* gradually changed. The film visibly warped in that small-town Montana theater. It was projected so many times that the images lost their pristine quality until they were overwhelmed with scratches. Through its repeated screenings, my local Cinema Paradiso unintentionally transformed Workman's film into a metaphor for an America degraded by the quagmire of the Middle East. It was as though the Hollywood sheen of the United States' righteous mission in the days following 9/11 became sullied by the nation's actions in its War on Terror. By the time graphic photos were released from Abu Ghraib in 2004, where U.S. soldiers were revealed to have tortured Iraqi prisoners, I paid less attention to the romantic images of Matt Damon in uniform than to the also-featured news anchor from Sidney Lumet's *Network* (1976) shouting, "I'm as mad as hell, and I'm not going to take this anymore!" I began to notice Workman's references to Hollywood's revolutionary fury. I wondered, what might these 9/11 reenactments reveal if I looked at them again with a skeptical eye? Perhaps I would find scratches that tarnished and muddied their presentation of a post-9/11 spirit of America.

So, in the spring of 2020 I conducted an impromptu 9/11 film festival for an audience of one. The reenactments were indeed far stranger and more ambivalent than I expected. As I watched, I felt myself both destabilized and implicated, even pushed to ask unsettling questions about the spectacular movies that so fascinated me. Seeing the Arab-as-enemy in *United 93* brought to mind the brown bodies destroyed in Jon Favreau's *Iron Man* (2008). But as a scholar of Arab heritage myself, how could I relish movies that trade in images of my own destruction? How do I reckon with my own privilege as a film critic? The way in which my impromptu "festival" generated such unnerving, implicating questions recalled my equally destabilizing visit to the 9/11 Memorial Museum in 2017. There, too, the collision of entertainment and mass suffering left me curiously at odds with myself and my own position as a spectator. As I toured the space, I was made aware of the intersections of my identity and the perceptions (both my own and those of others) of those intersections. I was treated as an enemy of America (I passed through machines signaling state sanctioned suspicion), as a victim (I was facing the wreckage of the towers), as a movie and pop culture fan (I contemplated old posters of Superman), as a critic (I was given space and opportunity to take copious notes while George W. Bush pontificated on the big screen), and as a secular hedonist (nothing prevented me from relishing a fine sandwich in the café).

In this introduction, I deploy different portions of that museum visit as springboards to reflect on key Hollywood films that attempt to recreate the day and its aftermath. These include *United 93*, *World Trade Center*, Adam McKay's *Vice* (2018), and Michael Winterbottom's *A Mighty Heart* (2007). Close inspection brings out moments when these films gesture to their inability to grapple with the event they work to fully capture. The museum's own pointed references to Hollywood indicate the presumed value in perceiving the spectacular attacks through the kind of violent, seemingly apolitical spectacles examined in this book. The site's permanent film presentation—two documentaries in which world leaders discuss the impact of the attacks—hints at how film can act as a tool for state power during times of emergency. And in positioning its screening room near the café, the museum forces a confrontation with the privilege of pop culture consumption and the fraught insights offered by such a vantage point. As visitors consume their sandwiches paired with a grand view of the memorial and the wider city, their sensory pleasure coexists with a simultaneous empathy toward and distance from those who suffered in the attacks. Ultimately, the museum evokes the "untidy" hall of mirrors that I explore in this book on post-9/11 genre film and law—in which the imagined boundaries between perpetrator and victim and between our geopolitical realities and our onscreen fantasies break down.

Passing through X-Ray Machines and into the Security Theater

The 9/11 Memorial Museum opens with an eerie reenactment of one of the consequences of the attacks. All attendees walk through a metal detector, and those who set off the alarm must submit to a pat down. Although I passed through without incident during my visit, I had been worried that my prosthetics would inspire the usual rigmarole that occurs in airports. When alarms are set off, the metal in my arm and leg braces provokes a frisking by bored security attendants. With clinical detachment they handle my right hand and leg, atrophied since birth due to cerebral palsy. Our interactions last far longer than those allotted for able-bodied persons who move through the machines without being stopped. The extended duration gives me time to ponder the perception of my disabled brown body in a post-9/11 context, not only as vulnerable but also as a potential threat. So my visit to the museum started with the now typical reflection on myself, a French Arab American, as principally an object of suspicion. In this way, the place felt less like a memorial to a major historical catastrophe than a monument to the Transportation Security Administration (TSA).

The entrance offers attendees a taste of what Bruce Schneier describes as "security theater," a space designed to evoke the feeling of security without actually having any tangible effects (Schneier 2009). Visitors dutifully took part in the performance, slipping off their bags and coats without question. My non-normative body exposed the strings of this puppet theater (at least in my own mind) by underlining my role as an antagonist in this drama. The theater demands the performance of vigilance on the part of security forces against the bodies falling under their gaze. Such "neutral" screenings tend to adopt an ableist stance, since those in wheelchairs or wearing prosthetics are often singled out. The exceptional treatment of those with disabilities draws attention more broadly to how this theater depends on and reinforces difference, be it bodily or racial. I feel, in these spaces, the intersections of my own identity that mark me as outside the norm, as worthy of scrutiny. Even though it is the metal in my brace that sets off alarms, I cannot help but consider my outward appearance. Indeed, I often sense myself as a brown body when walking through such machines, and that sensation was particularly palpable at a museum where in the formal displays Arab men are explicitly labeled as the enemy. Security theater intentionally or inadvertently depends on and implicates certain kinds of bodies, characters who fit a type.

Just as the museum's starting point drew attention to my visible Arab-ness, Greengrass's *United 93* traffics heavily in visions of the terrorist enemy as stereotypically Arab and quintessentially Muslim. Greengrass presents a reenactment of United Airlines Flight 93, where passengers allegedly resisted hijackers until the moment of the crash. The film recounts much of the story chronologically, in real time. It opens with a recitation from the Quran, the words heard first against a blank screen and then against a tight shot of the holy book. The recitation continues over images of New York City seen from above. The un-subtitled verse sounds like an incantation that looms menacingly over this metropolitan space. A supposedly incomprehensible Islamic threat thus floats above, permeating the American setting. In this way Al Qaeda members are reduced to their religious beliefs, acting without what they might consider to be their political logic. Soon the set design emulates an imagined radical Islamist view of the United States. Several of the hijackers enter the airport, passing by a pair of fake fashion magazine covers, "The Shape Issue" and "The Bust Issue," each of which features a seductively posed woman, one of them with a phallic Popsicle resting on her lips. Although the shot lasts only a second, it frames the enemy's perception of American media as prurient and obsessed with the female body. The set decoration, featuring such an objectified, hypersexualized femininity, implies that these enemies are driven either by misogyny or by regressive attitudes about sex and the body. *United 93*'s camera operates with an eerie prescience, continually falling on the Arab hijackers, even before the plane's takeoff—visually engaging in a kind of racial profiling. Greengrass's docudrama, where history seems inevitable, leaves little room for nuance.

"Don't think!": Looking at the Collapsing Towers

Following the security check that crystallized my "marked" status, and feeling scrutinized by museum personnel much in the way that Greengrass's camera was scrutinizing the Arab figures in *United 93*, I moved into the main atrium of the museum, a space in which the event is depicted as a sublime and overwhelming catastrophe. It presents actual warped steel beams of the World Trade Center. Through such a staging, the museum pushes visitors to inhabit a state of silent, unquestioning reverence. The melted and twisted debris suggests that the attack lies somewhere outside a rational understanding—these monumental disasters obliterated not just human life and architecture but the conceptual armature that supported the edifice of the nation. Even as the exhibit's construction shut down questions, it provoked them: What could a visitor of Arab descent, a young man who had just passed through a security screening, say that would be acceptable to other visitors in the face of these ruins? Moreover, what is he allowed to say about his own dehumanizing typecasting in the aftermath of such devastation?

Films that directly represent 9/11 often reference the inability of those affected to contextualize or make sense of what happened. They invoke that sense that I had too, of being speechless. In Greengrass's portrayal, when government officials realize that Flight 93 has been hijacked, they immediately struggle to recall when a hijacking last occurred. The camera hangs close to officials during an FAA briefing, the tightness of the shot evoking the claustrophobia inspired by the revelation of the hijacking, as though the state is becoming trapped by the unfolding attacks. For a moment, the officials are somewhat like the victims ensnared in the towers. Soldiers at the North American Aerospace Defense (NORAD) Command Center are similarly flustered by the hijacking and debate whether it is a simulation or "real world." The excited camera, bobbing around and punctuating the dialogue with rapid zooms, further frames a military institution struggling to find a vantage point from which to understand, let alone fight the situation.

Stone's *World Trade Center* portrays New Yorkers facing the attack in similar confusion. The film centers on police officers who become trapped under the rubble of the towers. From the bus shuttling them to Ground Zero before the towers' collapse, they catch a confusing glimpse of the smoking buildings far in the distance. They are unable to agree on which tower is smoking. Further illustrating their feeling of disconnection, one officer's cell phone has no reception. The bus then swerves wildly as it speeds around a corner, physically rattling the men. In this literally disconnected and shaken state, the officers see one man lying on the sidewalk, many blocks away from the World Trade Center. Stone deploys an editing technique from horror films—first presenting the shocked onlookers' reaction before cutting to the object of their gaze. Here the camera catches the dismayed officers staring out the bus windows and then shows the body that grabs their attention. Paramedics surround the victim, a middle-aged professional, his untouched appearance implying that he has most likely suffered a heart attack. It is a notably banal and distinctly non-catastrophic demise, lacking the overwhelming scale that commonly defines the attacks. However, somber music and slow motion draw attention to the significance of the law's first encounter with death on the monumental day. Stone's use of horror film convention in this encounter, from its visual style to even the officer's disconnected cell phone, underlines that state representatives confront an uncanny, dread-inducing challenge. The single death of a businessman, seemingly from shock, frames 9/11 as itself a lethal psychological shock to citizens. The police officers face the unnerving possibility that they cannot protect their charges from such terror.

When the heroes rush into the base of one of the towers, they hear blasts offscreen and briefly crouch down. Their leader, Sergeant

John McLoughlin (Nicolas Cage), shouts, "Don't think! Keep moving." To survive catastrophe, the film's A-list star is reminding us, we need to dissociate from our critical faculties, even shut them down. The scene ends with the sergeant urging his men to stay focused. With that directive, the lights of the downbound elevator briefly come into view. A deafening siren fills the soundtrack before a cut to black. Stone thus illustrates the difficulty of staying focused on the trauma. The film evokes this focal challenge again when the towers collapse. The implosion is seen from the limited perspective of the responders. Through a point-of-view shot, from McLoughlin's perspective, the film shows the lobby crumbling. Emulating his frantic head tilts, the camera whips from people running to shop windows shattering and the ceiling cracking. The quick succession of images fleetingly highlights only parts of the set design. While perhaps a necessity for economically capturing the large-scale event on film, the staging metaphorically reduces the World Trade Center to a claustro-phobic set where a macro-level view is impossible. The first responders rush toward the safety of an elevator shaft. Then, another cut to black. These parallel sequences where the image cuts to darkness signify the possibility of a conceptual oblivion. To confront the event directly may require a relinquishing of sight.

Both the museum and the films about the attacks feature clips of shell-shocked reporters, denoting how the mass media played a key role in representing the disaster for a global audience. *United 93* even presents a government relying on news coverage for information on the unfolding attacks. The din of phones ringing above the pulsating score creates a soundscape of confusion in the NORAD Command Center. Greengrass's camera wanders around the setting. Only the announcement of breaking news from the Pentagon slows the camera to a halt and brings quiet. News footage of a smoking Pentagon takes up the frame; however, the enlarged image appears blurred, as though such reporting cannot offer granular detail. Echoing Stone's insinuation that a focus on disaster leads to a shutting down, the reportage on the devastation causes the soldiers to fall silent. For a moment, they are unable to react. The sequence ends with the reporter's booming voice proclaiming, "There's a lot of confusion here at the Pentagon." By freezing the state representatives in silence, Greengrass's media outlets contribute to mass confusion; indeed, they are clearly framed as producers of confusion rather than conveyers of information.

In *World Trade Center*, news reports sometimes dominate as well, but the film also features citizens reacting to the shallowness of the ad nauseam coverage. In one sequence, a news report showing the collapsing towers ends with a handheld camera falling to the ground. When the announcer says that "officials seem simply stunned by the scale of the losses," Stone's camera pans from the television and through a living room. It lands on the disgusted wife of one of the first responders, who complains, "They keep showing the same thing over and over and over." Stone once more presents the footage from the news camera shaken by falling debris, centering it in the frame as the reporter calls the scene "complete chaos and utter hell." The volume of the rumbling is heightened so that its roar intrudes into the home. The sound design makes it seem as though the media contracts space and renders the living room into an annex of the World Trade Center. Watching the scene, another of the wives in the room cries out in terror, "Oh, my God!" Unlike her more frustrated friend who desires more information from the media, she appears ever more shaken by the images. For some, rhythmic repetition of the attacks on television, without any added context, further buttresses the event's traumatizing power. Stone's film thus indicates that spectacular images of 9/11 on (limitless) repeat, a refrain of the media's melody of devastation, can dull a critical ability to see wider systemic forces at work.

"Like watching a Hollywood blockbuster": A Memorial Calls Out to the Movies

Such a critical ability is a vital resource for those who would work to understand 9/11. The 9/11 Memorial Museum implies that the movies offer a space to do that work. Testimony from survivors is broadcast on loudspeakers, and their images are projected onto the museum's pillars. One of the first accounts visitors can hear and read states that, upon first seeing the attacks broadcasted, one witness "thought we were watching a Hollywood blockbuster." The word *blockbuster* is simultaneously projected on to a pillar. The prominent reference on the museum's wall also suggests a very different possibility: 9/11 has always been understood through the lens of popular cinema. The attacks represent America's cinematic dreams weaponized against itself, a disaster movie brought to life. As to the thin boundary between movies and life, media scholar Stephen Prince has argued that the limited popularity of films such as *World Trade Center* "suggest[s] that viewers are rejecting the role that popular cinema might claim in bearing witness to atrocity" (Prince 2009, 305).

Films about 9/11 sometimes share Prince's viewpoint that we do not want to glimpse atrocity in our entertainment. Stone features the frightened wife of one of the trapped first responders catching her daughter watching the television cartoon *Ed, Edd n Eddy* on a neighbor's sofa and laughing. Although the cartoon can only be heard and is not seen onscreen, the soundtrack reveals that the child giggles at a scene from the episode "Urban Ed" (2000) where a character's homemade cardboard city collapses. The city's downfall is met with the snide comment from an onscreen character, clearly audible in Stone's film against a shot of the concerned mother looking into the home: "Ceaseless toil and broken dreams are the essence of urban living." With its presentation of a pre-9/11 cartoon that stages a 9/11-like catastrophe as fodder for kids' entertainment, the film critiques Hollywood consumers as callously oblivious to the broken dreams of the citizenry who experience urban death. Moreover, even the most direct media parallels to our real-world traumas may refuse to be seen. The child's mother looks directly at the camera, thus at the film viewer, so that we are made to feel like her naive children, judged for our desire to be amused in a moment of crisis.

In his Dick Cheney biopic *Vice* (2018), Adam McKay is more explicitly skeptical about entertainment's relationship to recent history. As Cheney mulls over the opportunity to consolidate his power on 9/11, the dispassionate narrator notes, "As the world becomes more and more confusing, we tend to focus on the things that are right in front of us while ignoring the massive forces that actually change and shape our lives." The film punctuates this assessment with photos of a man golfing in front of a forest fire and a woman mowing her lawn in the path of a tornado. The narrator continues, "When we do have free time, the last thing we want is complicated analysis of government, lobbying, international trade agreements, and tax bills." His words are overlaid against a mid-shot of young people dancing—one shuts her eyes and another's mouth hangs grotesquely open. Our fantasies might reflect an urge to dance blindly. Are they a sign of our refusal to bear witness and engage systematically with not only a trauma like 9/11 but also the political order emerging from it, and the one from which it emerged?

For all their ostensible suspicion of escapism, reenactments of the attacks echo the museum's call out to the movies. They take seriously the role of cinema in comprehending what is posed as an inherently cinematic catastrophe calibrated to draw the world's eye. *Vice* metaphorically stages its indictment of our tendency to disengage during our free time just before its narrator announces the film's intention to capture the "ghost" of American power who revealed himself after 9/11. Popular cinema, productions designed for our entertainment and not featured at the 9/11 Memorial Museum, also might make us face the ghosts of our politics that we would otherwise be afraid to confront, as we will see later in this book.

On a more literal level, Stone's *World Trade Center* references Hollywood in the seconds before, and just as, the plane hits the first tower. A Port Authority police officer passes by a statue of 1950s sitcom star Jackie Gleason, jokingly warning loiterers to get away from "my statue," claiming this benign bit of popular culture as his own. At the precipice before a twenty-first-century trauma that will dramatically transform law enforcement practices, when, in the words of former director of the CIA's Counterterrorist Center, Cofer Black, "the gloves come off," the law seeks out a smiling mascot from the prosperous postwar years (Priest and Gellman 2002). When the plane strikes, we see it via a point-of-view shot from the officer's perspective (Fig. I.1). He watches the shadow of the plane pass over a billboard for Ben Stiller's slapstick

Fig. I.1. The shadow of a plane about to crash into the World Trade Center passes over a *Zoolander* (2001) billboard, a metaphoric gesture to how 9/11's shadow may fall over all of Hollywood. *World Trade Center.*

comedy *Zoolander* (2001) atop a Manhattan Loew's movie theater. At the moment of impact, the lawman is looking toward the movies. *Zoolander* was roundly criticized both for its irreverent attitude in a time of mourning and for ultimately editing out the towers from its New York City skyline (Jones 2016). Rather than position the cinematic junk food as separate from the American trauma, however, the shot composition leaves open the possibility that 9/11's shadow falls over all of Hollywood. Audiences can look for its presence at oblique angles and understand how deeply the attacks are embedded in the culture, bubbling up in benign stories ostensibly designed to help viewers ignore what the *Vice* narrator calls our "more and more confusing" world.

"The World Trade Center in the Popular Imagination": Finding Superman at the 9/11 Memorial Museum

The museum ultimately makes viewers confront the Trade Center's presence in Hollywood productions. A room presenting "The World Trade Center in the Popular Imagination" (as it is described on a very small plaque adjacent to the display thanking donors) contains bright posters showing characters such as Superman and Godzilla atop the towers, directly linking the skyscrapers to power fantasies, placing the site in the realm of superheroes and Eastern monsters.

Sarah Senk, in her study of the museum, frames the room as a site for a forbidden pre-9/11 nostalgia and notes that this is the only place in the exhibit where survivor testimony is not broadcast. Senk points out that on the official map of the collection, the pop culture–centric room is "marked only as an empty square" (Senk 2015). In her reading, the museum thus enacts a disavowal of its own archive. Senk's understanding of the room as a place of myopic nostalgia that pushes the attacks out of sight brings to mind Hollywood productions such as Robert Zemeckis's *The Walk* (2015), which chronicles Philippe Petit's famed high-wire walk between the towers in 1974. Zemeckis's film, on the surface at least, constructs a blissfully innocent time when authorities had only to worry about individuals turning the towers into spectacle for artistic performance rather than for deadly political statements. However, the film's dramatic impact depends on a thorough knowledge of a post-9/11 world. For instance, Zemeckis plays with the shock of seeing a lackadaisical American security system wherein U.S. Customs lets travelers pass into New York with equipment that they admit is designed to infiltrate the towers. The film appropriates the iconography of the famed "Falling Man" photo, where a citizen jumped from a tower before its implosion, for a sequence where Petit's shirt falls harmlessly from the towers. Even the film's final image, in which the hero claims that he (and implicitly the viewers he speaks to) will have access to the towers "forever," seems to visualize the shadow of the attacks. The shimmering towers in the morning light shine brightly as the image fades out, so that they seem to become overwhelmed by darkness.

The way I sense *The Walk* as a film that troubles pre-9/11 nostalgia, recognizing that it demands a recognition of the trauma in order to function, points to how I experienced "The World Trade Center in the Popular Imagination" differently than Senk. There, where the loudest of pop art is presented in silence, I found a space to reflect on cinematic myth after 9/11. Although the towers have fallen, the featured icons such as Superman, Godzilla, and Spider-Man remain. Perhaps their adventures, like the room itself, exist in an empty square in our imaginations, both outside and within the memory of the attack.

An allusion to pre-9/11 genre media is found in the wreckage of Stone's *World Trade Center* as well. Trapped under the rubble, the film's protagonists discuss their pop culture heroes. Officer Will Jimeno (Michael Peña) cites the televised police procedural *Starsky and Hutch* from the 1970s as the reason he wanted to become a police officer. He recounts that when he heard the television show's theme song, he would perform a mock arrest on his sister. In humming the theme song from the old program when faced with the destruction of the towers, the officers resemble George W. Bush, who invoked the western when he declared his War on Terror. Not only do law enforcement actors mobilize the popular stories of Hollywood in their rhetoric, but also Hollywood's example shapes conceptions of how to wield their power.

Like a Hollywood Superhero Blockbuster?
Finding Spider-Man in *World Trade Center*

Stone's film presents two different kinds of stories that became synonymous with the 9/11 attack—one religious and the other superheroic. A vengeance-seeking rescuer speaks with the rhetoric of Christian retribution that marked Bush's speeches. More strangely, under the wreckage the police officer who had professed to be a fan of *Starsky and Hutch* hallucinates Jesus Christ. In a time of trauma, he thinks about his heroes from both popular culture and his religion. Captured against a bright white light, Jesus appears in silhouette, the Sacred Heart wrapped in thorns on his chest. From the perspective of a pop culture fan, Jesus looks like a superhero, the Sacred Heart akin to the spider symbol on Spider-Man's costume. This portrayal of Christ foreshadows the film's homage to post-9/11 superhero movies at its climax. When the trapped Sergeant McLoughlin is pulled out of the rubble, the film alludes directly to Sam Raimi's *Spider-Man 2* (2004), evoking a sequence where the superhero is saved by New Yorkers, too.

To understand the full implications of the surprising gesture to the superhero figure in Stone's film, we need to linger on the vexed relationship of Spider-Man media to the World Trade Center. In the 9/11 Memorial Museum, the superhero appears on a poster for the 1978 Spider-Man television show. He stands in the front of the towers at midday, so that they seem to arise out of him. Raimi's *Spider-Man* (2002) similarly correlated the site and the hero in its advertising campaign. In its first trailer, released in the summer of 2001, Spider-Man catches bank robbers with a web he strings between the buildings. The towers are also reflected in the superhero's eye, reinforcing a visual link between Spider-Man and the New York landmark. Following 9/11, as with *Zoolander*, all traces of the World Trade Center were removed from the film. For some, that might exemplify how these genre movies merely enact erasures of troublesome history. Stone's key reference to Raimi's superhero film troubles this idea, however, showing how spectacular genre movies, even those scrubbed of the towers, may lead viewers back toward Ground Zero.

The specter of the superhero emerges from the rubble of the World Trade Center in Stone's film as McLoughlin, rescued, is lifted over the heads of emergency medical technicians. A shot from above shows him surrounded by a mass of caring citizens that extends to the horizon. Similarly, after Raimi's Spider-Man exhausts himself when stopping a speeding train, a band of commuters lift his unmasked body over their heads. Framed from above exactly as McLoughlin is, the composed superhero emphasizes that he is supported by ordinary New Yorkers. *World Trade Center* and *Spider-Man 2* convey a similar message with this portrait of a wounded hero surrounded by citizenry—disaster inspires compassion. By evoking the superhero film so directly in its final moments, *World Trade Center* highlights how audiences return to 9/11 not through meticulously detailed reenactments but through fantastic stories. It is striking that the first and only clear view of Ground Zero in Stone's reenactment is steeped in the imagery of a post-9/11 superhero film. Earlier in the film, describing the blinding smoke that rises from the site, an evangelical rescuer notes, "It's like God made a curtain with the smoke, shielding us from what we're not yet ready to see." The final moments of Stone's film inspire a question: Do superhero movies, a genre featuring the divinely powerful, offer us the strength to look at what we would otherwise not yet be ready to see?

"Welcome to a world without rules": World Leaders as Movie Stars

After passing through "The World Trade Center in the Popular Imagination," I encountered Arab faces in the museum's archival photos of the 1993 bombing of the World Trade Center. Senk finds that this exhibit is the only one that muddies the museum's rupture-oriented "before" and "after" presentation of the attack: in "a space otherwise dedicated almost entirely to the exceptionality of '9/11,' the brief inclusion of 1993 reveals at least a partial interest in thinking about 9/11 as something that was neither as singular as the dominant public discourse would suggest, nor without concrete historical 'causes' " (Senk 2015). She argues that the 1993 incident is presented in a way that makes it seem like a logical predecessor to 9/11. The narrative of somber inevitability is further reinforced in reenactments such as *United 93*, when the plane's initial taxi down the runway before takeoff is accompanied by foreboding and somber music.

The placement of these photos near "The World Trade Center in the Popular Imagination," filled with ephemera from pre-9/11 popular culture, also suggests the wider history of the Arab as an enemy in the popular imagination. He had long signaled fanatical menace in Hollywood films such as *Black Sunday* (1977), *Back to the Future* (1985), *True Lies* (1994), *The Siege* (1998), and *Rules of Engagement* (2000). The animated television program *South Park* gestures to how entrenched the archetype of the Arab terrorist is in a 2007 story arc entitled "Imaginationland," where terrorists attack the titular site, the literal home of all of humanity's imagination. The threatening Arabs coexist with and terrorize pop culture icons from both the twentieth and twenty-first centuries. The deadly bombing that heralds their arrival in Imaginationland visually mirrors the D-Day sequence of Steven Spielberg's *Saving Private Ryan* (1998), thereby suggesting that they act as a proxy for the Axis Powers in World War II. Like the figure of the Nazi, the terrorist can easily be slotted into viscerally satisfying narratives of exceptional catastrophe, comprising pure evil and assailing unimpeachable goodness. After watching a hostage video that ends with the beheading of a Care Bear, a happy cartoon character from the 1980s, a military general pauses the tape. He turns to his men and somberly remarks: "Terrorists appear to have complete control of our imagination." With a grotesque absurdity, *South Park* underlines that these figures hold a very real sway on the public and the state's thinking.

Following 9/11, the Arab has been represented as an enemy not only in the geopolitical world and reenactments like *United 93* but also in popular fantastical movies. He has controlled the imagination of Hollywood. For instance, villains linked to the desert land of Mordor in Peter Jackson's *Lord of the Rings: The Return of the King* (2003) are brown-skinned and dressed in robes that evoke the stereotypical image of Bedouins. *South Park* reinforces this reading by presenting its contemporary Arab terrorists running amok in Mordor. *Iron Man* (2008) reduces Middle Eastern men to cannon fodder for its superhero, an embodiment of the American drone program. With perfect aim, Iron Man separates the civilians from the enemies. The latter do not even get a label in his electronic sights—they are nameless, killable objects existing without clear definition, like the "enemy combatants" of post-9/11 law.

Remembering this scene amid the many photos of brown enemies at the museum, I wondered: Do these pop dreams that I love watching offer me only visions of my own inhumanity? How can I make sense of my torn allegiance between the heroes and their enemies? And how can I manage to genuinely love these films?

I think my love stems, in part, from their disruptive potential. Paul Pope's *Batman: Year 100*, which influenced the aesthetic and themes for Nolan's *The Dark Knight*, encapsulates my sense of how these tales of the (super)powerful can productively speak for the powerless. In a key moment in Pope's comic, the masked superhero is caught by the police in a rundown high rise. He hides in an apartment and is helped by a black child who leads the police away. "You see anybody come this way? Guy dressed like Dracula . . . ?," an armed officer asks the boy. The child sits in the foreground with his back to the reader, squeezing a Superman action figure. In the background of the panel, we see the militarized police leaning into the living room. Batman hides behind the door. In Pope's composition, the superhero stands over the child's head—the objects of the state's gaze are visually linked (Pope 2006, 9). After they are left alone, the boy gives the wounded hero his Superman toy, as if it were a protective talisman. The scene reveals how figures like the superhero give the marginalized the strength to look upon power directly and to be critical of those whom authority labels as monsters to be hunted down.

At the same time, Pope's focus on the black child who hangs on to his beloved superhero for strength stands at odds with how typical representations of Batman indulge in his privileged status as the white male industrialist Bruce Wayne. Pope told me in a personal interview: "My Batman is essentially an accidental home-grown terrorist against the state. My Batman isn't a billionaire. He's an Everyman [*sic*] trying to do good, maybe or maybe not Bruce Wayne, who gets sucked into the machinations of the state apparatus" (Pope 2017). In other stories, Batman usually directs his violence and his surveillance equipment against those in impoverished communities. Comparing Pope's rendering of Batman supported by a person of color who loves superheroes against more standard representations of the character draws attention to how such stories invite their consumers to wander between subject positions. Through them, we might hold the weapons of the state and take aim, even as we taste the fear of those targeted. Just as the black boy holds on to a superhero to give himself courage, we might also find new founts of bravery to resist. These spectacles break the "us-versus-them" mentality George W. Bush often evoked. In some ways, they allow us to be both "with us" and "against us," victim and victimizer, simultaneously.

The poster for *The Dark Knight* sharply exemplifies how pop heroes help us to sense the victimizing side of the authorities, undermining our allegiance with those conventionally presumed good. If the museum were to have an exhibit entitled "The Burning World Trade Center in the Popular Imagination," it could be a centerpiece. Batman stands in the foreground. Behind him looms a tower with a flaming hole at its center. Its structural wound forms the shape of the Bat symbol: this devastation appears to be Batman's doing. Combined with dust in the background that resembles the plumes from the imploding World Trade Center, the poster suggests that our heroes lie at the root of our terror. They are akin to the terrorists who linger on the periphery of our political imagination. At the top of the poster is the film's tagline: "Welcome to a world without rules." Such a story promises to show how violence can obliterate the ethical and legal rules of the established order.

While the Batman poster informs viewers of its intent to destabilize established Manichean frames in a world defined by a burning tower, the film component of the 9/11 Memorial Museum presents the trauma in simplistic good-versus-evil terms, as an exceptional moment outside of history. On the upper floors of the museum, an auditorium constantly plays two short documentaries featuring world leaders attesting to 9/11's impact. In *Facing Crisis: A Changed World*, President Bush testifies that he was horrified when he saw the TV footage of the attacks. Bush goes on to declare that the event showed that "evil is real" and that it "was brought home on that day." Displaying such a leader on the big screen, speaking with disbelief about the changed world, labeling the attacks as an ahistorical cataclysm in a way consistent with much of the museum's explicit presentation, implies that film can act as a tool for those in power to shape policy. Within its dark, subterranean levels, the museum shines a light on the ability of cinema to help audiences understand the attack. On the upper floors, it reveals how cinema can serve state interests by framing Western nations as righteous victims of "evil" enemies.

The Hedonist's Eye:
Eating a Sandwich and
Glimpsing the Nation's Enemy as a Mirage

Following their stroll past images of mass death, visitors have the chance to grab lunch at the café adjacent to the museum's cinema. The eating area sits next to huge glass windows that offer expansive views on the reflecting pools where the towers once stood, along with the wider city. When I ordered a sandwich, I thought of my own position of privilege. Michael Rothberg refers to "privileged consumers" as implicated subjects, "participants in and beneficiaries of a system that generates dispersed and unequal experiences of trauma and well-being simultaneously" (2019, 12). The museum offered an estranging space to contemplate myself as imagined enemy of the state, and as a disabled body attracting scrutiny. Sated from my sandwich while looking out at the memorial and New York City, however, I also sensed myself as a privileged consumer who has the luxury to muse about historical tragedy through the lens of enter-tainment. At the museum, my trauma and my well-being commingled.

Richard Rorty has argued that empathy emerges out of both "secu-rity and sympathy" (1993, 128). The latter feeling might arise only after the former is obtained. Emotional connection with those different from ourselves is possible only from a position of comfort. To be capable of compassion, Rorty suggests, is to be privileged. One filmmaker has crafted both direct and very indirect portrayals of the War on Terror: Michael Winterbottom. One of his films in particular encapsulates the tensions in my own identity that I felt at the museum café, with the remains of the World Trade Center somewhere far beneath my feet.

Winterbottom has directed several post-9/11 documentaries and reenactments, most notably *A Mighty Heart*, which chronicles the kidnapping of Daniel Pearl by Al Qaeda and the struggles of his wife, Marianne Pearl (Angelina Jolie), in the immediate aftermath. Many of the aforementioned themes of *United 93* and *World Trade Center* can be found in this film. With the assistance of a pulsating score and shadowy staging, its brown inhabitants of Karachi persistently exude menace, similar to Greengrass's hijackers. The film also narrativizes the struggle to look directly upon trauma. When the video of Daniel Pearl's beheading is played, the film shows only a montage of shocked faces reacting to the scene. Like Stone, Winterbottom is concerned with the struggle to directly face violence. He presents many shots through multiple panes of glass, which add a layer of illegibility. That visual remove accentuates the distorting power of the news media often referenced by Marianne Pearl and her peers. Finally, the film posits the difficulty of engaging in, and the temptation to withdraw from, the ethical ambiguities of the present moment through news reportage. One scene presents a friend of Marianne lying on the couch in a fetal position. As she nestles in her arm, as if on the verge of drifting off to sleep, a news anchor discusses the "renewed concern over how the United States is treating its detainees." Winterbottom, who also directed a documentary about Guantánamo prisoners, reveals the struggle to confront the inhumanity of one's own state and contemplate the humanity of the alleged enemy.

Within *The Trip* series of films (2010–present), Winterbottom proposes that the privileged consumer of cinema has the perspective necessary to accomplish such critical work. The series follows two hedonists, actors Steve Coogan and Rob Brydon, playing caricatured versions of themselves. They go to the finest restaurants while cycling through a Rolodex of celebrity impressions. As they eat and banter, they touch on different historical traumas, from Pompeii in Italy to the Spanish Inquisition and the Spanish Civil War. For these men, traumatic history and Hollywood cinema are inextricable. They mention both in the same breath as they feast on the most exquisite food. These pop-culture aficionados always appear to be on the border between complicity and insight. *A Mighty Heart* can only gesture to the guilt of its heroes within a broader political system and hint at how they rhetorically demonize nonwhite citizens around them, as when Marianne Pearl rants about Pakistanis as "psychos and liars" while her Pakistani allies look on. Although her insults are ostensibly directed toward those with knowledge of her husband's abduction, the camera hangs on the "friendly" Pakistanis present in the room. How they meet her hateful words only with a stunned silence implies that Pearl is painting all Pakistanis with a dehumanizing brush. *The Trip* series has the remove necessary to more pointedly lodge such indictments against its heroes and its viewers. Moreover, the films' mockumentary form calls attention to and hangs on the fulcrum between reality and fiction, providing viewers the chance to meditate on the fictional aspects of the enemies that terrorize our political reality.

The phantom of ISIS, radical Islamic terrorism, haunts the last moments of Winterbottom's *The Trip to Spain* (2017). One of the men looks at the perpetrators of traumatic violence, the phantoms of our time, directly. Without the context offered by Winterbottom's earlier work, such as *A Mighty Heart*, the suddenly political finale can seem inscrutable. Coogan goes to North Africa to meet his partner at a high-end resort. Although he appears to have met her, he wakes up at daybreak stranded in his Land Rover on a desert road. The idyllic reunion is revealed to be a dream. The roused comedian is framed through the shimmering reflections in his car window, recalling similar compositions in *A Mighty Heart*. Then the film cuts to an extremely wide shot of Coogan's Land Rover, so that it appears minuscule against the desert setting. Coogan discovers his gas tank to be empty. The hedonist, a man of cafés and cinemas, is alone and vulnerable. After he sips his last drop of water, he sees a car coming in the distance. He approaches the camera and smiles. When the car emerges out of the desert heat, his smile fades when he sees that it is the iconic white Toyota pickup of ISIS. As he stares at it, the cry "Allahu Akbar" can be heard. The film ends with the freeze-frame of the pleasure seeker staring at a geopolitical nightmare. Unlike the news media viewer from *A Mighty Heart* who seems to be near falling asleep on her sofa, Coogan, the consummate movie viewer and our hero in *The Trip to Spain*, remains frozen in contemplation, caught in the act of seeing.

Whereas the previously discussed reenactments often uncritically present Arab enemies, the Arabs' appearance in *The Trip to Spain* is troubled with a song choice. The Arabic cry of "God is great" is placed against the Michel Legrand song "The Windmills of Your Mind" whose English lyrics were written by Alan and Marilyn Bergman. The circular theme is the anthem for the film, lustily belted out by the comedians during their journey. They dub it alternately "a postmodern manifesto" and "a lovely song from the seventies." The tune first appeared in *The*

Thomas Crown Affair (1968) over a scene where Steve McQueen flies in a glider above Faye Dunaway, who looks up in wonder—one A-List star gazes in awe at another. Such cinematic origins imply that the comedians' beloved song acts like a melody for a Hollywood looking at the very dreams it produces. The final image of Coogan in *The Trip to Spain* facing the band of fighters is overlaid by the words (originally sung by Noel Harrison): "Round, like a circle in a spiral, like a wheel within a wheel. Never ending or beginning on an ever-spinning reel." At the mention of a film reel, the image goes black. An encounter with a real-world threat imbued with racist undertones is situated within a melody that references the movies and the hallucinations of the mad knight, Don Quixote, whom Coogan dressed up as earlier in the film. The song reminds us that such antagonists, windmills turned dragons, might be a mirage, a part of a never-ending movie that we screen for ourselves.

Legrand's lovely song could feasibly serve as a manifesto for *No Jurisdiction*, about the stories we tell ourselves in a time of emergency. Paired with *The Trip to Spain*, where history is constantly confronted through its reflections in Hollywood, the melody heralds my own investment in teasing out moments where we see the tales of our political order as part of and superimposed upon genres that continue into a pleasurable eternity. In my reading, genres are fluid storytelling modes that evoke dissolution of borders. Like *The Dark Knight* poster that promises to bring us into a world without rules, I unveil the stories of a lawless post-9/11 world where the boundary line between our realities and our fantasies is lost and we can no longer separate our heroes from our villains. Together, we peer into a hall of mirrors and fall ever deeper into, as the song puts it, "a tunnel that you follow to a tunnel of its own."

1

"It was like a movie!"

Theorizing the Eerie Symmetries
of a War on Terror

THE 9/11 ATTACKS INSPIRED a common refrain—onlookers who watched the towers crumble declared that it was "like a movie" (qtd. in Nacos et al. 2011, 25, 26).[1] Resembling a Hollywood disaster movie made real, complete with explosions and plumes of overwhelming dust, the scene became fodder for the mass media. Again and again, audiences around the world were exposed to the sight of the overwhelming devastation. Years later, victims of a mass shooting during a screening of Christopher Nolan's 2012 Batman film, *The Dark Knight Rises*, expressed their own confusion about the line between real violence and its cinematic depiction. One bystander said: "We thought, 'Special effects! Midnight showing! That's awesome. What theater does *that* any more?" (Breznican 2012). For a second, the carnage seemed indistinguishable from the superhero film being presented.

Ordinary citizens in the post-9/11 period were not the only ones who seemed to have difficulty parsing the line between the real and the fake, between violence as it is and as it is imagined. State leaders also spoke of such symmetries. In 2011, members of President Barack Obama's team described a key victory in the War on Terror in cinematic terms. Referencing the footage of American soldiers entering Osama bin Laden's compound, one Obama official declared, "It was like a Jerry Bruckheimer movie!" (qtd. in Bergen 2012, 228). Secretary of State Hillary Clinton similarly relied on media analogues to make sense of the action on screen, noting, "This was like an episode of *24* or any movie you could ever imagine" (qtd. in ibid., 220).

There would be grave human consequences from this imbrication of the War on Terror with the movies. The 2016 Chilcot report on the Iraq War found that one source cited in the British government's case for war may have been inspired by a plot detail from 1996's *The Rock*, directed by Michael Bay and produced by Bruckheimer (Walker 2016). Although the source asserted that the Iraqi government had placed chemical agents in glass containers, the report noted that "glass containers were not typically used in chemical munitions; and that a popular movie [*The Rock*] has inaccurately depicted nerve agents being carried in glass beads or spheres" (qtd. in Walker). The seemingly silly concoctions of a Bay-Bruckheimer film contributed to very real wars that are still being fought.

All parties in the War on Terror—terrorists, citizens, and governments—thus conceived of the conflict through the distorting lens of the movies. *No Jurisdiction* listens to the echoes that reverberate between our global state of emergency and the spectacles produced within it, where the violence of war is so intimately tied to our most beloved imaginaries. These eerie symmetries suggest that the stories we tell ourselves and the stories those in power want to tell us share a common thread. A supervillain offers a pathway to the connection between the stories told in films and those mobilized in political rhetoric.

The Joker's Lesson:
A Time of Law and Genre Cinema without Jurisdiction

In Christopher Nolan's 2008 Batman film, *The Dark Knight*, the supervillain Joker (Heath Ledger)—a terrorist caked in clown makeup—teaches a band of mobsters, as well as film viewers, a valuable lesson in the law.[2] In the scene, the mob's Chinese accountant, Lau (Chin Han), has escaped from the United States and video conferences with his criminal employers from a private jet bound for Hong Kong. Speaking with great confidence, Lau proclaims himself outside the jurisdiction of American law enforcement. Just then, the Joker barges uninvited into the criminal headquarters, laughing at Lau's sense of impunity. Looking directly at Lau's face projected on the monitor, the Joker replies, "Batman has no jurisdiction! He'll find [Lau] and make him squeal!" The Joker knows that the superhero's grasp in a post-9/11 era is global.

The Chinese fugitive abruptly cuts off the video feed of the conference call, thus becoming a stand-in for a cowardly kind of viewer. Lau, like so many of us, chooses to turn away from a world defined by an amorphous War on Terror where borders have lost their significance. Nolan's camera, by contrast, does not turn away from the Joker; the viewer must sit with the invocation of the hyperjurisdictional law and its permission to eliminate targets abroad without due process. The transnational staging of the scene, where a terrorist in a domestic setting communicates virtually with a foreign criminal flying through international airspace, further illustrates how the contemporary battlefield elides any fixed definition.

With new perceived terrorist threats, evoked in *The Dark Knight* even through costuming—the Joker wears grenades strapped to his chest, like a flamboyant suicide bomber—9/11 facilitated the justification for boundless war as well as transnational impunity for the powerful. Batman's superheroic reach recalls the myriad tentacles of the U.S. government, which has adopted the use of extraordinary rendition and black sites and evaded all meaningful accountability. Both Batman and the state have the capacity to capture those they label their enemies anywhere in the world and deploy enhanced interrogation techniques designed "to make [them] squeal." The superhero and other cinematic heroes like him do not merely allegorically represent the kind of far-reaching authority that the American state might desire; they reflect the actual power it has exerted in the aftermath of 9/11.

The established genres valorizing those wielding violent force are often mobilized by state actors. Yet their formulas unveil the villainy beneath the mask of power. This fact was perhaps most sharply articulated through a surprising allusion to a Batman villain during President Donald Trump's inaugural address on January 20, 2017. The speech encapsulated the isolationist, antiestablishment rhetoric of his campaign, which called up the image of a threatened nation whose borders were undefended and whose previous elite leaders cared little for the needs of its citizenry. Internet commentators noted that his so-called "American carnage" speech bore an uncanny resemblance to an address given by the supervillain Bane (Tom Hardy) in Nolan's 2012 Batman film, *The Dark Knight Rises* (Tilo Jung 2017). Trump proclaimed, "We are not merely transferring power from one administration to another or from one party to another, but we are transferring power from Washington D.C., and giving it back to you . . . the people" (Trump 2017). In the film, the masked Bane stands on the gates of a prison in Gotham City as he announces, "We take Gotham from the corrupt! The rich! The oppressors of generations who have kept you down with myths of opportunity and we give it back to you . . . the people."[3] Further suggestive of the possibility that Trump's speechwriters were fans of the Nolan blockbuster, Stephen Miller, the director of speechwriting, was in his mid-twenties when the film was released, while chief strategist Steve Bannon had previously produced Hollywood films (Greenwood 2017). The latter even declared in an interview with *The Hollywood Reporter* during the 2016 Trump campaign, "Darkness is good . . . Dick Cheney. Darth Vader. Satan. That's power" (qtd. in Wolff 2016)—explicitly linking the villains of American popular culture to American political leaders before helping to pen Trump's inaugural address.

While perhaps our first reality star president, Trump was not the only politician touched by the shadow of Hollywood and its superheroes. Post-9/11 genre films such as *The Dark Knight Rises* engage in a complex dialogue with more or less authoritarian visions of power and the state. One such vision was most starkly realized in the Trump administration's rhetoric. Chuck Dixon, co-creator of Bane and a Trump supporter, also saw the equivalences between his comic book creation and the politician but made sure to point out the villainous aspects of Trump's supposedly more progressive predecessor, noting: "Is [Trump] like a Batman villain? In many ways he is. But our last guy in that office often reminded me of a Bond villain" (Couch 2017). Thus Dixon pushed his audience to perceive the often-obscured violence that was couched in a cosmopolitan elegance.

At the 2009 White House Correspondents Dinner, a tuxedoed Obama jokingly warned the boy band the Jonas Brothers to stay away from his smitten daughters: "I have two words for you—predator drones" (qtd. in O'Connell 2011, 25). Legal scholar Mary Ellen O'Connell ends an essay on drone warfare and the "growing complacency with respect to drone attacks" by meditating on this presidential quip, as it reveals a broader societal comfort with the targeted killing of those the administration considers to be threats (O'Connell 2011, 2). Obama's attitude reflects a wider acceptance of this new type of warfare, echoed in the February 2013 Pew poll showing that a majority of Americans support drone use overseas ("Continued Support" 2013). Drone warfare, because it extends a state's right to use lethal force internationally, ignores fundamental human rights such as due process and has accelerated since 9/11. Could such growing complacency be due in part to Hollywood genre cinema, which has often depicted as exhilarating the kinds of deadly force the state has sought to normalize through the global War on Terror?

Stories matter and have an impact, be it in the world of entertainment or in geopolitics. Successive American political leaders often justified their policy shifts by invoking 9/11, so that the attacks were like the opening shot in a narrative of foundational rupture. By labeling 9/11 as a moment of supreme national vulnerability, the Bush administration expanded its power and transformed the legal landscape. The spongy language of trauma bled into the ill-defined laws that were created to fight the terrorists wherever they were, leading to an unprecedentedly broad war that spread from the military occupations in Iraq and Afghanistan to domestic counterterrorism efforts at home. America's post-9/11 laws created a paranoid shield that privileged security over individual liberty.

It becomes easier to sense genre stories' close ties with our political moment if we understand 9/11 itself as a genre, a kind of story that the nation tells itself. The attacks were of course not a fabrication, but they function as a climactic event in the popular imagination. Stephen Hutchings and Kenzie Burchell argue that an always renegotiated "terror attack genre" exists, in which both the media and the state frame attacks as exceptional but also able to be processed through the memory of previous experiences with terrorism (Hutchings and Burchell 2018, 183). More broadly, sociologist Jeffrey Alexander contends that cultural traumas are formed through an elaborate process that begins with speakers from the victimized group connecting the violence that befell them to the wider culture (Alexander 2004, 12). Events effectively identified as cultural trauma permit groups to "redirect the course of political action" (ibid., 27). A cultural trauma such as 9/11 is a constructed phenomenon, a narrative underlying a group's or a culture's identity that can be exploited by state actors to further their own political agendas. Expansive policy shifts sparked by 9/11 reveal how states deploy such discourses to achieve systemic change domestically. Popular genre forms play a role in substantiating such narratives and legitimizing policy changes.

This understanding of cultural trauma as a "socially mediated attribution," one whose mediation is a contest with political stakes, breaks away from understandings of trauma that propose events to be inherently traumatic (Alexander 2004, 8). Alexander saliently describes two schools of lay trauma theory: the Enlightenment approach and the psychoanalytic approach. The Enlightenment approach suggests that the parameters of what constitute a cultural trauma are clear and the response of actors to the trauma is "lucid, and the effects of these responses are problem solving and progressive" (ibid.,3). The psychoanalytic approach, as espoused by scholars such as Cathy Caruth, is more focused on individual experience and how healing occurs by recognizing and working through the trauma within one's self. Alexander highlights Caruth's deployment of objective language when describing traumatic symptoms, which in Caruth's estimation reveal "a reality or truth that is not otherwise available" (qtd. in ibid., 7). For Caruth, even if the trauma cannot be located by the victim, there is a fundamental reality or truth to it. Alexander argues that both approaches ultimately ignore what he dubs "the trauma process," the way a trauma is established (ibid., 11). Therefore, neither school can quite answer why certain violent events resonate widely and are understood as culturally significant (such as 9/11) while others are simply forgotten or are only remembered by a small few (like the Rape of Nanking).

In line with this study's interest in the way popular cinema sustains and responds to narratives of cultural trauma espoused by the state, Alexander links the trauma process to storytelling. He notes, "Representation of trauma depends on constructing a compelling framework of cultural classification. In one sense, this is simply telling a new story. Yet this storytelling is, at the same time, a complex and multivalent symbolic process that is contingent, highly contested, and sometimes highly polarizing" (Alexander 2004, 12). Each proceeding chapter highlights how the trauma of 9/11 is revealed to be a social phenomenon within the cited films and political discourse.

Unlike Alexander, this study privileges allegorical representations of the trauma of 9/11 that are presented in contemporary genre storytelling. When discussing the mass media's role in the discursive formation of cultural trauma, Alexander speaks only of news coverage (Alexander 2004, 18) and direct cinematic representations of violent cataclysms like the Holocaust and the Serbian War (ibid., 16). *No Jurisdiction* highlights genre cinema's role in the complex and multivalent symbolic process that Alexander describes. Genre film is a highly contested battleground. Through it, artists can critique the political transformations in an alleged moment of cultural trauma. At the same time, state actors may deploy its conventions for their own ends. Alexander describes the formation of cultural trauma as "deeply affected by power structures and by the contingent skills of reflexive social agents" (ibid., 10). I find that such power structures include those belonging to the state as well as media industries such as Hollywood. Reflexive social agents can be politicians seeking public support following an alleged trauma or filmmakers who can spark critical reflection in audiences through their self-reflexive, often violent films.

The Undercover Cop's Lesson:
The Power in Playing the Victim

While Alexander gestures toward how events labeled cultural traumas can aid the interests of the powerful, allowing for redirection of the course of political action, Vanessa Pupavac more fully articulates how such seemingly benign, even humanitarian frameworks have functioned as a tool for states' neoimperialist ambitions—for the insidious creation of modern-day empires. Focusing on the Balkan states and Rwanda in the 1990s, Pupavac argues that such rhetoric served Western superpowers who proclaimed themselves therapeutic agents (Pupavac 2004, 150). The result is that a country labeled by the international community as traumatized—such as Bosnia—would be forced to give up its sovereignty in the name of healing (ibid., 160). The language of trauma, she reminds us, can serve the powerful and harm the marginalized. The conflicts of the 1990s, marked by genocidal violence, gave the officials of Western nations such as the United States "a feeling of authority and legitimacy that they experience as lacking at home" (ibid., 165).

9/11 thus presents an important twisting of Pupavac's frame regarding the ways that cultural traumas advance national interests. The leadership of the United States claimed the nation to be traumatized, thus legitimating its increased authority at home. It also claimed that the rest of the world shared in this trauma and needed to change laws accordingly. The United States could position itself as both victim and healer. Violent, overwhelming force wielded without any jurisdictional limitations was the antidote it offered to the trauma of transnationalism terrorism.

In the above-mentioned scene from *The Dark Knight*, the Joker calls the gangsters' daylight meeting a "group therapy session." The supervillain's insult connecting the criminal with the therapeutic recalls Martin Scorsese's 2006 noir *The Departed*. Presenting several scenes where cops, as well as undercover cops masquerading as gangsters, attend therapy, the paranoid film offers a resonant critique of how the language of trauma and healing can be co-opted by perpetrators. The victim subject position can exonerate those with blood on their hands.

The Departed signals skepticism toward the spirit of unity and healing that emerged after the attacks. Its Boston setting is filled with patriotic iconography associated with the post-9/11 United States—a victimized nation. When the undercover cop Billy Costigan Jr. (Leonardo DiCaprio) has his fists up in the air ready to pummel a gangster, a bumper sticker with the phrase "UNITED WE STAND" looms near his enraged head. Performances of solidarity inspired by 9/11 only accentuate the nation's violent divisions.

While Costigan is tested as an exam-taking recruit on his understanding of his authority's limits, later in the film, as a jaded undercover officer in the field, he understands how trauma offers authorities pathways to act with largely unlimited violence. In a psychiatrist's office, Costigan lambastes police officers who cry in their therapy sessions. He scoffs when the therapist tells him that some weep after having to fire their guns and replies, "Let me tell you something. They signed up to use their weapons—most of them, all right. But they watch enough TV, so they know they have to weep after they use their weapons." *The Departed* establishes that the discourse of trauma, particularly displays of remorse associated with Post-Traumatic Stress Disorder, is a gift to perpetrators who represent a state that has been attacked. This gift has been passed to them through popular culture that seeks to humanize the violent.

While the Joker references Batman's lack of jurisdictional boundaries in the present day, *The Departed* even more directly underlines that 9/11 gave the United States the opportunity to deploy far-reaching legal powers. The police of *The Departed* never cite the Massachusetts State Police Policies and Procedures handbook that Costigan is tested on early in the film; however, they do visibly relish post-9/11 federal law. During a sting operation, a police captain informs his team: "All cell phone signals are under surveillance through the courtesy of our federal friends over there." A brief shot then shows suited government officials benignly smiling as they huddle over computer monitors. Basking in the extent of their new legal surveillance power, another police officer then proclaims with glee, "PATRIOT Act! PATRIOT Act! I love it! I love it! I love it!" In his ecstasy, the white officer briefly places a Black officer sitting beside him in a chokehold. The scene not only reflects the broader powers offered by such key post-9/11 legislation but also, in depicting a white officer choking a Black man, alludes to how such laws created in a state of emergency disproportionately affect minority populations (Kampf and Sen 2006).

A genre film such as *The Departed* literally cries out about the changes in legal structure made possible by 9/11 and the ensuing War on Terror. The executive branch of a nation that could now portray itself as a righteous victim further expanded and consolidated its power. Entrenched national myths became a key means to render the amorphous conflict palatable to the American populace.[4] Led by George W. Bush, the administration echoed the language of westerns and the "noble cowboy" in claiming that Osama bin Laden was "Wanted: Dead or Alive" ("Bush: Bin Laden" 2001). Karl Rove's underreported meetings with Hollywood executives shortly after the attacks point to an administration fully cognizant that cinema could play a role in mediating its policies (King 2001). The narrative of a traumatized and frightened culture helped to establish a neoconservative agenda whose legacy extended into the Obama and Trump years. The consequences of expansive laws, including the PATRIOT Act and the infamous Torture Memos, legal memoranda that provided the policy framework for the actions of soldiers in the Abu Ghraib prison scandal, put a spotlight on the excesses of executive power. With each photo of torture and leak of domestic surveillance, the foundational myths of a morally superior American national identity were being eroded. Public criticism made its way into post-9/11 genre films as well, where Americans were confronted with the sharp disjuncture between the state's ideals and its actions.

In the slipstream between mythic visions of power and the rhetoric of the powerful, George W. Bush's gunslinger was replaced by the self-professed superhero fan Barack Obama, who was then followed by the supervillain-quoting Donald Trump. This structuring imbrication of myth and political power highlights the importance of such spectacle as a potential site of critique. For example, Eve Sedgwick argues that our attentions are misdirected if we seek only to uncover invisible state violence. Instead, more focus needs to be placed on "forms of [state] violence that are hypervisible from the start [which] may be offered as an exemplary spectacle" (Sedgwick 2003, 140). We need new ways to "*displace and redirect* (as well as simply expand) its aperture of visibility," to change our perspective (ibid.; emphasis hers). By bringing victim and perpetrator into the shot at the same time, these genre films' spectacular mediation of inherently spectacular violence reframes the state's violent practices and encourages empathy toward its victims.

These sometimes hyperviolent films will be considered against a cultural backdrop where hypervisible forms of state violence, from torture to targeted killings, saturate the mass media and have become largely accepted by the general public. Although this study operates with a wide historical awareness, the genre films examined here negotiate these consequences of 9/11. The core chapters, focusing on the border western, film noir, and the superhero film, show that myths contain the potential to normalize state violence. At the same time, these genres challenge the distinction between perpetrator and victim that often frames discourses of human rights and cultural trauma. They allow us to more fully reckon with our complicity in the opaque operations of state violence.

Thus, these films productively counter the "empty empathy" that E. Ann Kaplan argues mass media reportage of the Iraq War cultivated. In *Trauma Culture*, Kaplan finds that such reportage presented viewers with a momentary and easily forgettable suffering. By depicting the birth of empathy with the victim as a painful process in and of itself, certain films in this study invite viewers to sense their de facto distance from the victim and their underlying closeness with the perpetrator. More broadly, these films answer Kaplan's call to "invent other strategies for communicating and understanding trauma" (Kaplan 2005, 100). They cultivate a strategy of self-reflection and an understanding of the ways binaries of victim/victimizer that are endemic to narratives of cultural trauma might be instrumentalized to spark policy shifts at a national and even global level.

These films are never quite comfortable being vehicles that catalyze self-reflection and empathy through stories that luxuriate in acts of violence. For instance, with a chief gangster villain that draws on familiarity with Jack Nicholson's Joker from Tim Burton's *Batman* (1989) along with a fleeting allusion to Wolverine, *The Departed* plays on my (and similarly inclined viewers') own love and knowledge of genre forms. It shows these stories to be a particularly perverse site of education. The film begins with Jack Nicholson's crime lord Frank Costello—whose ever-present grin recalls his iconic turn as the Joker—describing the history of racial tensions in Boston and the rise of contemporary organized crime families in the city. Commenting on the lack of Black dominance of both criminal enterprises and the state itself, Costello remarks in voice-over: "If I got one thing against the Black chappies, it's this: No one gives it to you, you have to take it." His steps, taken in deep shadow, are accompanied by the sounds of the Rolling Stones' "Gimme Shelter." Then the film cuts to Costello's point of view as he wanders into a corner store to collect his protection money. Mick Jagger's first few verses are clearly heard, "Oh, a storm is threat'ning / My very life today." Scorsese thus allows his viewers to feel the power of being a shadowy crime lord, a threatening storm of hate and appetite.

A disturbing testament to the scene's affective success was how I felt chills every time I re-watched the scene while writing the above paragraph! The overt racism did not overwhelm my giddiness in partaking in the gangster's sublime confidence and selfishness. I, too, craved to be the threatening storm.

Through its staging, which introduces a child's gaze into the scene, the film then marks its awareness of the potentially naive veneration of such a figure. Costello's next set of actions are scrupulously watched by a boy who sits drinking a Coke at the counter. Costello shakes down the store owner while verbally and physically assaulting his teenage daughter. Seeing the child as a future employee, he plies him with treats from the store. He asks him, "You like comic books?" A nod from the boy encourages Costello to thrust a copy of *Wolverine #11*, published just months after *Batman*'s release, into his overflowing paper bag. Since the boy will grow up to be Costello's mole in the police force, the film presents a criminal allegiance sealed not by blood but with a comic book. Scorsese thus hints that comic books teach hateful lessons to audiences turned gawking children. They glorify perpetrators, transforming them from men into forces of nature. At the same time, they offer a front-row seat to witness the suffering that perpetrators inflict and, as with Costigan's discussion of violence disguised with tears, to learn the strategies by which power maintains itself. James Mangold's 2017 genre-crossing superhero film *Logan*, featuring Wolverine, more directly comments on such comic book heroes.

Logan's Lessons: Learning Cruelty, Compassion, and History from (Super)Heroes

The Dark Knight reminds us of the porous boundaries between our politics and our stories while *The Departed* speaks to the porous boundaries separating perpetrator and victims. For its part, *Logan* frames the porous boundaries between genres that allow us to find our historical bearings within the present paranoid political moment and the way (super)heroes teach about cruelty and compassion. This tale about an aging superhero features the arid landscapes of the border western, the glaring neon of film noir, and the kinetic physicality of the superhero film. The titular character (Hugh Jackman) stands between a painting of a cowboy and a neon sign (Fig. 1.1). Framed in this fashion, he appears as a fulcrum between the western and noir, standing somewhere between the United States' dream of itself and its nightmare.

The image also emblematizes how post-9/11 genre cinema makes use of genre pastiche or blending. The border western often brings

Figure 1.1. The superhero stands between the neon of a noir motel sign and the cowboy of the West depicted in a painting. *Logan*.

together the visual conventions from noir movies and classic westerns. In a film such as *Logan*, set in a U.S.-Mexico borderland depicted as a space of death, two typically antithetical genres merge and inform each other. Later chapters of this book show how noir films allude to the superhero when they represent militant visions of the femme fatale capable of upending the stifling patriarchy of the state. The superhero film can in turn become infused with a noir despair when it depicts an American city transformed into an inescapable prison.

Logan offers a dystopic vision of 2029 America, which has been marked by some unmentioned cataclysm. Working as a limousine driver, the superhero Logan, also known as Wolverine, lives a domesticated life at the beck and call of nationalists. When passing through a border patrol checkpoint, partying white American men in his limousine chant "USA!" at nearby Mexican migrants. Such a scene of xenophobia implies that the unnamed cataclysm was not some superheroic battle but a political shift. In the film, the exploited Mexican youths whom the hero begrudgingly shepherds across borders seek sanctuary not in America but in Canada. For refugees, a complacent American nation has been transformed into a figurative no-man's land.

Produced in the last years of the Obama presidency and released in a time when the executive saw only carnage at the border, this "first blockbuster of the Trump era" suggests that a shadow has fallen over the United States (O'Connor 2017). By aligning the superhero with bigots in the opening scene, it reveals the complicity of powerful figures in breeding an inhumane and indifferent public. At the same time, ultimately linking the hero with Laura (Dafne Keen), a superpowered Mexican migrant whom he assists across the border, *Logan* posits the ways such icons might bring the public closer to the hated and the marginalized. As the film vacillates between generic visions of bigotry and ignorance on the one hand and compassion on the other, it shows how genre is a self-contested mix of discourses that both exposes and wallows in tremendous power disparities.

Via a demented hero's reference to a pre-9/11 *X-Men* film, *Logan* frames the post-9/11 era as a confused and forgotten time of violence in which the United States became an inward-looking and hate-filled nation. Logan works his menial position as a driver to earn enough money to bring his mentor, Professor Charles Xavier (Patrick Stewart), out of the country. A shell of his former self, the telepathic professor speaks in a drug-induced fugue about times past. After being injected with a sedative to keep his mental impulses from lethally consuming those around him, the decrepit telepath tells Logan, "They're waiting for you at the Statue of Liberty." Logan replies, "The Statue of Liberty was a long time ago, Charles, a long time." In his mental fog, Professor Xavier references the climactic set piece at the New York monument from Bryan Singer's 2000 film *X-Men*. From atop the statue where Logan battled the supervillain, the glittering towers of the World Trade Center were visible. The sequence does indeed seem to be a long time ago, a memento of a faraway world where the towers stood. *Logan* never explicitly discusses the intervening post-9/11 period, which thus becomes a structuring absence in the film. The Marvel Studios logo sequence at the very beginning of *Logan* heralds the film's investment in forgotten histories. It features a comic book page on which an abandoned home is described as "just a storehouse of memories and regrets!" The allusion to *X-Men* comic books signals that this film chronicles a nation that resembles an abandoned home, where our memories have been left to fade. At the same time, the briefly glimpsed comic book page also suggests that the superhero genre acts as a storehouse for such histories. Its heroes can wander through them, able to uncover the culture's buried memories and regrets.

By explicitly connecting the superhero with the gunslinger, the film encourages us to see how genres such as the western perform similar remembrances. Logan is often linked to the hero of *Shane*, George Stevens's 1953 western. *Shane* appears on the television in *Logan* just as the hero discovers that Laura, the superpowered girl he protects, carries around a bundle of old X-Men comic books (Fig. 1.2). Logan is framed beside a television that features a scene where Shane (Alan Ladd)

Figure 1.2. Connecting two genre heroes: a superhero reading of his exploits in glamorizing comics stands next to a TV, projecting an image of a young fan of the western gunslinger Shane. *Logan.*

demonstrates his own superheroic prowess, shooting multiple assailants before putting his gun back into its holster with a signature twirl. While Shane holsters his gun, Logan brandishes the comics he finds. He then expresses disgust about these tall tales of his own exploits, claiming that "in the real world, people die!" He tosses the comics aside, calling them "ice cream for bed wetters!"

The film then issues what might be read as a counterargument to Logan's dismissiveness of these stories by presenting the final scene of *Shane*, with the image of Shane's young fan Joey tearing up at the thought of losing his hero. Laura watches with rapt attention. Mangold's camera gently zooms in on both Laura and Joey, signaling that they see their heroes with similar wonderment.

Logan implies that these kinds of stories offer audiences the chance to safely face the suffering that permeates the everyday, a palatable means to confront death. After viewing *Shane*, Laura, who is later revealed as Logan's clone, joins the superhero in eviscerating an unnamed assailant. With its representations of enemies reduced to cannon fodder, *Logan* also suggests these media forms may teach as much about our capacity for cruelty as about compassion and empathy.

When the superhero dies, Laura recites, with some alterations, Shane's final speech to his young worshiper before riding off to his death, written by the screenwriters A. B. Guthrie Jr. and Jack Sher: "A man has to be what he is, Joey . . . can't break the mold. There's no living with the killing. There's no going back. Right or wrong, it's a brand, a brand that sticks. Now you run on home to your mother. You tell her, everything's all right. There are no more guns in the valley." Mangold's appropriation of the speech ironically breaks his own film's generic mold while poignantly suggesting a unifying truth between these genres—their brand of heroism built on violence can ultimately hurt those who subscribe to it. The film moves from appropriating an icon of entertainment to, more blasphemously, appropriating an icon of religion. Laura takes the Christian cross on the grave and leans it on its side to form the "X" of "X-Men." The camera slowly zooms in on this symbolic shift, emphasizing its importance. These tales are the faith of a troubled secular era.

The very nature of the texts that I consider here, which feature sometimes ultraviolent characters, pushes us to consider the blurred lines between perpetrator and victim in a time shaped by a catastrophe. Some scholars have suggested that the study of trauma has suffered from a victim-centered bias. This view is best articulated by Debarati Sanyal in her work on the poet Charles Baudelaire. She laments that an exclusive focus on the victim's subject position "fails to address how literature might engage with specific forms of power through dynamic relations of complicity or resistance" (Sanyal 2006, 10). Baudelaire's poems permit us to move beyond privileging that position by offering the perspective of both "victim *and* executioner . . . beckon[ing] us to consider how poetry responds to historical processes through active forms of resistance and critique" (ibid., 6). As suggested by *Logan*, genre films similarly can vacillate between the position of the victimizer and the victim, the all-powerful and the powerless. These films productively frame man as a dissensus, what philosopher Jacques Rancière calls a "putting [of] two worlds into one" (Rancière 2004, 304).

Such genre films are what I call "perpetrating cinema," playing on Raya Morag's term "perpetrator cinema." Morag developed this concept in her study of New Cambodian documentary created in the aftermath of the Cambodian genocide under the Khmer Rouge regime. These films, she argues, explore in part the "sudden closeness of both the director and the spectator to the perpetrator," cultivating "an intimidating intimacy" between the parties (Morag 2020, 9). Through their subtextual cinematic language, the Cambodian films create a duel between the survivor and the perpetrator. Moral resentment toward the perpetrator offers a response to the past the pushes beyond mere reconciliation, which can close wounds and ultimately diminish victims' suffering. Morag writes, "Cambodian perpetrator cinema is first and foremost a cinema of survival that keeps the wound open" (ibid., 186–87).

The pleasurable perpetrating cinema of the films in *No Jurisdiction* proves more troublesome. We are not (only) asked to resent those who commit violence but also shown how much we enjoy it. Through the complicitous intimacy the films cultivate, we relish a dehumanizing drone view and enjoy the firing of a superhero's missile, even as we hear the screams of targeted victims and empathize with their fear. These films push viewers to resent ourselves, our appetites, and the institutions we uphold. Perpetrating cinema is a genre of simultaneous exhilaration and repulsion—of fraught pleasure. Pleasure, notably, never enters Morag's discussion. The closing line of her work wonders how the imbrication of studies of the victim and perpetrator reveals the "new challenge faced by spectators of the perpetrator era," a period following the genocides of the twentieth century that extends into the twenty-first (Morag 2020, 187). *Logan*, along with the various genres it embodies, unveils the nature of this challenge, where to identify with the perpetrator means (the chance) to thrill in power, and to identify with the suffering victim means (the possibility) to be open to empathy.

The very pleasure these genre films induce in viewers creates a place to confront one's complicity that never is foreclosed. This is a cinema that keeps wounds open, one that savors the cutting. *Logan* offers a metaphor for this possibility when it presents the image of Laura cutting into her own wrist with her claws. While she tears into her skin, it quickly seals up. The power of super healing allows the caged Mexican girl to keep cutting and to contemplate her wound. Through fantastic figures who are insulated from hurt yet may themselves be from marginalized populations, such films invite us to examine our own culture's wounds.

Mangold's defense of genre through his central allusion to *Shane* also reveals the dissolution of the boundaries between perpetrator and victim and between past and present. The link between the heroes Shane and Logan illustrates genre's unique capacity for multidirectional memory, what trauma scholar Michael Rothberg describes as "dynamic transfers that take place between diverse places and times during the act of remembrance" (Rothberg 2009, 11). The post-9/11 superhero text reaches back to a McCarthy-era western to place these two traumatic moments in American history into dialogue. Their respective paranoid political discourses exist on an underexamined continuum, operating as timeless scripts for the powerful. The fearmongering tropes used to sustain states of emergency, their respective controlling policies, and the underlying fragility of state institutions are revealed when their respective pop stories are brought together.

Without the comparative framework that *Logan* both enacts and encourages, a subversive western such as *Shane* might easily be perceived as a simple valorization of existing institutions of power. Film scholars such as Stanley Corkin have read the classic western as a negotiation of the Korean War, which was being fought during the film's production. Corkin interprets *Shane* as a metaphor for a militaristic, unilateral United States asserting itself within Korea, with strong "leaders [who] vanquish the forces of chaos and enable the social development of 'normal' Americans and their communities" (Corkin 2004, 15). The hero Shane, according to such a reading, acts as a proxy for an American leadership that might be able to model self-sacrificing citizenship, offering the possibility to bring Americans into "the family of civilized, socially responsible humanity" (ibid., 152). However, Mangold's frequent depiction of the grotesque consequences of Logan's exceptional superhuman power and the impotence of the state actors he fights against encourages a new understanding of the threat inherent to a hero like Shane in such chaotic times.

Mangold encourages a similar reading of Shane's disruptive potential. He shows that the gunslinger does not merely save the American nuclear family but reveals its underlying weakness. Corkin notes that *Shane*, and Fred Zinnemann's narratively similar 1952 *High Noon*, "despite their appreciation of the idea of the common good, ultimately suggest that such a social state can be catalyzed only by the acts of an extraordinary individual. That individual is marked by his capacity or willingness to exercise violence—however lamentable the necessity for such action may be" (Corkin 2004, 153). Whereas Corkin sees wielding violence as necessary for preserving the American community, *Logan* draws attention to how exceptional power challenges that community. The scene that follows the presentation of *Shane*, in which the outlaw Logan (and his clone/daughter Laura) easily kills security forces frozen in place, echoes how *Shane* undermines existing institutions in his unwavering pursuit of justice. By his mere presence, Shane completely rattles the foundation of the institution of the family. He works as a ranch hand for and ultimately saves the Starrett family from predatory cattle barons with his gunslinging prowess. The hapless father seems rendered impotent by Shane's overwhelming strength, reduced to poring over the lingerie section of the Sears catalogue. The mother discovers in Shane a virility that leaves her in a state of unfulfilled longing. Their boy, Joey, discovers a man who overwhelms him with his heroism. The child will shout Shane's name in vain as the cowboy rides off into the sunset, pleading with the hero to stay with them. Through its canny comparison of (super)heroes across different troubled times in American history, *Logan* underlines how the "normal" American status quo during states of emergency rests on a fragile foundation.

Disrupting a post-9/11 public discourse shaped by Manichean divisions, these films provoke productive estrangement, challenging us to see the resonances between this cultural moment and past traumatized moments in U.S. history. The genre form allows for discursive fluidity, with recognizable tropes and figures such as the femme fatale, cowboy, or superhero that remain singularly malleable to those who mobilize them within the political or the cultural sphere. Recent speeches by U.S. presidents show how genre modes hold sway in executive discourse. I probe the cross-sections, slippages, and conflicts within the ongoing dialogue between Hollywood entertainment and political discourse in the creation of competing visions of power to frame genre as a contested critical site, of equal interest to politicians and to critically inclined filmmakers. My analysis both reveals and wrestles with genre's multivalent purpose: sometimes as a tool to normalize state violence and at other times as a potential mode of human rights critique.

In *Orgies of Feeling: Melodrama and the Politics of Freedom*, Elizabeth Anker has pinpointed the generic dimensions of post-9/11 political discourse by situating it in relation to the genre of melodrama. Through a form that privileges the retribution of a righteous victim against evil forces that have done it harm, Anker finds that "the nation's terrible injury becomes the foundational justification for violent and expansive state power" (Anker 2014, 3). Anker extends the work of scholars such as Michael Rogin, who has framed the executive discourse of President Ronald Reagan and its relation to the personas he inhabited in his career as a Hollywood actor. Rogin found a subject "replacing history by visionary myth" who "was soaring above the real" through continual citation of his own and other cinematic analogues (Rogin 1988, xvi), responding to a "shift in American politics from appeals to history (however mythicized) to the more immediate power of the screen" (ibid., xviii). By the post-9/11 period, this shift to the screen was well established.

Looking at post-9/11 presidencies, I find an executive overwhelmed by the ambiguity of genre myths, unable to cleanly co-opt the stories for self-valorizing purposes. For George W. Bush, the West was at first a place of absolute moral clarity that transmuted into an impossible dream, a place outside the realities of Washington, D.C. Asked in a CNBC interview whether or not he used Google, Bush replied that he used Google Maps, "In fact, I kind of like to look at the ranch, remind[s] me of where I want to be sometimes" ("George Bush uses 'The Google' "). For his administration, the idea of the superhero became a kind of insult to its own limited capacity to seek out its enemy, Osama bin Laden. For Obama, the superhero framed not simply the possibility of his ideals but also their eventual erosion—reflecting his shifting representation from photographs taken during his tenure as a U.S. Senator to official White House photos. The former presented Obama posed in front of a Superman statue to link him to the superhero; the latter playfully depicted him as a supervillain being caught in the web of Spider-Man played by the masquerading child of a White House staffer. For Trump, the discourse of the supervillain spoke to what critics perceive as his malignant intentions. I expand upon Anker's and Rogin's studies by drawing together the language of state and mass art, framing the intersection between them as crucial and contradictory, mediated within the spectacular genre films themselves.

At the same time, I move beyond Anker's emphasis on melodramatic modes that invite unity between the citizen and the nation-state to focus on genre forms that stress and codify hierarchies of power. Such films, promoting disunity, offer a destabilizing individuality, at times (super) empowered and at other times isolated. The legally unbounded ideals present in such stories contain the possibility to express the limits of state power, not only to defend against transnational threats but also to sustain a legitimizing monopoly on violence. These tropes suggest how "great criminals," such as the figure of the terrorist, might co-opt the state's violent power for themselves.

The genre films under review are allegories, extended metaphors that concretize the abstract systems that govern everyday life. Fredric Jameson finds that "we map our fellows in class terms day by day and fantasize our current events in terms of larger mythic narratives" (Jameson 1995, 3). These narratives as modes to comprehend the present geopolitical moment are harnessed and constructed by the state, its citizens, and its artists. Allegory can represent change within systems, thereby bringing into view broad transformations of the governing legal apparatus, what Raymond Williams describes as structures of feeling, "a social experience which is still in process" by which state violence and extralegal practices are normalized (Williams 1977, 132).

9/11 reveals that perceived cultural traumas and their associated policy transformations are negotiated by politicians, artists, and audiences through allegorical storytelling forms. Such allegorical modes resting on violent actors can be adapted to valorize leaders and lend their policies moral weight and mythic comprehensibility. These storytelling modes also contain the possibility for the films (and their audience) to critique such power, as they effectively frame the suffering caused by actors even as they expose the viewer's potential complicity. The exhilarating pleasure of this brand of perpetrating cinema opens vexing questions about viewers' relationship to the violence of their heroes, questions that might be foreclosed if not seen through a distancing allegorical lens.

Placing key genre works in direct dialogue with the transformed legal landscape, *No Jurisdiction* makes films often perceived as merely apolitical fantasies newly relevant. Similar to the harsh post-9/11 legal reality that promised an easy though brutal solution to transnational terrorism, these genre films privilege violent enforcement of conflicts through the western sheriff, the noir private eye, and the crusading superhero, both reinforcing and critiquing the discourse of trauma manifest in muddled post-9/11 law.

These varied productions show that genre film holds an influential and indeed determining sway over the conceptualization of how crime should be fought, in the minds of the public and in the views of the executive. Silver screen heroes contribute to a view that limits critical assessment, encouraging suspicion toward legal strictures, a traditional check on executive power. And yet, via the inherent multiplicity of meanings possible within such allegorical forms, these films also reflect on the ways such valorizations of the extralegal emerge and can be resisted. The work of Siegfried Kracauer and Fredric Jameson has been crucial in positioning mass art as a lens into the economic and political forces that shape society; I extend their views by arguing that such texts not only provide a systemic view of existing legal frameworks but also articulate minute shifts in the law's particularities.

No Jurisdiction probes the stakes of a discursive synergy that continues to reemerge in modes at once enamored and skeptical of great power. Zack Snyder's 2016 *Batman v Superman*, a film saturated with 9/11 imagery, links the superhero with the terrorists behind the attacks. The supervillain Lex Luthor (Jesse Eisenberg) tells an American senator, "We know better now, don't we? Devils don't come from Hell beneath us. No. No, they come from the sky." The valences of this linkage are manifold. The film encourages seeing the superhero as an extralegal transnational threat akin to the terrorist, yet Superman as a quintessentially American icon also pushes us to contemplate the spectacular kind of violence practiced by Obama's United States that came from the sky—drone warfare. *Batman v Superman*, like so many other genre films, leads viewers into a productive space of ambivalence toward such vigilante icons associated with extralegal power and the state forces they have come to represent.

Remaining attuned to the shifts between perpetrator and victim depicted in these films that implicate the viewer, *No Jurisdiction* is meant to be a particularly disordered and messy study. It is not a traditional "semantic" distillation of genre forms, to use genre scholar Rick Altman's influential terminology, that systematically frames the "building blocks" or conventionalized elements in these kinds of stories (Altman, 31). Neither does my study take a rigid "syntactic" approach that methodically explores how each genre's building blocks are structured together (ibid.). That said, we will see how previously set genre conventions have shifted since 9/11 and how the relationship between those conventions is changing. For instance, a genre-crossing variant of the western, the border western, that privileges the U.S.-Mexico border and responds to changes in immigration policy after 9/11 has emerged. In post-9/11 noir, the once oppressive setting of the city seems newly fragile. The post-9/11 superhero film often frames its protagonists as proxies for U.S. military and executive power. Global popular and art cinema skeptically co-opt elements of these Hollywood genres as they reference the attacks and the War on Terror. The borders between genres are not set. By simply cataloguing the building blocks of each genre and their relationship to one another, we would lose sense of the crucial porousness of these storytelling forms.

Instead, this book takes as a starting point that genre forms are fluid within both political and aesthetic representation. The study creates a catalogue of my readings of these films, attendant to how stories told within the political sphere often harness Hollywood genre tropes and to how such political narratives become reinscribed in contemporary films in those genres. Such stories implicate the viewers, revealing them to be "privileged consumers," to use Michael Rothberg's expression, who benefit from and take part in systems based on inequality (Rothberg 2019, 12)—forcing them to contemplate the contradictions in their own allegiances and subject position. My own contemplations result in this intersectional record of an American of French Arab descent's perception of genre as a site of critique and normalization of state violence. This study thus echoes the structure of Kaplan's *Trauma Culture*, a "personal account of experiencing 9/11 that will illustrate the complexity of a catastrophe as registered through one consciousness, with its unconscious substrates" (Kaplan 2005, 2). More broadly, the implicated structure of my analysis, where I lie at the center of my theorization of trauma, takes inspiration from Lauren Fournier's conception of auto-theory. Fournier's feminist practice springboards from "theorized personal anecdotes" where "embodied experience becomes the primary material for generating theory, foregrounding disclosure and ambivalence as that which enhances critical rigour and relevance" (Fournier 2019). As a critical viewer and a conflicted fan, I stand between and amid the brown victims and the often-white victimizers in these films. The very contradictions these works highlight within me also point toward the complexities of narratives around the cultural trauma of 9/11, in which all manner of jurisdictional lines are blurred or erased, be they legal, aesthetic, or ethical.

Using my own idiosyncratic experiences with the featured films as a model, this record exposes how the disordered, violent stories, which reveal and revel in audience complicity, allow us insight into how our own hands are sullied by state violence. They also offer privileged yet marginalized persons like me new avenues of empathy and resistance. Each chapter opens with short epigrammatic passage wherein I discuss my personal experiences with the fraught ideals of these genre forms. Using such a disordered framework, interweaving autobiography with analysis and shifting between a pre-9/11 and post-9/11 world, *No Jurisdiction* can ultimately answer a question: How do I, a disabled child of immigrants, justify my love for the very (super)heroes that destroy brown persons who look like me on screen?

Responding to a Challenge to Complicate Histories of 9/11

On the tenth anniversary of 9/11, media historian David Slocum wrote a salient breakdown of media scholarship. He challenged those investigating the subject "to historicize analyses of 9/11 film and media productions, to address the extraordinary transformations in the media ecosystem of the early 2000's, and to provide rigorous and specific cultural ground-ings for studies" (Slocum 2011, 187). *No Jurisdiction* contributes to our understanding of the impact of 9/11 on the media according to these three key critical imperatives.

First, my analysis, resting between legal, trauma, and film studies and between the humanities and social sciences, historicizes post-9/11 genre films. Through this interdisciplinary framework, a film that has existed outside the purview of any post-9/11 study, such as Robert Rodriguez and

Frank Miller's film noir *Sin City* (2005), is shown to be a canny response to the Abu Ghraib scandal and the visions of militant, perpetrating femininity that flared up in the torture episode and the exploits of female soldiers on the battlefield across the last two Iraq wars.

Second, by incorporating a host of different media forms—speeches by state leaders, comic books, viral advertising on the internet, and video games—I situate these Hollywood and international films firmly with a wider media ecosystem. The subtleties of these texts' political critiques most sharply emerge when viewed within such a cross-media spectrum.

Third, in synthesizing international law and international genre cinema, I illustrate how genre texts frame the shifting meaning of the War on Terror and its discursive impact across borders and cultures, reaffirming genre as a site of ambiguity and tension. Slocum, like many post-9/11 film scholars, assumes a tendency for such entertainments to provide "coherent stories with clear resolutions" (Slocum 2011, 189).[5] But I find that in their vacillation between the subject positions of victimizer and victim, and between skepticism toward state power and exhilaration about its usage, these texts engage in a productive incoherence wherein viewers' presumptions become destabilized and their potential collusion with structures of political violence might be exposed. My analysis of Nolan's *The Dark Knight* trilogy, which has been criticized in previous scholarship for its political ambiguity, frames how its inherent tensions and lack of overriding clarity create much of its decentering critical force. I investigate the fraught ways that audiences might be able to confront political violence and find new routes toward compassion through genre spectacle.

Ultimately, I construct a new filmography that pairs canonical post-9/11 texts with some that have received little to no sustained attention while creating an interdisciplinary critical frame that allows scholars to "open outward to complex and contradictory readings, rather than closing in on themselves and reinforcing selective interpretive and political positions" (Slocum 2011, 192). Through such work, *No Jurisdiction* not only responds to Slocum's call for scholars to complicate histories of the post-9/11 decade but also points to new ways of considering art and law in times marked by states of emergency.

The second chapter focuses on the border western and considers Denis Villeneuve's *Sicario* (2015), Tommy Lee Jones's *The Three Burials of Melquiades Estrada* (2005), and Ridley Scott and Cormac McCarthy's much-maligned *The Counselor* (2013). Their position as genre films about the borderlands is crucial to comprehending the interrelation of trauma, genre, and the law in the U.S. context: following 9/11, few spaces were as affected on either the discursive or the political level as the U.S.-Mexico border. Saturated with surveillance imagery, *Sicario* frames a panoptic border wherein the state's eye acts as a kind of haunting phantom that reduces the humans it surveys to little more than specks and blurs. Historian Mae M. Ngai identifies the illegal alien as an impossible subject—one stripped of all rights who exists within a legal limbo where his immigration status denies him his humanity.[6] In *The Three Burials of Melquiades Estrada*, Jones visualizes this limbo to articulate the psychological toll of such a status. Examining the film against the fear-filled discourse surrounding immigration after 9/11, which often conflated the Mexican and the terrorist, I show how *Three Burials* exposes the discursive process by which the undocumented migrant is transformed into a potential threat. *The Counselor* extends these concerns, framing the U.S.-Mexico border space as a kind of broken mirror in which contemporary American anxieties are refracted. These films that merge the tropes of film noir and the western use genre as a vital critical mode to confront suffering and revolutionary violence.

The third chapter, on Robert Rodriguez and Frank Miller's *Sin City* (2005) and David Fincher's *Zodiac* (2007), uses Paula Rabinowitz's concept of a "pulp politics," in which a noir mood emerges within paranoid political discourse, to offer entirely new insights into the political critiques made by both texts. Disrupting traditional readings of *Sin City* as a chauvinistic fantasy, I place it against the Abu Ghraib torture and prisoner abuse scandal to reveal how the film visualizes a destabilizing potential in the "female perpetrator," a militant version of the femme fatale. Few have read the 1970s-period film *Zodiac* against the political climate in which it was produced. Concerned with the failed search for a killer who encroaches upon the everyday through his pervasive presence in the mass media, *Zodiac* cannily allegorizes the bureaucratic failures in the lead-up to 9/11 and the search for the United States' chief menace of the 2000s, Osama bin Laden. Yet even as these texts capture how myth can haunt, they also show that only in such a violent, often spectacular mode can the phantoms of public discourse be detected.

Focusing on Christopher Nolan's *The Dark Knight* trilogy in the fourth chapter draws out the nuances of Nolan's critique to uncover the depth of his indictments of the American executive during a state of emergency. I find the muddy definition of "enemy combatant" within the amorphous terrorist threat of the Joker and excavate the Black bodies of Hurricane Katrina in Batman's Gotham City. Nolan is invested in symbolic fluidity between hero and villain, perpetrator and victim. The Batman films position the superhero's exploits as a spectacular "show" for the executive—legally unbounded and intoxicating, turning excessive force into fodder for collective fantasy. However, Nolan also frames genre as too volatile to be entirely co-opted by the state, calling attention to both the terrorizing power of such genre myths and their resistant potential.

Through a discussion of UNSC Resolution 1373, which made the laws of the War on Terror global, the final chapter features a brief exploration of other national cinemas and their allegories of a changed post-9/11 landscape. Just as the Bush administration transformed domestic law, it also created global security law via this far-reaching resolution, binding on all member states. Its poorly defined key terms, such as "terrorism," mired UN partners in the dangerous muddle of meaning emblematic of so much post-9/11 law, in which fundamental human rights were subordinated under the rhetoric of increased security (Scheppele 2013 "The Empire," 265; 267).

Just as American policy since 9/11 has shaped international law, so too has the shadow of America's global War on Terror extended to international cinematic works. Considering a range of films that either inhabit or comment upon genre types, my conclusion uncovers echoes of these American productions in works compelled and repulsed by the exhilarating modes of Hollywood spectacle. These international films contain key disorienting moments that articulate regional concerns and reflect on the ways their respective governments have responded to America's wars. An emblematic Japanese example is Kiyoshi Kurosawa's *Tokyo Sonata* (2008), about a Japanese youth joining America's conflict in Iraq. A nightmare sequence of his homecoming, shell-shocked in his military fatigues, employs a noir staging to reflect a home space invaded by American political forces. In France, in Nassim Amaouche's *Adieu Gary* (2009), a banlieue western, the French Arab protagonists negotiate mass media envisionings of the "terrorist" in ways that highlight the pressures the controversial resolution placed upon Arab and racially mixed populations. *Adieu Gary* subversively refashions the western aesthetic and its iconic heroes to signify not strength but weakness. In its appropriation of the ghost town convention, the film articulates the psychological disempowerment of an ethnic group framed in legal terms as a potentially violent threat.

The final chapter is a first step within an emergent dialogue that aims to situate local cinematic texts within transnational frameworks to help clarify and critique states' responses to terrorist threats. Through such work, we might bring what Paul Giles describes as a "critical transnationalism" to contemporary genre studies (Giles 2003, 65). Giles finds that to "reinscribe classic American literature in a transnational framework is to elucidate ways in which it necessarily enters into negotiation with questions of global power" (ibid., 72). Doing the same with American genre cinema allows us to appreciate the ways filmmakers negotiate and question a geopolitical terrain shaped by American visions of power. In moments of enigmatic and compelling ambiguity, the global films that deploy and comment on these Hollywood genres show the ways such fraught visions might also be appropriated by those rendered Other and relatively voiceless within post-9/11 political discourse and law, to express and potentially transcend their marginalized condition.

On the Frontier between Hate and Empathy

The Post-9/11 Border Western

"I am not a cowboy": Finding My Selves in the Western

IN FIRST GRADE, I WROTE A short report on Montana, my home state. It begins simply: "In Montana, there are cowboys." Although we lived on a suburban street in the small town of Sidney, my immigrant family was often invited to attend various cowboy events, including the annual cattle branding. Although my sisters eagerly participated in the spectacle, one even carting about a bucketful of freshly castrated bull testicles, such outdoor events were anathema to my couch potato ways. I sat on the sidelines with my parents, overwhelmed by the odor suffused with a fecal pungency. Oh, how I begged to be brought back home!

The second page of my report attests to this distaste for cowboy culture and my urge to position myself outside of it: "I am not a cowboy." In the original, "not" is underlined not once but three times. The realm of ranch hands and bull riders was emphatically not my world.

The final page features the declaration: "In Montana, they sell black-and-white movies. That's good." The movies were my lifeline. On that last page, I drew a very rough rendition of the poster for my favorite director Alfred Hitchcock's *The Birds* (1960). My anti-cowboy report on Montana contains a strong allusion to a Hollywood director who, in Pascal Bonitzer's estimation, finds "a stain" in picture-postcard visions of America (Bonitzer 2002, 20). Although Hitchcock's spectacle about a malicious natural world was filmed in Technicolor, not black and white, I notably privileged a film that framed small towns and their schoolhouses as spaces of threat. Hitchcock movies uncovered something wrong underlying America and its prevailing social order. My report, positioning cowboys against Hitchcock, implied that the stories of cowboys featured none of that compelling ambivalence. Where could I, a disabled boy of French Arab descent, find myself in tales about white men who resembled the gruff attendees of our town's most pungent gatherings? Only over many years did I come to appreciate how the western genre could also capture the stain of traumatic histories and speak to my own sense of not belonging.

In adolescence, I first gleaned a resonant weakness in these tales about hardbitten men on the range. My late childhood best friend, and conveniently next-door neighbor, had a little hideaway in his basement. His rumpus room was our mediatheque and was close to his father's gun room where ammunition would be prepared for weekend hunts. The smell of pets and gunpowder seeped into our insulated media bubble—the potent sensorium that was Montana could never be fully escaped! One day we watched John Sturges's 1960 *The Magnificent Seven*. I expected nothing but tired bravado, given my long-standing antipathy to all things cowboy. To my shock, I saw myself on screen.

In the film, Lee (Robert Vaughn) is a broken Civil War vet. At one point, he wakes up from a nightmare, jumps out of bed, and barricades himself in a corner, desperately trying to find shelter against the vastness of the southwestern night. Two Mexican villagers, men Lee is ostensibly meant to protect, tell him to have no fear. Now fully awake, Lee wanders from the corner of the room and sits at the dinner table. Staring at a candle, he explains that the gunman's life is nothing but fear. He speaks of waiting "for the bullet in the gun that is faster than yours . . . and the lies you tell, to fool yourself."

As I stared at the glow of my friend's large CRT television, Lee, sitting in a chair in the dark and staring at the lone flame, seemed like my proxy. Lee was transfixed by the candle's flame; I was transfixed by him. Our shared subject position made me begin to realize that the western, which I had long discounted, could help frame the lies we tell about our nation and ourselves. The genre and its faux majesty could be a means to sense the lies I told about myself and my own exclusions in a community in the West.

As Lee's monologue continued, it cut deeper still. He comes to contemplate his own declining body. With an atrophied right hand and limping gait from cerebral palsy, I took the cattle brandings of eastern Montana to be an estranging parade of the aloof and the able-bodied. Lee's self-reflection left me uneasy but fascinated.

His musings about fear are broken by three flies sitting on the table. A cut-in on the insects is paired with a harp's melody, marking this moment as a shift in the troubled man's thinking. A wide shot then shows Lee grasping at the insects. He moves with a quickness that the camera cannot catch, and he becomes a blur. A point-of-view shot follows, and his hand opens; a single fly flutters out. His hand fills the wide frame of the epic film, typically used to accentuate the grandeur of the western landscape and the smallness of man. Such a wide framing is instead brought to a body, making its tremors appear monumental. His human frailty, not some landscape or spectacular duel, is rendered sublime and overwhelming. His aging body is marked as worthy of contemplation. A wider shot shows Lee looking down at his hand in resignation. He laments, "There was a time when I woulda caught all three." His exceptional act of speed is positioned as a failure—even a movement that is faster than the camera's eye heralds his growing weakness rather than his undiminished strength. He ends the scene alone and in silence, contemplating his fear by candlelight.

The broken Lee promised me a different kind of western hero—one who recognized the illusion of his own grandeur and who looked critically at himself, even if such a self-critical gaze encouraged others to turn away. Encompassing both the lies of the West and its discomfiting truths, for me, Lee redefined what freedom in the West meant: not the ability to dominate others with one's strength but rather the capacity to sit with one's weakness and fear. In inviting viewers to experience the perspective of a man who fully recognized himself and his decline, Sturges showed me that through these spectacular and hypnotic films we can begin to recognize our different selves and our pasts that we bury.

Growing up, I regularly faced resistance from others when naming historical realities head on, without the metaphoric gloss offered by films such as *The Magnificent Seven*. In the fifth grade, I challenged my teacher's efforts to present an off-curriculum unit on patriotism in which she described the first Thanksgiving as a happy one between "the pilgrims and the Indians." She gave us handouts featuring cartoons designed for much younger children. Raising my hand, I held open our American history book and asked her to explain the cited Trail of Tears to the class. I wondered aloud: Were the tears of Native Americans forced to migrate to Oklahoma happy ones? In lieu of an answer, I was sent to the school counselor for a psychiatric evaluation. Raising the true history of America was made to seem, in my school's eyes at least, a sign of madness.

On the surface, the western genre often propagates palatable national myths that would fit nicely into my teacher's rogue patriotism unit. But self-critical westerns such as *The Magnificent Seven* suggested how this seductive and seemingly naive genre might bring audiences to witness past sufferings they would otherwise refuse to see. With our defenses lowered, we open ourselves to the possibility of generative conflict with the mythologies that would seem to inhibit critique.

At the same time as I was encountering such films, I grew aware of Sidney, Montana's own unspoken history of violence against minority populations. Six miles out of town there had been a Japanese and German prisoner-of-war camp used during World War II; its prisoners had worked for the local sugar beet factory. A small plaque marks its location on the side of the road. Although my father introduced me to this past, the camp was never mentioned in our classrooms. My middle school Montana history textbook did, however, contain a veiled reference to the lynching of East Asian immigrants shortly after our town was incorporated in 1911. A Korean family owned a restaurant in Sidney; under threat, the textbook said, they disappeared into the night.

Recently, I reached out to the local heritage center in Sidney to confirm the truth of this unsettling but increasingly muddy memory. Administrative assistant Leann Pelvit confirmed: "[T]here was a Korean restaurant in Sidney. . . . The story about them leaving in the middle of the night is correct, they left everything in the restaurant. It was speculated that they had been threatened. . . . Unfortunately, that is all of the information I have. No name or names are included" (Pelvit 2021). She attached to her email a photo dated 1916 of the unnamed and now largely forgotten family in their restaurant. Staring at the image of a meticulous eatery with white tablecloths, my eyes were drawn toward the right side of the frame. Near the counter lies a crate emblazoned with the words: "YELLOWSTONE MERC SIDNEY, MONT." This aspect of the photo leaped out at me. While the Korean family was lost to time, Yellowstone Mercantile was a local store that continued to thrive throughout my childhood. The store even gestured to its early-twentieth-century founding with a quaint cash carrier system where invoices and dollars would zoom on wires over the heads of patrons. The crate in the photo underlined that certain businesses could survive and thrive in Sidney—especially, or perhaps exclusively, if their founders were white.

The threatened Korean family captured my attention because they put into relief how privileged my immigrant family's life was in Sidney. As the local orthopedist for more than three decades, my father seemed to have replaced the knees and hips of much of the town. My joyful French mother charmed the community, distributing boxes of baklava from Shatila, the famed Lebanese bakery in Dearborn, Michigan, and introducing our neighbors to all manner of European gastronomic delights. My sisters left their mark on the quintessential American high school by becoming homecoming royalty and, in the case of my oldest sister, an Olympian. Her photo is prominently displayed near the school's entrance. Even I was chosen to be prom prince in 2004—I was so close to the king's throne!

9/11, which marked a new chapter in the country's Arab-as-enemy saga, somewhat troubled Sidney's near-total acceptance of me. A few times, a bullying classmate would launch the epithet of "terrorist" in my direction. One time a teacher invited me up to their desk and showed me their drawing of angry eyes. They remarked, "These are the eyes that the terrorists would see before I kill them." So foreign to me was this animosity that I barely recognized its violence. Some days later, I told the story in passing to my physical therapist while she massaged my leg, and she reported the incident to the school. This led to a tense meeting with the school administration where they offered their full assurance that such incidents would not happen again. The teacher in question never apologized for their behavior and never mentioned it to me again. Over time, I began to wonder how and whether I was accepted by the town's less overtly intolerant. During a meeting of an afterschool club, on the eve of the Iraq War, our faculty adviser referred to Arabs as "camel humpers" and remarked that the desert of Iraq should be "turned into glass" by a nuclear explosion. I wondered why they did not seem to factor me in among those they hated. It was as if gaining their acceptance meant accepting the literal obliteration of a part of myself. Only much later did I understand my inability to confront the way my teacher targeted me as a sign of my own complicity in this process of obliteration.

During my high school career in Sidney from 2001 to 2005, when authorities so heavily foregrounded Arab identity, George W. Bush performed the role of the wartime president as swaggering cowboy. It was difficult to fully embrace the western movie then, in part because of how the rhetoric of this nation's leadership encouraged a view of the Arab as the new enemy on the frontier. Many of my high school peers, including my late best friend, enlisted in the wars in Afghanistan and Iraq. It was difficult not to imagine his rifle pointed at someone like me as easily as John Wayne would target a Comanche on the horizon. However, the longer I stayed out of Sidney, moving between college on the East Coast and graduate school on the West Coast, the more the West became an ever more abstract, largely cinematic idea. During this time, I immersed myself in what I categorize as border westerns, the kind of films that make up the rest of this chapter. Through such a cinematic lens, I could see the disquieting lies about the border and migrants presented in political discourse and mingled with truths about their suffering.

Although I saw myself somewhat in these films about migration and disillusionment, it was not until 2017 that I again fully identified with a western. Chinese filmmaker Chloé Zhao's 2017 *The Rider* is set on the Pine Ridge Indian Reservation in South Dakota and focuses on a young rodeo star who suffers a traumatic injury after falling off his horse. Brain damage creates a nonvisible disability that keeps him from realizing his rodeo dreams. Zhao's camera, like that of Sturges in *The Magnificent Seven*, centers on the clenched hand of a cowboy. The image emulates how the cowboy's world narrows, from the vast and familiar expanses of the prairie to the unrecognizable geography of his injured body. As mentioned, my own cerebral palsy atrophies the right side of my body and warps the fingers of my right hand. A western film again pushed me to see my own non-normative body, which I often disassociate from, covering it up with braces in public. In *The Rider*, the hero comes to see that his changing body offers him new routes for empathy to connect with his fellow cowboys. The film ends with the character holding the hands of a quadriplegic friend and former rodeo rider, pantomiming being his horse. Holding each other, the injured men close their eyes and ride together on some imagined prairie. Zhao thus positions the West as a place of connection to one's self and to others who exist on the edges.

In a personal interview, Zhao noted that as a Chinese person raised abroad, she does not understand herself as rooted and has "a liquid sense of identity" (Zhao 2018). She had come to feel "in between worlds," and thought of her filmmaking as an opportunity to find a sense of belonging (ibid.). She saw in the West a place where one could crystallize the very instability of her self. This in-betweenness, this liminality is key for exploring how such a set storytelling genre can speak to those whose stories are often unheard. In westerns by filmmakers like Sturges and

Zhao, I found the many fissures of my identity that lie across cultures, somewhere between privilege and disempowerment. In such tales, the western becomes a cry not by the strong but by the weak, the wounded, and the different. Through such films and the border westerns discussed in this chapter, we can glimpse the stains of suffering that emerge out of beautiful landscapes.

So, in learning to love the western, have I become a cowboy?

Unfortunately, as I have never quite fit convincingly in a Stetson hat, I cannot claim such a mantle. However, through cowboy tales, I have been made more aware and accepting of the wounds with which I ride.

When Texas Stands in for Iraq: Introducing the Border Western and Its Ever-Shifting Boundaries

In the opening stages of the War on Terror, President George W. Bush configured the conflict in terms of the western—less as an abstract transnational conflict and more as a metaphorical showdown between the sheriff George W. Bush and the outlaw Osama bin Laden. On September 17, 2001, responding to a reporter's question about whether he wanted the Al Qaeda leader dead, Bush responded, "I want justice. And there's an old poster out West, I recall, that says 'Wanted: Dead or Alive'" ("Bush: Bin Laden" 2001). Bush spoke in the present tense, as though the West that he referenced still existed, its values well suited to the complexities of the contemporary political landscape. Moreover, the president seemed to want to transform himself into a mythic hero, operating with as clear and stark a moral code as a western gunslinger who would save the terrorized town that was post-9/11 America. Bush employed the language of genre to frame his administration's acts, placing the far-reaching executive and legislative response to the attacks in a "larger mythic narrative" (Jameson 1995, 3).

Cultural commentator Tom Engelhardt finds that Bush's remarks referencing the "Wanted" poster typify an establishment shaped by such pop cultural visions. Previous presidents, most notably Ronald Reagan, employed the western myths of Hollywood in both their language and their self-fashioning. However, Bush and his neoconservative peers never had direct combat experience. Engelhardt suggests that this allowed Bush and many within his administration to remain "screen warriors," who "never left the confines of those movie theaters where American war was glorious, our military men always bravely patrolling the frontier, and the Indians, or their modern equivalent, always fell before our might" (Engelhardt 2007, 313). This chapter will consider visions of a modern-day frontier shaped by a post-9/11 discourse and law—the U.S.-Mexico border—as well as the modern equivalent to the American Indian of the western—the Mexican migrant. Like Engelhardt, I see such images in film as valorizing and reinforcing contemporary political forms; I am also attuned to the counternarratives such genre films might offer.

These ambivalent stories about the frontier were created in decades when the border was often marked as a national vulnerability by the executive branch. These post-9/11 films offer a vantage from which to critique the western-infused language of not only George W. Bush but also his successor Donald Trump, who highlighted menaces at the border both in his campaigns and during his time in office. When announcing his candidacy in 2015, he claimed, "When Mexico sends its people, they're not sending their best. . . . They're sending people that have lots of problems, and they're bringing those problems with us. They're bringing drugs. They're bringing crime. They're rapists" (Trump 2015). In the same speech, he suggested that such migrants had ties to terrorism, declaring, "It's coming from more than Mexico. It's coming from all over South and Latin America, and it's coming probably—probably—from the Middle East" (ibid.). His commentary helps frame a core motif of the border western, where the drone-surveyed U.S.-Mexico border is conflated with the drone-surveyed battlefields of Iraq. As a candidate and echoing the rhetorical strategies of his predecessors, Trump instrumentalized the trauma of 9/11 and the threat of terrorism to strengthen his claim about the ongoing crisis at the border and the implicit need for a strong executive to control it.

Trump's always-bombastic rhetoric around the border also reinforces how cultural traumas, be they around attacks or states of emergency, are narrative forms. In 2018 and 2019, Trump declared national emergencies in response to caravans of migrants heading to the Mexican border from Central America. In contrast to the Bush-era claims about Iraq's weapons of mass destruction, which were often uncritically supported by news organizations whose journalists were embedded with the military, Trump's claims were often treated as suspect by the mainstream American news media. In a fact check about his speech on the caravans, the Associated Press declared, "He's wrong" (Yen and Long 2018). However, such claims continued to electrify Trump's base. The mixed success of Trump's storytelling about the border highlights how cultural traumas are socially mediated attributions, to use Jeffrey Alexander's formulation discussed in chapter 1, that can resonate differently across a culture.

As a rhetorical mode that might validate state violence by rendering it spectacular, the border western genre provokes the spectator to reckon with his or her own attraction to, or even collusion with, the kind of spectacle proposed by leaders such as Trump, where the border is a threatening site and those who cross it are criminals. Border westerns are an undertheorized and underexamined form of storytelling that emerged after 9/11. The three films that compose the core of this chapter—Denis Villeneuve's *Sicario* (2015), Tommy Lee Jones's *The Three Burials of Melquiades Estrada* (2005), and Ridley Scott's *The Counselor* (2013)—visualize and critique a dehumanizing public discourse. They are all deeply self-reflexive, meditating upon the disquieting allure of genre and how its viscerally satiating qualities might be both commented upon and challenged. Border westerns can use the violent form of genre as a vital critical lens through which suffering might be confronted and a "revolutionary" violence conceived—a lens defined by a greater humanity because it reckons with our own proclivity toward violence.

Although media scholar Camilla Fojas has previously identified the conventions of recent westerns about the borderlands, my conception of the border western stresses its role as an aesthetic response to the War on Terror and the ensuing transformations in immigration policy.[1] It is a particular storytelling form that has emerged in the last two decades. Delineating this subgenre may seem unnecessary, in part because of the western genre's root preoccupation with the frontier. Constraining our focus geographically, however, permits a more incisive exploration of such films' representations of contemporary political discourses surrounding the U.S.-Mexico border space. My analysis of the border western also emphasizes the formal features of often generically unstable films that both visually and figuratively bring the shadows of noir to the sweeping landscapes of the western.

Noir (the conventions of which will be further defined and explored in the next chapter) is traditionally understood as a storytelling type antithetical to the western in both theme and style. While classic westerns ostensibly represent the heroic settling of the frontier during the nineteenth century, noir is a despair-laden genre that represents a claustrophobic modern city. Westerns typically take place in vast, sunlit terrain while noir films often inhabit cramped, dark spaces. In the latter genre, shadows on the exterior of the world reflect the psychological darkness of its broken heroes. By exploring the merging of divergent genres in border westerns, we can sense how they articulate a metalevel anxiety regarding the ability of such storytelling modes to engage the viewer with the political Other—in this case, the Mexican migrant—and insist that audiences contemplate their own complicity and pleasure in that subject's suffering.

The disquieting self-reflection encouraged by the border western is facilitated through various kinds of slippage. These films often visualize a geographical muddling between the Southwest and other global sites of violence and terror that have been a motif in post-9/11 political discourse. *Sicario* opens with an overtitle stating, "The word Sicario comes from the zealots of Jerusalem."[2] Then these explanatory words appear: "Killers who hunted the Romans who invaded their homeland." Before introducing the setting, the film gestures to a historical vision of the Middle East, just as other border westerns might nod to today's Israeli-Palestinian conflict.[3] Finally, the last line appears: "In Mexico, *Sicario* means *hitman*." The opening then fades to an establishing shot of Chandler, Arizona, overtaken by a SWAT team sneaking toward a suburban home. Through this brief evocation, the film links the United States to the Roman Empire, an invading force whose presence inspires violent resistance. The Mexican cartel members are positioned as radical combatants fighting imperial power. Calling upon a kind of prototypical Zionism, the film troubles the delineation of the Mexican hit man as a kind of criminal outlaw without an agenda. The overtitles frame such border violence as inherently political, a response to an American superpower's invasion of its southern neighbor. *Sicario* thus establishes that the setting's violence needs to be understood within the broader context of U.S. wartime endeavors.

When performing this correlation of geographies, viral ads for *The Counselor* (2013) formally and covertly transpose the U.S.-Mexico border setting to the Middle Eastern site of America's war, capturing the uncanny sense of estrangement when the two locations become conflated. The videos feature mundane conversations among the film's central characters interrupted by the radio chatter of the police and aerial footage from drones surveying the scenes. The coordinates presented in the drone view of a Texas highway correspond not to the film's border setting but to the very center of Iraq. Such geographic dislocation makes clear that the state connects the border space of *The Counselor* with the Middle East.

Notably, this cartographic play is hidden as an Easter egg in *The Counselor* ads, legible only to geographically savvy viewers or those (like me) who have the urge to uncover any secret meanings that lurk within scenes. Do these coordinates gesture to the limits of the public's understanding (or willingness to face) the true symbolic meaning of the post-9/11 border? Do the filmmakers believe that few will bother to uncover the significance of that particular latitude and longitude, instead unquestioningly accepting the drone footage? The advertisement clearly frames its intent to critique the viewers' allegiance by taking the vantage point of the state's distancing drone eye; however, the full force of its indictment only becomes apparent if we happen to uncover the hidden meaning. Once the visible yet initially illegible Texas/Iraq conflation is revealed, the ad makes the critical project of all post-9/11 border westerns fully apparent. These films push us to question our ignorance and even tacit support of the policies that make those inhabiting the border resemble enemies in the Iraq War—not subjects to be empathized with but rather objects to be surveyed, tracked, and then potentially destroyed.

This is perhaps why, given the profound dehumanization of brown communities from the Middle East and Latin America in the War on Terror, the films are permeated with death in a way that is even more stark, terrifying, and extreme than the violence of classical westerns. Traditionally, the western genre has been conceived as an epic form devoted to depicting the founding of the American West upon the silver screen. André Bazin described the genre's hero as resembling "our knight [who] must now pass through a series of fabulous trials" (Bazin 1971, 143–44). The post-9/11 border westerns present knights in the form of cowboys and law enforcement actors who begin to question their own mythic stories—who realize that their triumph on the frontier necessitates the death of others. In an essay discussing key texts of the border western, Camilla Fojas further contextualizes the shift toward explorations of mortality. Due to increased militarization of the space, "the borderlands, which are typically associated with risk, are now associated more often with death" (Fojas 2011, 97).

Just as border westerns depart from the western genre in how they both visualize and weaken the thin line between living and dying at the border, given the perceived disposability of migrant populations, they also destabilize geographic, political, and generic lines. Through such blurring—wherein the space resembles the front line of the War on Terror, its inhabitants akin to enemy combatants and disposable subjects who die spectacular deaths—the films blend the archetypes of the western genre with the shadowy form of film noir. The border western thus hangs on the edge between America's dream of itself and its nightmare. The films under review all perceive the western with what we might call a kind of "noir skepticism," considering the genre of John Wayne and Gary Cooper at an ironic remove. In doing so, they position the Western myth as inherently kitsch; its dangerous malleability comes from its image as an innocuous, highly commodified vision of American ideals and history.

Sicario performs the cross-genre commentary emblematic of the border western to underline how the ostensibly moral and principled form of the western is made suspect and estranged within a noir universe. It presents the FBI Agent Kate Macer (Emily Blunt), who loses faith in the moral righteousness of the United States' mission on the border. When she questions whether her interagency drug task force operates within the law's boundaries, her superior answers, in a phrase that might very well be a mission statement for the border western more generally, "The boundary's been moved." One shot in particular, in which Macer visits the Wild Pony Bar with her partner, dissolves the boundaries between seemingly antithetical genres, bringing noir and the western together in a critical dialogue. She is bathed in purple neon light as the silhouette of a stallion-riding cowboy looms in the background. In disbelief, Macer later asks her partner, "Where have you taken me? What is this place? . . . It's full of cowboys!"

Later, a key prop further places Macer in the logic of the western while establishing that she holds the status not of the classic hero but of the villain. She smokes a cigarette after being set up by her peers and attacked by a corrupt policeman that she met at the Wild Pony Bar. A cut-in on her hands shows a pack of Indian Creek cigarettes, whose box features the profile of a Native American chief. The fictional brand suggests the border western's interest in interrogating and reframing our view of the traditional enemies of the frontier space. Macer resembles the Native American in the western, at once a threatening witness to the state's extralegal violence and a potential object of that violence. More often in these films, however, the Mexican—as migrant or drug cartel member—fulfills the Native American role. Film scholar A. J. Prats writes that the classical western genre is distinct in that it "must produce an Other whose destruction is not only assured but justified," allowing for the forgetting of indigenous genocide (Prats 2002, 2, 14–15).[4] While border westerns may similarly produce and destroy the Other, they crucially question whether such destruction is justified.

Drones over the Frontier:
Sicario and the Panopticon Border

Understanding the attitude of westerns toward the borderlands is crucial for comprehending the interrelation of trauma, genre, and the law, since few spaces were as affected on either a discursive or a political level following the 9/11 attacks. Border scholar Tony Payan notes that "no other geographical area of the country underwent the intensive and extensive changes that the U.S.-Mexico border did" (Payan 2006, 100). The years following 9/11 saw a rise in border militarization as well as interior enforcement. A security fact sheet from the 2002 federal budget stated, "The massive flow of people and goods across our borders helps drive our economy, but can also serve as a conduit for terrorists" ("Securing America's Borders" 2002). Somewhat irrationally, as Payan finds, the border has often been cited as a central reason for the attacks and an ever-present vulnerability, so that the state of the border "represented a national security threat" (Payan 2006, 94). Emblematic of this fear-filled rhetoric, and despite all evidence to the contrary, U.S. Representative Sue Myrick claimed in 2005 that "terror was spilling across the border" (qtd. in ibid., 2). More recently, U.S. Congressman Duncan Hunter disseminated unfounded reports that "at least ten ISIS fighters" were caught by Border Patrol agents while moving in from Mexico (qtd. in Parkinson 2014). Meanwhile, President Trump declared in a press conference, "We have terrorists coming through the southern border because they find that's probably the easiest place to come through. They drive right in and they make a left" (Trump 2019). The aftermath of the attacks both exposed and exacerbated the marginalized position of the undocumented migrant, who was conflated with the wartime enemy. Reflecting upon the shifting conceptions of the Mexican worker, an El Paso community organizer found that "[f]rom [9/11] on everyone who crossed the border was a potential threat" (qtd. in Jones 2012, 109).

Within this paranoid climate, policy changes transformed the border into a hyper-surveyed space akin to a post-9/11 war zone. As mentioned, border westerns merge the home front and the war front, thematizing the omnipresence of police surveillance. In these films, the state's sight acts as a kind of haunting phantom over the border. They emblematize Tony Payan's view that the policy related to the War on Drugs and the War on Terror has created a "Panopticon Border": "[T]he U.S. government is waging a war to surveil and control all border crossers" (Payan 2006, 114). The Panopticon, a prison model first proposed by Jeremy Bentham in the eighteenth century and later theorized by Michel Foucault, imagines a prison wherein the jailers have a constant, yet unverifiable view of their prisoners. Saturated with distancing drone imagery and featuring an extensive sequence of interrogation, where waterboarding is heavily implied, *Sicario* contemplates a border space where the controversial policies that have marked America's foreign wars come home, where the border has become a Panopticon guarded by the military. What, *Sicario* asks, are the costs and impacts of such an effort to transform the border into a figurative Guantánamo?

Villeneuve frames the jailer's perspective throughout the film, while acknowledging a fraught possibility to empathize with the prisoner. A tense scene at a U.S.-Mexico border crossing is presented from the paranoid point of view of the agent Macer and her American colleagues. They have been sent to Juarez to extradite a drug cartel leader to the United States, so that they can question him using enhanced interrogation techniques. The scene's momentum builds as the government's vehicles move quickly out of Juarez, until a lengthy pause at the border as Macer and her team are trapped between other cars coming in from Mexico. The camera's position in the car emphasizes Macer's claustrophobic perspective. Sharing the road with emigrants, the heroine gazes out at row upon row of Mexican profiles. She is looking for cartel members who may be seeking to rescue their crime boss, though every surrounding Mexican person seems to be a threat. Performing a kind of racial profiling in this border-crossing sequence with an ironic wink via its composition, the film pushes audiences to adopt a suspicious perspective on the agents of the state.

Sicario not only has the viewer experience the state's suspicion toward the migrant but also encourages them to inhabit the state's deadening distance vis-à-vis its play with differing surveillance filters. It later presents a magisterial set piece that cycles through surveillance footage from the FBI's night vision, the army's infrared, and the CIA's drone view. This final action sequence features Macer, along with CIA agents and soldiers, clandestinely crossing into Mexico at night using the drug cartel's tunnels. The disorienting scene creates a visceral appreciation of the kind of spectacular distance that reduces humans on the border to little more than specks and blurs.

The sequence begins by establishing that the U.S. government agents monitor their surroundings and each other with surveillance technologies—every gaze is paranoid and detached. Before Macer and her peers' trek into the tunnels, the camera faces the heroine in a mid-shot through the military's infrared filter, so that she visually resembles a gray form, as if hollowed out by her experience, estranged from her own country's political regime (Fig. 2.1). The soldiers in front of Macer then engage the cartel members in an offscreen firefight. When one of the soldiers approaches the tunnel, the film presents a highly abstracted view through his night vision goggles, drained of color and marked by obscuring grain. Before the infrared camera arrives at a dead body killed in the exchange of fire, the camera pans down to traces of footsteps on the ground, confirming the capacity of the surveillance state to achieve a superhuman vision. When it finally encounters the corpse, the face of the dead cartel member is entirely obscured in the white light of his fading body heat, underscoring the material erasure of the state's penetrating sight. *Sicario* thus shows an awareness of what (and who) is lost in this spectacular, panoptic vision of the border.

The violence of the border is compared to a frivolous spectacle when a soldier asks Macer, "You like fireworks? Want to see something cool?" He then takes her to the rooftop of a military base adjacent to Juarez; from there, the cartel violence is abstracted and reduced to a sequence of distant explosions. The jailors see only plays of fire and light, detached from any human impact in a way that seems to mirror the journalistic myopia referenced in the film. After the shootout in broad daylight at the border crossing, one agent worries that the violence will provoke nationwide media scrutiny and appear "on the front page of every newspaper in America." A wizened colleague replies, "It won't even make the papers in El Paso," offering a commentary on how neither the general

Figure 2.1. The disillusioned FBI agent seen through infrared—drained and hollowed out. *Sicario*.

public nor the media are willing to acknowledge the human suffering of the War on Drugs, to say nothing of their potential complicity within it.

Villeneuve often ends his action sequences, and in this case ends his entire film, by lingering upon the sight of Mexican victims, subjects seen as disposable. For instance, the border-crossing scene ends with a pan away from the moving federal government vehicles to the dead cartel member on the road. The camera then moves past the body to the Mexicans in their cars, looking on in silence. Visually linking the corpse with the concerned passersby, the film suggests that all Mexican subjects in this space might intimately understand the threat of this kind of death.

The Three Burials of Melquiades Estrada: Realizing the Impossible Subject's Humanity

Whereas *Sicario* only presents the fear-infused perspective of everyday Mexicans in brief, fleeting sequences, Tommy Lee Jones's *The Three Burials of Melquiades Estrada* more fully represents their point of view. Undocumented migrants in the film resemble what historian Mae M. Ngai identifies as an impossible subject—one stripped of all rights who exists within a legal limbo where his immigration status denies his humanity. Jones's film expresses the psychological toll of such a status. Against the fearful discourse surrounding immigration after 9/11, which often conflated the Mexican and the terrorist, *Three Burials* also exposes the discursive process by which the undocumented migrant is transformed into a potential threat.

Three Burials tells of ranch hand Pete's (Tommy Lee Jones) quixotic quest to bury his friend Melquiades (Julio Cesar Cedillo) back in Mexico after he was killed in Texas by a Border Patrol agent. Reminiscent of *Sicario*'s opening sequence, *Three Burials*' first scene following the opening credits presents Melquiades as a corpse. In so doing, the film gestures to how undocumented migrants are envisioned as dehumanized archetypes, known in the public discourse as "illegal immigrants" (Fig. 2.2). Filmed upside-down in the center of the frame, the dead worker appears on a metal slab in the county morgue. His milky eyes are turned away from the camera, rendering it difficult to perceive this figure on fully human terms. The inverted view of Melquiades points to a topsy-turvy world where such immigrants are viewed as fodder for the rifles of Border Patrol and agents from analogous law enforcement agencies. The edge of the film's sociopolitical commentary is further sharpened by the shot's color scheme. The blue hue of the scene, the dried red blood, and the dead man's stained white shirt sardonically echo the colors of the American flag. *Three Burials* thus issues its mission statement: to probe the border, where American ideals appear as inverted and skewed as this camera's initial view.

In this grisly image, *Three Burials* creates a visual metaphor for the disenfranchised condition of the illegal alien as described by Ngai—a "social reality and a legal impossibility—a subject barred from citizenship and without rights" (Ngai 2004, 4). Ngai argues that these impossible subjects linger in a limbo where their immigration status deprives them of not only their rights but also their very ability to be perceived as fully human. Since 9/11, Tanya Golash-Boza comments, a "heightened, yet unsuccessful frenzy to find dangerous people has created a climate of fear in immigrant communities across the United States" (Golash-Boza 2012, 8). Polls of Californians in 2010 found that a larger percentage of Hispanics than Arab Americans felt "less secure" after the attacks and attributed their decreased wages to 9/11 (Tirman 2006). Jones's film, with its nightmarish mise-en-scène against a more grounded depiction of Melquiades's alienation while alive, structures a macrolevel critique of border policy within a microlevel exploration of the anguish caused by societal and legal stigmatization.

The film evokes the feeling of being formally ostracized in scenes that situate Melquiades against the mass media. Ngai explains that the impossible subject is a person who, according to the state, "cannot be and [is] a problem that cannot be solved," antithetical to a migration

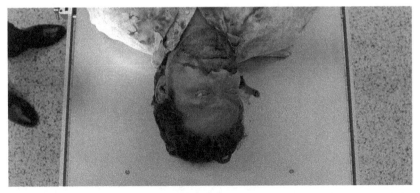

Figure 2.2. The corpse of an undocumented Mexican echoes the colors of the American flag: a bloody red, white, and blue. *The Three Burials of Melquiades Estrada.*

system defined by citizenship status (2004, 5). These individuals have been governed by immigration law, "where sovereignty, not the Constitution, ruled" (ibid., 90). Melquiades's own visible discomfort with urban spaces, which he expresses to the seemingly oblivious Pete when describing the threat of "La Migra" (U.S. Immigration and Customs Enforcement), highlights the toll of this demarcation of difference: the attention of the U.S. government represents, at best, the possibility of expulsion.

Melquiades's fractured psyche, cracked by fear and the label of difference, is revealed when he wanders alone toward a bank of televisions sitting in an electronics store's display window. The plasma screens present the blurred image of the finish line of a NASCAR race track, forming the dark visual pun that Melquiades is near his own finish line. His reflection in the glass shows a man in shadow. It appears as though Melquiades confronts his doppelganger, a silhouette that seems to radiate out of the television (Fig. 2.3). In this moment of literal reflection, we see Melquiades perceive himself as Other, an undifferentiated impression, less a human than a phantom that lingers within the media.

The scene poignantly articulates Melquiades's feeling of estrangement, even as its visual joke foreshadows his literal death. The scene ends with a shot of Melquiades coming out of his reverie when Pete sneaks up beside him to exclaim, "Could I see some photo ID, sir?," thereby situating the scene within a cultural context where Border Patrol could ask for such material based on nothing more than bias, on limited articulable facts. The ghostlike impossible subject is haunted by the state, whose very presence keeps him in a psychic and literal limbo.

Figure 2.3. Melquiades confronts his reflection in TV screens, less a human than a phantom that lingers within the media. *The Three Burials of Melquiades Estrada.*

To borrow Foucault's terms, "Visibility is a trap" for Melquiades (Foucault 1977, 200). The film shows how his white friend begins to empathize with the dead Mexican, coming to share his feeling of claustrophobia in a South Texas town. When Pete realizes that the local authorities will not investigate the circumstances of Melquiades's death, he no longer jokes about his friend's susceptibility to state scrutiny and sees the setting anew. Having decided to abduct Melquiades's killer, Mike (Barry Pepper), he sits waiting in front of the patrolman's home. The steel fences in the scene—when a nearby neighbor chains up her dog and then in the point-of-view shot where the Border Patrol officer's vehicle arrives—underline how Pete now perceives the American town as a stifling prison. Calling to mind the security fences across the U.S.-Mexico border, the scene shows Pete's visceral understanding of his friend's alienation. He comes to inhabit the subject position of those affected by what Gilberto Rosas describes as "policeability," which labels people such as Melquiades as "worthy of dying in the treacherous geographies of the border, or subject to militarized policing, or vigilante action, or daily forms of surveillance" (Rosas 2006, 413). With the new perspective of a policable subject, the Texan no longer sees a life within the United States as tenable.

The film continues to play with shifts in subject position to explore the Border Patrol officer's painful process of gaining compassion and empathy toward those made Other in the political discourse. In the early moments of the film, Mike treats the Mexican migrants brutally and is visually linked to a predatory hawk flying over the frontier. Throughout his abduction, Mike is equated with Melquiades's corpse, forced underground with the body and often occupying the same visual plane in the frame. Faced with the prospect of his own demise, Mike also begins to rot, bemoaning his disenfranchised status. The correspondences between Mike and the dead Melquiades continue to grow—both are made to swallow antifreeze by an increasingly deranged Pete; with Mike developing gangrene on his foot after a snake bite, the film evokes the despairing weakness of the migrant forced to navigate a treacherous border.[5]

Ultimately, the film renders Mike's increasing sense of impotence when Pete forces him to traverse the Rio Grande, the natural border between the United States and Mexico. Here, the film correlates Mike with a beast, just as it did Melquiades when confusing his presence with that of a coyote earlier in the narrative. Mike's screams and profanities are crucial because they linguistically mark the struggling person as American. In an essay titled "Humanity, Rationality, and Sentimentality," Richard Rorty writes how empathy for victimized others is constructed only when their story of suffering shows listeners how they are "people like us" (1993, 113). This scene operates in a parallel way: the disempowered individual garbed in the clothes of his Mexican victim but screaming in English makes comprehensible the plight of migrants whose foreign speech can mark them as insurmountably different. Mike tries to make a break for it at the river; however, his fight for independence is short-lived, as Pete easily catches him with his lasso, like a stubborn calf wandering away from the herd (Fig. 2.4). The camera first jerkily follows Mike's angry stumbling, then glides with Pete's horse in a way that signals the former's relinquishing of all power as he is dragged into the Rio Grande. As he is submerged, his cries grow distorted, resembling the bleats of an animal. The very incomprehensibility of his voice explains why Pete is so impassive to his charge's cry for help—in this scene at least, he does not see Mike as human. The perpetrator and victim subject positions have been inverted: now the grieving ranch hand operates with Mike's former detachment and the patrolman tacitly sympathizes with the dead man. The film confirms this with the first shot of the following sequence. Mike slumps across his horse, exactly echoing how Melquiades slumped across his donkey; the aggressor and the aggrieved have become one.

The scene in which the patrolman speaks to Melquiades at his final resting place conveys a dual recognition: Mike acknowledges both the humanity of his victim, the impossible subject, and his own role as perpetrator. The painful lucidity in the murderer's speech is denoted by the harsh lighting as he buries Melquiades for a final time, unlike the overwhelming darkness that surrounded the patrolman when he excavated the body in Texas. Forced onto his knees under the shade of an oak tree

Figure 2.4. A border patrol agent experiences the Other's plight when lassoed like cattle. *The Three Burials of Melquiades Estrada.*

where the Polaroid of Melquiades and his supposed family sits, Mike appears about to be executed. Whatever last bit of resistance he has is nullified when Pete then fires his gun. Through the use of slow motion, time becomes traumatically elastic, mirroring the patrolman's purgatory in this moment—trapped by his disempowerment as well as his own resistance to admitting guilt. The threat of death propels an apology as Mike's attention shifts from his present victimizer to his past victim. Through tears, he exclaims, "I'm sorry! I swear to God, I'm sorry . . . I did not mean to kill him." For the first time in the film, Mike refers to the migrant by name. With Pete off screen, Mike begins to speak directly to Melquiades, saying, "I didn't want it to happen. It hurts me, I regret it every single day. Forgive me. Forgive me, Melquiades."

Golash-Boza proposes that legal scholars pursue a "human rights analysis . . . to calculate the human, and not simply economic, costs of immigration policy" (2012, 4). Via the timeless tropes of the genre form, the border western *Three Burials* begins to perform such an analysis, demonstrating how crucial the aesthetic can be for coming to grips with the human impact of sometimes abstract political decrees. Waking up to the gentle prodding of Pete's foot, Mike expresses surprise that the ranch hand will not be killing him. Pete replies, "You can keep the horse, son," a gesture of goodwill that mirrors Melquiades's bequeathing of the animal to Pete. As Pete rides off into the morning sun in the film's retooling of a classic western trope, Mike yells, "You gonna be all right?"

The film ends on a moment of empathy, thereby illustrating that the journey has brought Mike to perceive the humanity of his victim, the impossible subject, and his victimizer. These roles are not mutually distinct. *The Three Burials of Melquiades Estrada* closes with a man accepting a dissensus, what philosopher Jacques Rancière calls a "putting [of] two worlds into one," the interweaving of perpetrator and victim (Rancière 2004, 304). The final, quiet moments thus testify to the possibility of a human rights analysis within the border western genre—the very violent form, where pleasure coexists with pain, encourages the spectator to understand his own complicity while also revealing his capacity for compassion.

The Noir Border in *The Counselor*: Where Economics Trumps Humanity

Three Burials, with its portrayal of emerging empathy, is counterbalanced by Ridley Scott's 2013 *The Counselor*, written by Cormac McCarthy.[6] If Jones's film tries to uncover the human lost within the discourse around a border tinged by post-9/11 fear and policy, *The Counselor*, infused with the generic tropes of noir, considers the era's inherent inhumanity. It too turns its gaze upon the viewer, forcing him to meditate upon his own depravity. Although *The Counselor* resembles both *Sicario* and *Three Burials* in its deep concern with the illuminating potential of genre, Scott's film touches the limits of the violent form's ability to enlighten. On a thematic level, while *Three Burials* examines the struggles of individuals crossing the border, *The Counselor* quickly evinces an overriding concern with the drug economy, which implicates those living far north of the Rio Grande. In this it resembles *Sicario*, which also explicitly positions American desire as a root cause of the drug trade and the War on Drugs.

The initial scenes of *The Counselor* present a surprising image of tranquility. The establishing shot depicts a traffic sign denoting that Juarez, Mexico, is straight ahead. Behind the sign lie a row of modern wind turbines, silently rotating. These elements undermine conceptions of the border space as wild; here, man has cleanly harnessed the energies of the environment. The camera disrupts this harmonious representation by jerking quickly to follow a motorcycle that races by and reveals another road sign, for El Paso, Texas. The very intensity of the camera pan echoes the narrative of conflict used by the American media when presenting the border space.

The film returns to the border environment during its opening credits, but this time the wind turbines have been replaced by cheetahs roaming the landscape, while the film's larger-than-life femme fatale, Malkina (Cameron Diaz), rides along on a horse, personifying the fusion of noir and the western (Fig. 2.5). Presenting the U.S.-Mexico border through this genre filter, the film focuses on discourses related to the War

Figure 2.5. A femme fatale rides the frontier, personifying a world where noir and the western are fused. *The Counselor.*

on Terror and the War on Drugs and how they sculpt the borderlands into a mythic space, a bricolage of the fears that permeate contemporary public debates.

A sequence directly following the opening credits also highlights how this cinematic representation of the border is complicated by the economics of the drug trade and is not expressly interested in the issue of migration. Tracking a shipment of drugs through an established point of entry, the sequence features a moment when the traffickers come upon a group of migrants wandering through the desert. The camera begins the scene first atop and then within the truck, aligned with the drug traffickers, before cutting to a wide shot where migrants cross a desolate highway, trudging along in silence. As one migrant catches the driver's eye, the trafficker exclaims in Spanish: "Illegals! Welcome to the United States." His dozing passenger stirs only to wave his hand with indifference, reflecting the film's concern with the free movement of illegal commodities that flow with perverse ease through official channels.

The Counselor chronicles the downfall of a criminal lawyer, known only as "the counselor" (Michael Fassbender), who mistakenly believes he "can live in this world and be no part of it." In this heightened setting that mirrors the inflamed rhetoric surrounding the border space, where cheetahs roam wild and razor wire extends tautly, a noir feeling of claustrophobia and menace emerges. The border space reflects a broader economics of desire, and through a simultaneous embrace and parody of genre, particularly noir's titillation and the western's core violence, the film metaphorically frames our own allegiance to it. *The Counselor* ultimately delivers a nuanced sociopolitical critique, exposing a social myopia toward the suffering engendered by material wants.

Screenwriter Cormac McCarthy similarly treats the border space as a reflection of contemporary fears in his 1985 novel *Blood Meridian*. Although set in the post–Civil War era, *Blood Meridian* establishes the symbolic role of the border that McCarthy continues to explore in *The Counselor*. In an attack by the Comanche somewhere between Mexico and Texas, "up . . . rose a fabled horde of mounted lancers and archers bearing shields bedight with bits of broken mirror glass that cast a thousand unpieced suns against the eyes of their enemies" (McCarthy 1985, 55). That the menacing riders' accoutrements permit them to both reflect and blind the Americans signals that the border operates like a broken mirror for the broader culture: our fears are projected onto it and take on a glaring shimmer.

McCarthy's configuration of the border as a site imbued with national anxieties resonates with sociologist Peter Andreas's view that the border acts as a powerful discursive tool for the state to symbolically express its continued fight against perceived menaces. Andreas finds that "the border functions as a kind of political stage," offering both politicians and police a prime performative space (Andreas 2001, 9). Former United States secretary of homeland security Michael Chertoff seemingly confirmed this view, admitting that a proposed U.S.-Mexico security fence was not really a practical measure against illegal immigration but instead had "come to assume a certain kind of symbolic significance" (qtd. in Jones 2012, 51). For Andreas, actual results matter far less than the pantomime of an engaged state relentlessly fighting the War on Drugs and vigilantly fending off law-defying immigrants. Any police actions such as drug seizures are primarily "ritualistic performance" in which the state acts out its "moral resolve" (Andreas 2001, 11). *The Counselor* builds on McCarthy's earlier work, finding new enemies emerging in the border's reflections.

Within a theatrical scene in which the symbols of the United States are central, *The Counselor* suggests the conflation of post-9/11 political discourses, in which the War on Drugs exists as part of the War on Terror. When Reiner (Javier Bardem), an associate of the titular counselor, speaks of the dangerous entities that lurk within the underground economy, he points toward the perceived threats to the nation in a time when the indigenous Comanche have been replaced by Middle Eastern terrorists. After describing the nefarious killing methods of the cartels, he notes that their new penchant for beheading is inspired by practices "blown in from the East." When the counselor asks him whether he intends to do business with the Arabs, the usually smiling Reiner grows serious and replies, "They don't need your money," implying that the forces of terrorism are somehow uncontrollable, beyond the governing equation of a place defined exclusively by economic exchange. For Reiner, a master of this domain, such individuals are troublesome because they operate as a systemic challenge with which he cannot engage.

Director Ridley Scott's surreal and stifling imagery harnesses the sense of unease within the official rhetoric. The presence of cheetahs, animals outside their natural habitat, reflects an interplay of the various anxieties at work in this setting, where the Middle East and the Southwest converge to the point of being indistinguishable. The scene of a hit man running nearly invisible razor wire across a highway underscores how treacherous the borderlands can be for the individual. Writings on classic Hollywood films that have blended western and noir have noted how the iconic, expansive landscape of the West sometimes nullifies noir's central emphasis upon individual weakness. Considering 1953's *Shane* in the essay "The Film Noir and the Western," Edward Recchia finds that "despite the dark, realistic interior shots and the understated dialogue, the grandeur of the exterior shots gives the film's characters a heroic stature that clearly overwhelms any vestigial *film noir* techniques that the film inherited" (1996, 609). By introducing displaced African beasts and razor wire, the film cannily exposes the seemingly liberating potential of the untrammeled border as deception. The border zone represents not freedom but a deadly trap.

A billboard near the Rube Goldberg–like contraption shows the scene's intended meta-register, in the phrase "aye have faith" (Fig. 2.6). In a direct address to the spectators, the film asks the viewer to trust in the inevitability of brutal death. As surely as the audience can anticipate rolling heads, the scene also offers a comic articulation of the inherent, if invisible, corrosive aspect of our wants. The counselor's position as a court-appointed attorney on the state's payroll draws attention to the issue of the corruption within the economics that drive the Drug War. A DEA survey of informants noted that those interviewed found corruption to be of paramount importance for the success of a drug-running enterprise (Redmond 2013). There would of course be no need for corrupt officials if the American consumer did not have an appetite for illicit drugs. However, end users' understanding of their role in this economy is tremendously abstract, since most "live away from the border. They have no incentive to reach into their consciences and consider the motivations of the drug lords and dealers . . . They are not in the trenches

Figure 2.6. An assassin prepares his decapitating death trap under a billboard reading: "Aye have faith." The words act as a promise to the viewer that soon heads will roll. *The Counselor.*

of the border; they cannot see. They cannot care" (Payan 2006, 139). *The Counselor* probes the role of genre in allowing the viewer to see the consequences of participation.

Via parody, particularly in relation to the femme fatale Malkina—Reiner's girlfriend, who masterminds the theft of the cartel's drug money, a betrayal that leads to the ruin of all those associated with the counselor—the film presents our absurd blindness to our destructive needs and the suffering we inflict upon others.[7] Writing about what he dubs a mature western with noir elements, Clint Eastwood's 1992 *Unforgiven*, Recchia observes that the film's "personalities veer, sometimes to seeming heroic heights, sometimes to levels of bestiality, sometimes in both directions at once" (1996, 611). *The Counselor* is similarly dualistic, encouraging a delight that coexists with repulsion toward its characters. Malkina serves as an exaggerated example of the ravenous bent of the neo-noir femme fatale, an expert in extravagant consumption, interested only in her pleasure. In one scene, she immediately appraises the value of a diamond with her naked eye. The cheetah-print tattoo running down her bare back is visible, making her a literal embodiment of the carnivorous capitalism that governs the border.

Malkina most explicitly functions as a subversive caricature of the femme fatale when, ostensibly for Reiner's amusement, she proceeds to masturbate herself to climax on the windshield of his sports car. Her lover sits in the passenger seat, looking on in a state of concerned confusion. As expressed by her superior positioning in relation to him, her body filling much of the frame, she destabilizes her role as a gazed-upon object, aggressively turning her position as the center of scopophilic pleasure into an opportunity to command the spectator. The scene plays with the classic femme fatale's sexual power over the males of her universe. Such a theme is saliently summarized by Frank Krutnik when he writes that noir tales typically present "the woman as erotic object, as a glorified body of awesome excitation (which poses [a] danger of overwhelming male rationality)" (Krutnik 1991, 43). Malkina employs her carnal capital to captivate as well as frighten Reiner and his proxy behind the screen, the film viewer. In a study on the psychology of sadomasochism, Gary W. Taylor and Jane M. Ussher note that female practitioners are often drawn to role playing since it permits for "parodying [of] sexual relations considered as traditionally subjugating, oppressive, and exploitative of women" (2005, 5). Parody, then, is power. After reflecting upon the experience, the counselor asks a clearly troubled Reiner whether he thought Malkina knew what effect her ride upon the car would have, to which he categorically replies, "Jesus, Counselor, are you kidding? She knows everything."

These two scenes—the extended presentation of the hit man's trap and Malkina's confrontational gyrations upon the glass—show noir and the western to be forms that serve our base appetites and perpetrating instincts, thus revealing our own capacity for violence. The final scenes of the film, where the counselor reckons with the blowback of his deal gone awry, show the possibility of genre to frame unseen human suffering while highlighting a wider culpability.

A bitter visual joke in the montage following the cartel's abduction of the counselor's fiancée, Laura (Penélope Cruz), reiterates societal indifference to the violence at the border. As Laura walks through an airport parking lot toward a flight that will take her to Idaho and, presumably, safety, an SUV slowly follows her. The vehicle crosses various parking lines, mowing over any markers of separation that frame the scene, introducing the lawlessness of the U.S.-Mexico border into the seemingly insulated American setting. Chased down by one of the gang's thugs, Laura falls to the ground. She is pulled up from the pavement and pushed inside the vehicle. The camera's vantage point from inside shows the whimpering woman pressed down into the darkness that dominates the frame. A gang member forces Laura's head into a seat cushion; then, a match cut goes to white children plunging into a pool. Laura is forced downward in complete subordination; the children leap downward in pure joy. This tonal and spatial juxtaposition articulates a larger psychic distance for contemplating border violence. Following the image of children playing in water, the film cuts to their father busily preparing a barbecue, unaware of the cheetah that has just wandered into his backyard. Comfort both juts up against and is dependent upon the invisibility of the gruesome reality.

Returning to the global orientation of the border western, the most explicitly violent scene in the film occurs in London, far removed from the chaos of the borderlands. There, Westray (Brad Pitt), one of the counselor's business associates, is beheaded in the street—an act of overwhelming violence from which the perpetrator maintains a total remove. Beginning with the marked man leaving what appears to be a Bank of America branch location, its sign partly obscured by the framing, the film signals that the execution takes place in a financial center. The brightly lit urban setting, defined by a regimented blocking of various businesspeople walking at perpendicular angles, appears to be at odds with the disorderly border. The assassins are disguised as joggers, creating a quotidian appearance that seamlessly blends with the surroundings. Although the scene begins in mid-shot, close on Westray leaving the bank, it gradually pulls away until the subject is in a long shot. This distancing draws attention not only to the world of finance in which he is currently enmeshed but also to the character's diminishing power. He comes to be dominated by the urban landscape in ways that harken back to man's smallness within the Western wilderness.

Only when the target is hooked with the deadly bolito, a mechanical garret that slowly tightens around the neck, does the camera draw close again. The film's gaze returns to the victim to expose, even luxuriate upon, his deepening wound. Several wide shots show the distance between the screaming man on the brink of death and the various financiers looking on. As the mechanism closes, the victim lets out a momentary laugh, perhaps at the very absurdity of these bankers who do nothing, refusing to get blood on their hands. The bankers' unwillingness to help the victim of cartel violence gestures to how established financial institutions sustain the drug cartels. The banking class unquestioningly accepts blood money of the drug trade—the violence that produced their capital is kept willfully out of sight.

Malkina's presence in the scene underlines the institutional collusion within the drug economy. Before the victim's ill-fated walk through the streets, the femme fatale sits at a café terrace, conversing with the woman she has hired to steal his identification. A sign for the London Underground hovers over them in the background of the wide shot, gesturing toward how the financial centers' dark side remains largely invisible and underground thanks in part to the ubiquity of these institutions within quotidian life. After one of the joggers places the assassinated man's briefcase in Malkina's waiting car, she removes Westray's laptop and proceeds to make bank transfers to her account. As she does, the transferred millions appear on documents featuring official bank letterheads on the dead man's computer screen.[8]

There exists a troubling auto-critical valence in the bankers' sustained gaze upon the second, excruciatingly slow beheading in the film. The first beheading, by razor wire, is notable for the cleanliness of the execution. Contrasting with the clinical air of that desert scene, an outpouring of blood defines the killing in the London street. Several features in the staging lend it a meta-register that comments upon the violent pleasure audiences derive from genre films. A crowd of bankers form a semicircle around the dying man, thus creating a kind of a theater, and the space on the sidewalk acts as a stage. Although the crowd screams as the blood gushes from his neck, the film shows no member of this onscreen audience looking away. Their pristine clothes are never sullied by the outpouring of crimson. Placing the camera among the onlookers, their heads in the extreme foreground of the frame while the victim's lies trembling in the mid ground, makes the film's viewers resemble the bystanding bankers. Both are spurred on by a morbid desire to witness extreme gore. That the victim happens to be Brad Pitt, among the most famous of film actors, suggests that part of the joy of genre is that it can reduce cinematic idols to mere fodder for imaginative killing devices. When the film cuts from an extreme close-up to a wider overhead shot, the width of the framing approximately matches the distance blood spurts out of Pitt's neck; the genre form's very materiality is dictated by violence. While gore lends genre its formal pulse, the gesture toward the audience during the death scene underscores that noir and the western are built upon the spectator's insatiable desire to be moved by such corporeal rhythms.

Through an analogy with the snuff film that follows the beheading, *The Counselor* posits that genre contains, by its emphasis on such violence, an illuminating possibility for viewers to realize their own involvement in inhuman economies. Westray told the counselor about snuff films, recordings released by the drug cartels that depict actual killings. He notes that "the consumer of the product is essential to its production. You cannot watch without being an accessory to a murder."[9] The snuff film's position in the dialogue of the border western aligns it with genre cinema itself.

In Mexico City, the counselor, having failed to convince a drug lord to grant him clemency, receives a DVD slipped under his door. It is the snuff film of Laura's murder. The two shots where he unpacks the film and realizes its awful significance merit attention. A crumpled-up newspaper lies in the background of the cut-in featuring the disc, a tacit repudiation of traditional news outlets unable to effectively show readers the full costs of the Drug War and their complicity in the economies that drive it.[10] Perhaps, in line with *Sicario's* skepticism about news outlets' interest in border violence, its crumpled state also marks the continued apathy of the media. The counselor's face is reflected on the DVD, creating a correlation between the two. He turns the DVD around to see written in marker the Spanish salutation "Hola," an address that acknowledges that he takes part in a familiar dialogue with the criminal parties. It reminds him of his role in their violence and that he has become an accessory to his fiancée's murder. Cutting to a low-angle mid shot of the hero against a black background reinforces his sense of isolation as he begins to understand the nature of the film he has received. Such high-contrast imagery is representative of noir; in the words of film scholar David Cook, it often "parallel[s] the moral chaos of the world they represent" (1981, 405). The counselor has fallen into a trap of his own making.

Just before the shell-shocked counselor receives the DVD presenting Laura's murder, he walks through the "moral chaos" of the Mexico City streets. Initially framed as a small silhouette against the vertiginous façades of the dilapidated buildings, he comes upon a group of Mexicans protesting the War on Drugs. Beginning in 2006, President Felipe Calderón endeavored to quell border violence and shake the hold of the cartels upon the north, a policy that led to the deaths of many thousands of citizens.[11] The president sent nearly fifty thousand troops to the border, which, as Peter Watt and Roberto Zepeda point out in an analysis of the war's link to neoliberal economic policy, equaled the amount sent by the British government to Iraq (Watt and Zepeda 2012, 2). Calderón's underreported War on Drugs shares many hallmarks with a large-scale armed conflict, and in its single scene of protest *The Counselor* attempts to bring the war's often unseen victims into view.[12]

In the very first shot of the demonstration, where the lead speaker cries out against those who have kidnapped the city's youth, the blue-and-red police emergency lights shine behind her. Lending a personal edge to the disappearances, the briefly captivated counselor walks by a sign with the photo of a smiling young girl. Next to her image is the question "¿Me has visto?," or "Have you seen me?" These criticisms of Mexico's War on Drugs (launched by Calderón and continued by his successor Enrique Peña Nieto) are softened by the linguistic barrier: all the signage as well as the scene's dialogue is in Spanish, and thereby largely incomprehensible to the English-speaking counselor and the quintessential white and Anglophone film viewer for whom the protagonist again serves as a proxy. Although central within the film's soundtrack, the speaker's fiery words are further obscured by the mechanical distortion caused by her equipment. As she speaks of injustice and killings, the film cuts to a shot from behind the police who stand in shadow, their machine gun perched atop a jeep pointed toward the protesters. Coupled with the flashing red emergency light, it helps further define the vehicle as both military and police. Pervasive shadows strip the onscreen officers of any identity, unlike the evenly lit protesters whom the film tries to individualize, creating a visual discrepancy that marks the police as inhuman. This noir staging obscures the particularities of the demonstrators' grievances while clearly pitting the angry citizens against the state; it allows the viewer to understand heretofore unseen suffering even if he or she does not fully comprehend the language in which it is expressed and, by extension, the contextual details.

The counselor, rather than being moved to action or even to wider empathy, wanders away from the protesters just as they become animated and start to chant for justice. His brow furrowed in agitation, he pushes past the camera, the photo of the victimized girl becoming lost as the film moves to follow him. The film ends not with the image of the broken hero in his hotel room with the cartel's DVD or the later shot of Laura's corpse among trash heaps, but rather with Malkina, who offers some unnerving musings about the animalistic, self-interested nature of man and his tendency toward self-deception. In keeping with the empowered variant of the femme fatale within neo-noir who thrives as all around her die, she ends the film dining with her banker. She notes that one of her cheetahs still roams the border, indicating that the space stands as a place of menace. Talk of her animals leads her to wax poetic about the grace of a hunter and its purity of purpose, then to speak with venom toward humanity defined by a hypocritical division between its ideals and its actions, claiming that "nothing is crueler than a coward." The film overlays these words on a close-up of the banker looking vaguely unsettled by her inconvenient truths. He responds, "I think you've told me more than I wished to know." The film ends with Malkina happily dropping the subject and asking in the film's last line, "Shall we think about ordering? I'm famished." For both the participants in the drug trade and the consumers of such a film, hunger and desire outlast and perhaps overpower any concerns about morality.

Conclusion: Finding (and Exploiting) the Divine Violence in Genre

Political scientists Guadalupe Correa-Cabrera and José Nava write that in the 2000s the border had been affected by cartels to such a degree that in some regions of Mexico, "organized crime groups have effectively supplanted local as well as state governments, and at times even federal dependencies, as the sole purveyors of legitimate means of violence" (2013, 12–13). Issues that arise in studying the western genre echo issues articulated in Walter Benjamin's "Critique of Violence," which probes the tensions in a legal order founded upon, sustained, and legitimized by violence. He argues that the legal order is established through the peace ceremony that ends an armed conflict, which demonstrates that peace's correlative is war, and its law-preserving mechanisms rest on corporeal punishment (Benjamin 1986, 283, 286). The three films in this chapter, focused on a border where the state's executive agencies have sometimes been challenged and replaced, highlight the violence and the tenuousness of law-executing institutions. Both *Sicario* and *Three Burials* portray what Benjamin calls "the great criminal," a figure whose pursuit of individual justice positions him as a dangerous alternative to the established order (ibid., 281). At the same time, *Sicario* and *The Counselor* foreground the root similarity between the criminal and the state within an economics of desire.

Benjamin also envisions what he calls a "divine violence," an expiating or atoning violence that can destroy the boundaries set by the law (1986, 297). The living are then freed from the rule of law and can face their own guilt, which the legal system has allowed them to ignore. Within sometimes fleeting moments of empathy or of self-understanding, these films point to alternative worlds that might exist beyond a law-preserving or law-making violence. To be able to envision a saving violence, the subject must interrogate his own natural violence and perceive the limits of the established legal order as well as his complicity within it. Genre films are uniquely positioned to perform and reflect on atonement because they can at once luxuriate in violence and provoke a vital calculus about the ethical stakes of viewers' relationship to it and, particularly, the pleasure they derive from watching it.

Sicario finds a heroine forced to witness the law's amorality and whose position as a critical outsider threatens the state. She moves from uncritical to disillusioned, losing faith in the state institutions that she once upheld. She comes face to face with a system governed by the military and what Benjamin calls the "formless" power of the police, capable of acting extralegally in the name of security (1986, 287). Benjamin argues that such a system is inherently vulnerable (ibid., 287); any external violence contains the capacity to nullify existing legal conditions (ibid., 282).

After Macer uncovers how the state works to sustain a violent status quo by clandestinely supporting a single cartel, Alejandro (Benicio del Toro), a mercenary agent of the United States, visits her home to force her to sign a report exonerating his team. After she resists, he brings his gun under her chin. While the legal document remains out of the frame, the shot's composition makes it appear as though the gun comes out from the contract. The staging literalizes Benjamin's statement that each legal contract operates through the possibility of violence or punishment

(Benjamin 1986, 288). She signs. As Alejandro leaves, he advises her: "You should move to a small town, where the rule of law still exists. You will not survive here. You are not a wolf, and this is a land of wolves now." The legal system appears as a kind of smokescreen for the state, used to attest to a governing humanity that no longer exists. Macer inhabits a position of total vulnerability, holding none of the disruptive potential of saving violence. Yet she still poses a threat of perception. Attuned to the hypocrisy of the state and the victims it ignores, Macer renders visible the state's hidden immorality as well as its precarious nature.

Three Burials more fully extracts the empathetic force of divine violence. "You gonna be all right?" Mike asks his victimizer, Pete, at the end of the film. After Mike has had to atone for his actions and accept the necessity of self-sacrifice, he can appreciate victim and victimizer as fully human subjects. This moment where Mike can sense the humanity of those he previously viewed as monstrous or subhuman illustrates that a truly transformative empathy must have at its center a reckoning with our own propensity for violence. Benjamin laments that the legal order is fragile because lawmakers have forgotten the violence intrinsic to its creation (1986, 290). No viable solution can be found if "violence is totally excluded in principle" (ibid., 293). Genre, especially a subgenre of the western, which itself is founded upon the tension between morality and the law, brings violence to the forefront, giving us a prime conceptual space to consider alternative forms.

Still, one of the villains in *The Counselor*, the head of the drug cartel that has had Laura killed, reflects quite directly on the difficulty of such a change. The counselor has called the drug lord to beg for clemency for his abducted fiancée; the relaxed criminal, with the camera lavishing attention upon him as a servant prepares hot chocolate in the background, subtly raises the question of the exploitative possibility of pleasure. Yet over a series of shots that oscillates between the drug lord, the servant, and a cut-in on the hot chocolate pot, the criminal notes, "Reflective men often find themselves at a place removed from the realities of life. In any case, we should all prepare a place where we can accommodate all the tragedies that sooner or later will come to our lives." He holds up two fingers, indicating the number of sugars he wants in his drink. The drug lord continues, "But this is an economy few people care to practice," his first words transposed over the film's final, very fleeting mid-shot of the servant.

In a moment reflecting on meaning, the genre film mingles visions of pleasure and pain, of exploiter and exploited. The drug lord narrates an anecdote about the poet Antonio Machado, who was inspired by his wife's death. The counselor replies that he will sacrifice himself to save his fiancée. The drug lord appreciates his willingness but suggests that this gesture is not enough. To achieve enlightenment, which can encompass life's tragedies, the drug lord says, one must experience a transcendent despair that leads to "the ancient understanding that the Philosopher's Stone will always be found, despised, and buried in the mud." This mud, suggested in the shadowy noir framing as he delivers this proclamation, may be genre itself. The dramatic irony of the drug lord's satisfied philosophical pontificating shortly after having ordered the brutal murder of Laura sparks skepticism and emphasizes the tensions of the genre aesthetic.

Even as the genre might permit filmmakers to destabilize boundaries of perpetrator and victim, to find the lost humanity of the impossible subject, the same narrative elements can be employed by the state in ways that efface ambiguity and distort reality. The films *Sicario*, *The Three Burials of Melquiades Estrada*, and *The Counselor* challenge even as they unveil the discursive processes by which the migrant becomes an Othered menace and the War on Terror becomes linked to the War on Drugs. The myth of genre has a very palpable weight upon state leaders and agents, which I will consider in more depth in the next chapter, on the western's thematic inverse, film noir.

Femmes Fatales as Torturers and Lost Detectives in a Fragile City

Post-9/11 Noir

"I hate this place!": Seeing a Noir City as a Dark Mirror

As intensely as I felt trapped in my small town on the Great Plains of eastern Montana, I longed for New York City. My parents had immigrated from Grenoble, France, to Flushing, Queens, in August 1977 for my father's medical residency. They arrived the week that Elvis Presley died. Their frequent conflations between the King of Rock 'n' Roll's passing and their arrival ensured that, for me, New York would be forever entrenched in and inextricable from pop fantasy.

In their stories, New York was a stranger, more perilous, more cosmopolitan place than the monotonous Sidney, Montana. With the unabashed glee of a spinner of a scary story, my mother would recount witnessing seemingly random acts of violence on the subway. The city brimmed with unknown threat. By contrast, my town felt fully and terribly known to me. I could only ever truly feel lost and exhilarated wandering the aisles of our two video stores or attending a matinee at our local cinema imbued with the scent of cigarette smoke and stale popcorn.

My mother experienced the city as an outsider; however, rather than feel alienated as I did in my Montana village, she thrived. Not speaking a word of English upon her arrival, she conversed with others in Spanish—the language of her parents, who had fled the Franco regime in the fifties. Her neighbors would respond in Italian or Portuguese and, according to her, many merry friendships were formed across linguistic divides. She even became a French tutor for children of the Vanderbilt dynasty. In my young mind, New York seemed like Babel before the tower fell: a place where all languages and people could coexist. Why, I often wondered, had we left this magical city? Why did we end up in the empty, homogenous Sidney, Montana, seemingly composed of only the most white and monolingual? My parents' explanations regarding the advantages of the citizenship process for rural medical doctors did little to satisfy me. I craved the city and reveled in its cinematic representations.

My childhood perception of New York was shaped by noir-tinged films, where shadows overwhelmed urban settings and cynicism reigned. Andrew Dickos saliently described the modern world presented in noir as "a sensorium of disillusionment" (Dickos 2002, 65). Noir films let me be immersed in spaces of lost ideals. Such despairing and often terrifying environments seemed antithetical to my hometown, whose bright blue Big Sky metaphorically signaled that all was sunshine and that nothing should be questioned.

Sidney in the 1980s and '90s shared all the tropes and charms of 1950s Americana, where almost exclusively white children were expected to earnestly pledge their allegiance to the American flag at the start of each school day. Because of my disability, I pledged with my left hand, an embodied indication of the skepticism I had long brought to such rituals. In contrast to the wide-open plains of western movies, cinematic noir cities allowed me to express the otherwise taboo disenchantment I often felt toward the United States and my own community. If the western was a place to sit with my weakness, noir offered a place to sit with my hatred and self-loathing. While the genre's celebration of misanthropy often felt liberating, post-9/11 noir revealed that my ever-present feelings of alienation could be self-annihilating.

My cinematic journey into the noir city began not with classics such as *The Naked City* (1948) but rather with a noir-tinged superhero film—Tim Burton's 1989 *Batman*. Its Gotham City was all vertiginous towers and gloom, so unlike the relative desolation of Sidney, where the horizon could never be escaped. Three-year-old me was spooked and thrilled. I watched my VHS copy so much the tape warped, and several sequences became a running joke in my family.

One much-quoted scene in our household was the opening, which presents a suburban family being mugged in an alleyway. The film begins with an establishing shot of Gotham City. Skyscrapers, silhouetted by moonlight, pierce the night sky. Police sirens wail—this is a place of constant emergency. After a cut to the crowded streets, the film presents the lost family stumbling out of a movie theater. Father, mother, and son all seem uneasy. The father cries, "Taxi! Taxi! Taxi!" Never does he secure the sanctuary of a cab. The map-holding son cries out, "We're going the wrong way!" The father yells back defensively, "I know where we are!" Their turn into an alleyway is captured with a Dutch or tilted high angle of horror film—the suburban family descends into an ever more dangerous world. Here, they are mugged by two men. Just before the father is pistol whipped, one of the assailants masquerading as a panhandler asks, "What are you, deaf? You don't speak English?" Any family overwhelmed by the city might as well be a group of suspicious foreigners. The mother screams as the father falls before her.

Notably, Batman does not save them from harm. Instead, he watches from the rooftops above, little more than a caped witness to the displaced family's pain. Batman's passivity toward the plight of outsiders left me feeling disenchanted. Instead of inhabiting a utopian Babel, those perceived as foreigners were targeted and objectified by both their attackers and those meant to protect them. If a bumbling white family on the street was not worth saving, what hope did we have?

When my family traveled to larger cities, my father would often playfully pantomime the role of the frazzled father in the film, yelling, "Taxi! Taxi! Taxi!" and "I know where we are!" The similarities between the two men made the gag more unsettling. Both wore trench coats with fedoras and looked like they had stepped out of a 1940s noir. My Arab father played the role of the overwhelmed patriarch with zeal. I sympathized with the son in the *Batman* scene, just out of the cinema and trailing behind his parents. Ignored by his family, the neurotic moviegoing child fears where they are headed. When coupled with my father's comic reenactments, the opening scene reinforced my view that a place like New York caused outsiders to lose their bearings. Under the threatening glares of urbanites, even the seemingly solid foundations of family could become unstable. The scene drew me in in part because it gave me permission to scream. It allowed for a child to be suspicious of where his parents had taken him, be it down a dark alley in Gotham City or into the void of Montana.

Later encounters with the city in film further solidified it in my mind as a place where one's own dissatisfaction could be freely admitted. The virtual city in the Wachowskis' influential sci-fi film *The Matrix* (1999) is a sprawling and often sinister American metropolis straight out of classic film noir. Like *Batman*, *The Matrix* inspired me to stress test my VHS copy of the film. If, in the late 1980s, I was the frightened filmgoing boy wandering the streets of Gotham, by the late 1990s I was becoming Agent Smith (Hugo Weaving), the *Matrix's* AI villain who despises the city, his home, and wants nothing more than to leave it.

Dressed as a federal agent in a dark suit, Agent Smith can instantly appear in any part of the urban environment; his long shadow heralds his arrival. He asks a resistance fighter whom he has tied up: "Have you ever stood and stared at it? Marveled at its beauty, its genius?" With his prisoner, he stares out an office window toward the metropolis. Sitting across from the prisoner, Smith then describes how he has come to be repulsed by such a marvel of steel and concrete. He later takes off his sunglasses and his earpiece—the parts of his uniform that flatten his individuality and tie him to others. Then he confesses, "I hate this place, this zoo, this prison, this reality. . . . It's the smell, if there is such a thing. I feel saturated by it. I can taste your stink, and every time I do, I fear that I have somehow been infected by it."

The frightful monologue by Agent Smith the torturer captured my imagination in part because I too felt trapped by my ostensible home-town—the city's pungency as distressing to Smith as the odor of cattle brandings was to me. However, this interpretation and affinity dangerously skirts the white-on-Black violence that is central to the staging. Smith is a white man who has trapped a Black prisoner. As he speaks of his pris-oner's "stink," staring him directly in the eyes, Smith swipes the sweat off the man's brow and forces him to smell himself. He asks, "It's repulsive, isn't it?" The film thus invited me to not only express my alienation but, more insidiously, to embrace the power of a racist authority—to inhabit the white gaze at its most obliterating, where people of other races are reduced to nothing but their smell.

After 9/11, views of the newly fragile city as captured in noir forced me to reckon with how I came to sense my own Arab identity as a putrid stink.

My high school's televisions broadcast and rebroadcast the footage of the attacks that day. New York had come to the small town of Sidney, though only in its most fragile state. In my world history class, we watched the North Tower collapse at 8:28 a.m. local time. The New York City skyline seemed to be encompassed in a storm cloud—the kind of huge cloud formations typically associated with tornadoes in Montana. Conceptions of New York as Gotham City or as a prisonlike matrix evaporated. Both skyscrapers and country homes could just as easily be swept away into the sky. I averted my eyes from the replays, refusing perhaps to implicate myself as a member of the town's sole Arab American family.

Just a year later, Spike Lee's post-9/11 noir *25th Hour* (2002) articulated the hatred that I feared might be awakened by the attack, which had exposed the American city as vulnerable to the effect of a perceived Arab threat. The hero of the film, New Yorker Monty Brown (Edward Norton), has been sentenced to prison for drug possession. The film chronicles his last few days of freedom before he must turn himself to the authorities. Standing in front of the mirror at his father's bar, Monty goes on a spiteful tirade about New York. Whereas my previous exposure to the city suggested a sprawling, endless place, the angry hero meticulously maps the city by the people and the institutions he despises. Lee stages a census motivated by xenophobic loathing. In so doing, he suggests how the post-9/11 city, both real and cinematic, had too become terribly knowable.

Beside the mirror in the bar hang emblems of the police and firefighting units as well as a stylized American flag carved up by the black outlines of the towers. A cut-in reveals graffiti in the corner of the mirror that says, "FUCK YOU!" Monty exclaims: "Fuck me? Fuck you, and this whole city and everyone in it!" He proceeds to insult various races, classes, and ethnicities, and each rant is accompanied by a portrait of a representative person. Some border on outlandish stereotypes while others are more earnestly portrayed. With a racist bile, he pulls out and tosses aside the individual ingredients from the city's signature melting pot.

His indictments move from an individual level to an institutional one before shifting toward the cause of 9/11. He critiques the police and the church. Finally, after presenting a cathedral in New York, Lee cuts to footage of Osama bin Laden. "Fuck Osama Bin Laden, Al Qaeda, and backward-ass cave-dwelling fundamentalist assholes everywhere. On the names of innocent thousands murdered, I pray you spend the rest of eternity with your seventy-two whores roasting in a jet-fuel fire in hell." His Islamophobic words sound over images of the *New York Daily News* front page that present the Al Qaeda leader in a Wanted poster, linking New York to the Wild West. Just as he fully embraces the logic of violence that inspired the attacks and defined its aftermath, wishing for another grand cataclysm to destroy the city, Monty turns against himself: "No. No, fuck you, Montgomery Brogan." His hatred comes from within. A cut-in shows Monty trying and failing to erase the small and very destabilizing "<u>FUCK</u> <u>YOU</u>!"—a signal that he may not be able to vanquish his self-loathing.

I first watched the scene in my basement's computer room—the darkest, most confined space of my childhood home. With its claus-trophobic dimensions, it was perhaps my best approximation of a noir setting. I felt targeted by the film's white New Yorker. The attacks not only crystallized a national malice toward the Arab but also exposed just how tenuous my place in the nation seemed. There was no room for Arab American citizens in such a wounded New York. Our only representative was the ultimate enemy, Osama bin Laden. Such an absence ensured that, even after Monty confronts his distorting prejudices, Arabs do not appear worthy of compassion. Moreover, the scene troublingly broke down the distance between my hometown and New York. Lee's inclusion of bin Laden in a Wanted poster highlighted that the dehumanizing logic of frontier justice had come to the metropolis. In the city about which I had long fantasized, would I be a terrorist forever consigned to being hunted by the law on some imagined prairie?

There was an even more disquieting valence to Monty's rant, one that further foregrounded my racist self-loathing that I had begun to glean in the interrogation scene with Agent Smith. Lee stages that scene so that Monty often stands absolutely still in front of the mirror, but his reflection inside the mirror is moving around, animated with anger. The surreal presentation of a broken reflection establishes that he will not express his true xenophobic thoughts during such a time of national unity. Underneath his calm exterior lies a secret and deadly white rage. The scene shocked me because of its demand that the viewer reckon with the trauma of 9/11 as a white man. In not allowing for the possibility of any other point of view, it exposed how I confronted my Arabness through a white gaze. Inhabiting angry white eyes, like those my teacher drew, the film helped illuminate my psychic split between cultures. Through it, I realized my own unspoken frustration with bin Laden, whose political actions thrust me out of my America. It was as if I pettily blamed him and his followers for making my life in Montana harder by being poor representatives of our ethnicity! Was I too creating an Islamophobic, racist correlation between the terrorist and the Arab?

Looking back in 2021 on the scene where Monty uncovers the depths of his own self-delusion, I found it further jarring because of how it frames the lies I have been telling myself about my past. By high school in the fall of 2001, I would not say the words of the Pledge of Allegiance. Instead, I would just mouth them with my left hand across my heart. Lee's staging of Monty in front of the mirror, where the angry reflection of his interiority clashes against his still exterior, uncannily captured how I felt after 9/11, when I was forced to perform citizenship in ways that felt inauthentic. While I often pushed against my school's authorities, I remember never speaking out against this ritual of patriotism. I silenced my own questions.

Or so I believed, until I told my mother about this preface after writing the above reflection on *25th Hour*. She revealed memories I had repressed of my earlier resistance toward such public displays of patriotism. In the sixth grade, after a unit on the Cold War and McCarthyism, I also refused to say the Pledge of Allegiance. My mother was called in to discuss my disruptive behavior. This repressed memory revealed the possibility that, in the autobiographical recollections presented in these chapter prefaces, I may subconsciously be framing myself as tamer than I was. It is as if my adult self cannot fully accept the force by which I once pushed against structures of authority. Am I afraid that my present relative docility would disappoint my younger, more questioning self? Would my younger self be the angry and judging reflection in my own mirror?

After 9/11, the noir city thus transformed from an overwhelming place to an intimate and brittle mirror where I could face the hatred I direct outward and within. The post-9/11 noir films discussed here present broken cities bordering on war and terror. Their denizens, like me, get lost in these newly vulnerable urban spaces, sometimes reflecting upon fantasies that can blind them from seeing their own privileged, even complicitous, position in the institutions they uphold.

As suggested by the frightened son of *Batman*'s opening, the resentful Agent Smith of *The Matrix*, and the hateful Monty of *25th Hour*, noir welcomes articulations of fear, skepticism, and self-loathing in the United States. Through the often-unbecoming reflections offered by these dark mirrors, I could sense how the movies that I love, which offered a chance to freely dissent, also taught me to hate and Other myself. Sometimes overwhelming and other times fragile, the city of such films offered me a space to be honest about my own destructive impulses and to reckon with my own (non-)belonging in a reeling nation that demanded my allegiance.

"Somebody's lying!":
Introducing Post-9/11 Noir and Our Paranoid Politics

Spike Lee's *25th Hour* contains an indelible image of the 9/11 trauma that has overtaken the noir form. As two men stand at a window discussing the fate of a mutual friend about to be sent to prison, Ground Zero looms in the background. Their conversation first confronts the reality of living next to the smoldering urban ruins. The visitor claims that *The New York Times* said the air quality around the site is dangerous, while the proud apartment owner declares that it passes Environmental Protection Agency standards. Commenting on the disjuncture between their sources, the visitor admits, "Somebody's lying!" Neither the mass media nor the government can be fully trusted, a skepticism inherent to the noir genre further explored in the core films of this chapter. The apartment owner states that he would never move even if bin Laden were to attack again, but the limits of his belief in an unchanging quotidian are fully exposed as a performance when he angrily reacts to his visitor's assertion that the relationship with their condemned friend will continue after he goes to prison: "Wake the fuck up!" A man who claims that he can live a normal life next to the ruins of the 9/11 attack appears insulted by the suggestion that their friendships will continue unchanged. The strong shift in his tone—from seeming indifference to anger—signals the shock of still-unresolved traumas and the frustration that their impacts are ignored. Shifting completely from the small-scale personal trauma to the site of the cultural trauma, Lee's camera then moves toward Ground Zero. The camera pan, accentuated by the soundtrack's pulsating drumbeat and lamenting choral chants as the wreckage comes completely into view, reduces the petty materialism and relationships of bourgeois New Yorkers to a passing dream. All need to be awakened to the consequences of this collective trauma.[1]

The wound at the center of New York City in Lee's film thus represents a post-9/11 noir vision of the American metropolis as a space of disillusionment. In *Film Noir and the Spaces of Modernity*, Edward Dimendberg argues that a later variant of the genre, the neo-noir, developed at "the end of the metropolis of classical modernity, the centered city of immediately recognizable and recognized spaces," shifting the genre's focus to reflect an American culture increasingly defined by sprawling suburbia and a more ambivalent, decentered city space (Dimendberg 2004, 255). In post-9/11 noir, then, as Lee's camera—transfixed by the urban wreckage—attests, the city reemerges as a dominant though unsettled trope. Whereas once the urban environment was an inescapable prison for its citizenry, it is now newly fragile. In an era that saw the discursive rise of transnational terrorism, a shift occurred in cinematic conventions: in classic film noir, the city was a threat to man, but in post-9/11 noir the individual came to stand as a threat to the city.

Denis Villeneuve, who previously depicted the homecoming of War on Terror policy in *Sicario*, visualizes the city's fragility in 2017's *Blade Runner 2049*. His sequel to Ridley Scott's 1982 noir features a scene where an android calls a drone strike on a Los Angeles junkyard while getting her nails done. Here, Villeneuve restages a sequence from the original *Blade Runner* where a detective pans over a still photograph in search of clues, calling out directions so that his computer changes his viewing angle. By contrast, in the sequel, the observer pans over a live drone feed. By simply uttering the word "Fire," she destroys what she sees. Footage of missile explosions is broadcast over the lenses of her sunglasses, and she looks upon the suffering with no expression. The bareness of the set where the android conducts her attack accentuates the fact that she acts alone. Without any effort, a single person can bring fiery devastation upon an American urban landscape. The films in this chapter show the shock of waking up to not only such sights of mass destruction but also the elastic legal frames and inflexible bureaucracies the destruction has exposed. The genre archetypes that permeate the dreams in the cultural imaginary can now taunt state actors and expose their weakness.

Although President Bush often adopted the rhetoric of the western gunslinger, a point alluded to in Monty's rant in *25th Hour*, he identified the post-9/11 world as a noir one. In line with Lee's camera, public policy pushed society's attention toward the rubble, turning Ground Zero into the embodiment of American fragility that justified a state of emergency. Literary scholar Paula Rabinowitz's concept of "pulp modernism," detailed in her interdisciplinary history *Black and White and Noir*, serves as an appropriate lens through which to consider the anxiety palpable in presidential discourse following the attacks. She describes pulp modernism as a "political theory of America's problematic democracy disguised as cheap melodrama," useful for considering the "hidden history of state violence" that has come to define American modernity (Rabinowitz 2002, 18). Rabinowitz explores how noir and pulp fictional forms manifest within the American political imagination and summarizes her argument: "Politics of twentieth-century America becomes pulp fiction; or, more accurately, pulp fiction leads the way in matters political" (ibid.). She goes on to underline that such narratives haunt the rhetoric and security theater that emerged after 9/11 amid the devastation of the attacks.

The Homeland Security Advisory System sought to gauge threat levels but also offered a barometer for national anxiety. The advisory system stood as a visual emblem of a key rhetorical trope within the Bush administration's narrative of a threatened nation. Its prognostications were born from the so-called Threat Matrix, a daily statement, prepared for the executive branch, of every potential menace to the nation. The Threat Matrix's logic of extremes of good and evil resonates with a melodramatic imagination. In a memoir on the Bush administration and the law, former assistant attorney general Jack Goldsmith argued that such lists of potential catastrophes caused those within the executive branch to "imagine a threat so severe that it becomes an obsession" (qtd. in Goldsmith 2009, 72).

Both publicly and internally, the Bush administration existed within and reinforced a climate tinged with the existential malaise so pervasive in noir. Former secretary of defense Donald Rumsfeld states in his memoir: "Major landmarks considered likely targets were watched with anxiety. Each rumor of another attack set people on edge" (2012, 349). Rumsfeld ironically identifies a link between this climate of fear and increased executive power. In justifying a full-fledged War on Terror, he writes that the terrorist can "attack any place and at any time," encapsulating how the administration positioned the transnational enemy as an almost existential threat (ibid., 362). Scholars across disciplines have recognized this essential quality of the "terrorist" in nations' policing practices. Jean Baudrillard argues that it was impossible to prevent the terrorists' 9/11 plot, which ensured that they achieved "a veiled form of perpetual terror" in the West, ultimately "forcing [it] to terrorize itself" via ever-increasing but futile security measures (qtd. in Toffoletti and Grace 2010, 70). Similarly, political theorists Michael Hardt and Antonio Negri find that, unlike the sovereign nation, terrorists belong to a distributed network defined by its lack of center (54).[2] This network cannot be effectively tracked and regulated, making it appear that terrorists are omnipresent. The effect upon the nation is tremendous, as those named terrorists and their unlocatable perceived threat can thrust the "old form of power into a state of universal paranoia" (Hardt and Negri 2004, 55).

The establishment visions of post-9/11 America resembled a world also frequently framed in film noir, where no one can be trusted and a sense of security is impossible. Rabinowitz argues that a "pulp politics" provides a ground on which to theorize American modernism "not as [a] seamless grand narrative . . . but as the chaotic repetition of the familiar" (2002, 22). The very conventions of genre, continually adapting to negotiate different points of history, force recognition of the recurring conventions of such political discourses. The Bush administration's use of the language of catastrophe to describe terrorism echoed past presidencies during their states of emergency (and foreshadowed the discourse of President Trump around the coronavirus), and in this sense the forms of noir and Bush's pulp politics have a long historical legacy.

As one example, Richard Kelly's 2008 sci-fi noir pastiche *Southland Tales* makes such a point through its many citations of Robert Aldrich's 1955 *Kiss Me Deadly*. The latter film, widely read as film noir's contemporary response to the possibility of nuclear annihilation, saturates the former.[3] The opening of *Kiss Me Deadly*, featuring a mysterious woman nearly colliding with an oncoming car, evokes an imagined pleasure of obliteration achieved by technological force. This scene plays on the television in *Southland Tales* while the narrator describes how the adult film star Krysta Now (Sarah Michelle Gellar) has co-written a "screenplay that foretold the tale of our destruction." The presence of *Kiss Me Deadly* foregrounds *Southland Tales* as a contemporary response to Aldrich's work. It draws historical connections between differing rhetorics of destruction, illustrating how Cold War hysteria centered on the nuclear bomb and 9/11 fearmongering focused on the terrorist share similar roots and generic conventions. By connecting a paranoid American past and present through an allusion to a noir classic from the 1950s, *Southland Tales* makes clear that cultural traumas are socially constructed phenomena built on narratives that have recurrent motifs. To borrow the narrator's words, such stories all follow the same beats of a stock screenplay that foretells our destruction.

The film's transhistorical linkage shows how noir films expose pulp politics and, by illuminating the present via an appropriation of tropes from the past, demonstrate the reiterated narrative structures of state-sanctioned national allegories surrounding cultural trauma. Post-9/11 noir films emulate the classically understood forms of Freudian belated-traumatic memory, where past fears stumble forth into the present, fostering a temporal breakdown. Such a blind spot in the historical memory appeared within the political discourse about 9/11, where the transnational nature of the attack fostered a narrative of absolute rupture in which previously established restrictions on executive power governed by the tenets of human rights law were rendered moot.

Southland Tales features a striking breakdown in imagery that signals that noir films can challenge the narratives of rupture created when traumas are mobilized for political gain. Playing a disfigured Iraq War veteran, pop singer Justin Timberlake drunkenly belts out a version of the The Killers' "All These Things That I've Done." After dancing with interchangeable uniformed nurses who appear to have stepped out of a World War II field hospital, he stares directly at the camera, then takes a sip of beer as the lyrics continue to play in the soundtrack. Thus, the film exposes not only the artifice of genre, whether musical or noir, but also that its well-worn conventions might have been rendered inadequate. Similarly, Spike Lee punctuates *25th Hour* with sequences where the images stutter, as if drawing attention to the hidden seams in the film's editing. These moments of a shaken diegesis, however, are always temporary. These post-9/11 noir films thus imply that to uncritically accept the story of an exceptional trauma perpetuated by the state may mean losing sight of the way national vulnerability fits in a very pernicious genre that cuts together citizens' fears into an overwhelming montage.

Indeed, state actors created policies after 9/11 within what one might call a "terrified public space" of suspended rationality. The policies were sustained via codified rubrics measuring the threat level. Traditional guideposts of conventional human rights disappeared from view in the context of this terror-built exceptionality. Similarly, noir often presents a clear vision of a nation in limbo. One can at times perceive forgotten historical resonances and witness, as in *Southland Tales*, the absurd paradox of the normalization of a state of emergency. The post-9/11 noir films under consideration in this chapter demonstrate how the tropes in noir, like those in the other genres featured, can be appropriated by the powerful even as they are harnessed by artists. When detailing Raymond Borde and Etienne Chaumeton's foundational writing on the genre, James Naremore writes, "Above all, noir produces a psychological and moral disorientation, an inversion of capitalist and puritan values, as it if it were pushing the American system toward revolutionary destruction" (2008, 22).

But what occurs when the state co-opts the language of revolutionary destruction to produce an exploitable disorientation within its citizens? The paranoid view espoused by the Bush administration, marking lone individuals as possible threats to the nation, led to a sort of state-sanctioned noir rhetoric that these genre texts both express and question. The two key films of this chapter, Robert Rodriguez and Frank Miller's 2005 *Sin City* and David Fincher's 2007 *Zodiac*, present the noir icons of the femme fatale and the detective within the newly fragile city to allegorically showcase executive actors both emboldened and oppressed by mythic archetypes. Even as these films identify the genre's potential contribution to the Threat Matrix, where reality is made into a foreboding noir, they also show that such films have the potential to expose the theater behind a culture of fear.

Sin City and the Militant Femme Fatale

Whereas the femme fatale is traditionally emblematic of a home front anxiety, Robert Rodriguez and Frank Miller's Sin City situates the femme fatale on the front line, offering insights into how archetypical violent femininities might sustain and buck against the state's wartime narratives.[4] I break away from the critical consensus on the film, which has not identified any underlying sociopolitical critique or sustained play with genre convention. Mark Bould offers a common and simplistic reading of Sin City when labeling the production a juvenile exercise in style that stands merely as an "expression of a cultural moment which shies away from exploring depth" (2005, 114). In contrast, I find that Rodriguez and Miller's black-and-white adaptation of the latter's comic-book series Sin City presents a shrewd representation of the femme fatale in her varying iterations within film noir, shifting from a passive object seemingly in need of male protection into a dominating force fully able and willing to protect her own autonomy.[5] The film builds upon a crucial facet of the neo-noir iteration of this female figure: her delight in violence. Ruby Rich argues that in recent examples of noir, femmes fatales grew ever more depraved and yet articulated "a new version (albeit warped) of female empowerment" (1995, 9). Her essay illustrates a key change in critical perception that informs my analysis—the inherent violence of the femme fatale has come to be seen not simply as a manifestation of male anxiety but also an embodiment of her liberated potential. Sin City probes the increased wickedness of these noir icons in its allegorical contemplation of women as both part of and potentially against a state whose wartime practice has become increasingly brutal and sadistic.

Although the noir genre is often criticized for its misogynistic tendencies, it is precisely because Sin City works to titillate that it is of such value, and able to expose structures of desire as well as expectations around gender and power.[6] Within this tension between the feminist and the chauvinistic, the film can explore the issue of collusion via the figure of the prostitute, an individual sometimes met with ambivalence or derision in mainstream feminist thought. Uninhibited by the constraints of a singular ideology, the film can explore the possibility of freedom offered by this position, taking a somewhat more radical view of sex work. Through a legally independent red-light district, Old Town, the film depicts a utopian vision in which a band of militant prostitutes operate within an organization that guarantees safe working conditions. Mindful of such individuals' complicity within an economy underpinned by male desire, *Sin City* unveils the power and powerlessness that come through the deployment of what Lynn Sharon Chancer, echoing Pierre Bourdieu, terms "sexual capital" (162). The pressures of such a dualistic position, teetering between empowerment and objectification, are articulated within a film enmeshed in a patriarchal mode of viewing. The organized violence practiced by the sex workers pushes the film's critical focus onto law enforcement actors, in particular the military.

On a broader political level, the female soldier's collusion with the male order has been the focal point of public debates. Although it would be too reductive to place the female characters of the film in one-to-one alignment with actual soldiers, their characterizations resonate with a public discourse both enamored of and repelled by such fighters. Kelly Oliver's essay "Women: The Secret Weapon of Modern Warfare?" repeatedly compares female soldiers to the femme fatale. The discourses depicting them, she claims, meld sexuality with brutality, an alignment highly prevalent within the cultural imaginary (Oliver 2008, 5–6, 13). *Sin City*, though, is precisely about the conflicting discourses surrounding these women.

In the post-9/11 period, *Sin City* proposed a new paradigm for the ever-more-empowered archetype, wherein such women form a militant community independent from patriarchal structures. This paradigm articulates a fear of a femininity that exudes not only sexual power but also the powers of violence. The heightened anxiety expressed in the film takes on an added contextual specificity within the contemporaneous public discourse shaped by two very different militarized visions of femininity during the Iraq War: the female Rambo turned damsel in distress Jessica Lynch and the Abu Ghraib torturer Lynndie England. Examining analogues to both figures in the film alongside contemporary debates surrounding women in the military and developments in military law, I see *Sin City* as a dynamic work that touches on antifeminist and feminist discourses concerning a transformed femininity in war. The female roles are neither wilting damsels nor fully "gender decoys" that buttress the established masculinist structure through their violent acts; the noir where "the ladies are the law" presents women actively resisting discursive and legal strictures that would either rob them of their violent potential or cast them as scapegoats who distract from the malignancies within the military bureaucracy.

In order to wrestle with *Sin City* and its negotiation of a geopolitical landscape defined by war in the Middle East, we need also to consider the original comic book series by Frank Miller. The series debuted in 1991, mere months after the end of the first Persian Gulf War, an American conflict where an unprecedented number of female soldiers served in combat situations. Media scholar Lynda E. Boose conceptualizes the war as a reassertion of American masculinity undermined by the failure of the Vietnam War (1993, 68–69). Even as the ideal of a supplicating, vulnerable femininity was key in constructing a narrative that helped garner public support for the war, Boose argues that the presence of American women on the battlefield defied the military's framework that implicitly posited women as victims and men as their saviors (ibid., 77–78). There existed a challenge to the male warrior. One of the most infamous female American soldiers to take part in combat, Private Melissa Rathburn-Nealy, was captured by Iraqi forces, and, according to official accounts disseminated within the military, "she had been raped and/or found 'slit from [her] crotch to [her] neck'" (qtd. in Pin-Fat and Stern 2005, 38). The soldier in fact experienced no such assault at the hands of her captors; what mattered was that the narrative effectively reduced the female fighter to a victim.

The reductive military discourse echoes the process of female objectification that gender scholar Sharon Marcus argues occurs linguistically within publicly prevalent rape narratives.[7] Marcus concludes that the codified roles of woman as victim and man as victimizer only perpetuate the vision of women as powerless and rape as inevitable. This rape script is one of the "microstrategies of oppression" that validate the patriarchy while feminizing women (Marcus 1992, 391). In order to resist the "gendered grammar of violence [that] predicates men as the objects of violence and the operators of its tools, and predicates women as the objects of violence and the subjects of fear," Marcus argues, women can challenge the rape script by developing their own "capacities for violence" (ibid., 393, 397). In this way, they move from a position of passivity into one of active resistance. Marcus also calls for new ways to represent militant femininity, in which the female body becomes the "potential object of fear and agent of violence" (ibid., 400). *Sin City* functions as a cinematic depiction of Marcus's vision for perpetrating femininity. The film shows women transcending their objectified state through violence to ultimately challenge the patriarchy, which, in its official rhetoric, conflates femininity with weakness and vulnerability.

Rathburn-Neely's trials during the Persian Gulf War foreshadowed the plight of Private Jessica Lynch during the Iraq War more than a decade later, pointing to a profound institutional suspicion about the very idea of a female soldier on par with her male counterparts. An epidemic of sexual assaults followed the unprecedented infusion of women into the male-dominated system. Although rates vary depending on the study, it is estimated that from 52 to 70 percent of female veterans have experienced some form of sexual trauma while serving (Middleton and Craig 2012, 242). Sexual assault in the military flared into the public eye most infamously in the Tailhook Scandal of 1991 where, at an annual convention of aviators in the navy and marine corps, eighty-three female soldiers were alleged to have been sexually assaulted. *Sin City*, then, makes a spectacle of a war in which women were shown to have violent strength yet were either rhetorically marked as victims or reduced to sexual objects by their brothers in arms.

Jessica Lynch Comes to Sin City: The Damsel in Distress as Female Rambo

Sin City in its original and adapted iterations contains depictions of women in command of men who operate in a space linked with the conflict in the Middle East. In the first tale of the series, a bouncer describes Marv, the hulking hero of the story, as looking like Baghdad (Miller 1991, 6). Marv longs to return to "the old days, the bad days" of war. *Sin City* represents an American urban reality haunted by conflict, much as Lee's New York City was haunted by Ground Zero, and presents a fusion of the home front and the front line. Like Marv, the Old Town women share a predilection for conflict and always seem primed for a fight. Gail, the head of the Old Town, responds to a potential threat to her territory by exclaiming, "We'll go to war!" In the comic, the lettering of the word *war* is exaggeratedly large and breaks out of the speech bubble (Fig. 3.1). War cannot be contained. This forthcoming battle represents the femmes fatales' chance for full violent liberation from the male order, but also the possibility of their annihilation.

In the opening stages of the Iraq War, the story of Private Jessica Lynch, who was taken hostage by Iraqi forces, thrust two sharply disparate popular visions of femininity into the public discourse. Susan Faludi, in her overview of post-9/11 national identity within the mass media, *The Terror Dream*, describes this rhetorical reshaping of Lynch, a process that she argues reveals the establishment's discomfort with a

Figure 3.1. The word *war* breaks out of a speech bubble. In Sin City, the women's war cannot be contained. Frank Miller's *Sin City: The Big Fat Kill #3*, 2.

fully militant female soldier emerging in a time of expansive conflict. Initial reports of the Lynch incident described her as a "female Rambo" who took a lone stand against enemy fire and shot her weapon until no bullets remained (qtd. in Faludi 2007, 175). In cold desperation, one official said that she was "fighting to the death. She did not want to be taken alive" (Schmidt and Loeb 2003). These accounts constructed the soldier as a ruthless fighter, completely liberated from feelings of fear or even a sense of self-preservation.

In later reports of the kidnapping, the conception of Lynch's battle prowess changed entirely, as expressed by *Time*'s Nancy Gibbs: "Everyone around her . . . may have been fighting heroically, but she couldn't do a thing" (qtd. in Faludi 2007, 175).[8] The media portrayed her as a helpless young girl. While recuperating in the military hospital, she is reported to have sat "clutching a teddy bear," an image that erased any trace of her former physical power and transformed her into a passive entity dependent on the masculine establishment for protection (qtd. in ibid., 183). In this enfeebled and infantilized state, Lynch was refashioned into a vital cog that propelled the war machine forward: as an archetype of the asexual, virtuous white woman who needs to be saved from foreign barbarians, Lynch provided the moral justification for the invasion of Iraq (Feitz and Nagel 2008, 206). She served the same rhetorical purpose as Rathburn-Neely before her: helpless women in distress who supplicated and validated the male order, weakened females who provided a moral gloss to America's present conflict.

Sin City contains an analogue to Lynch in the form of Nancy Callahan (Jessica Alba), a woman tortured by an ostensibly Oriental threat. She entirely subverts the damsel type, ultimately pulsating with the destructive potency that Lynch the soldier was briefly said to possess. In the process, she frames the need to define her as a vulnerable woman as a sign of the male subject's impotence. First seen as a scared eleven-year-old sent into the hands of a pedophile (Nick Stahl)—a deranged son of a U.S. senator—Callahan is initially portrayed as a victim, framed in a subordinate visual position to her seemingly gigantesque captors (Fig. 3.2). The sequence ends with Nancy being pulled from their hands and huddling in the arms of her savior, Detective John Hartigan (Bruce Willis). When Hartigan comes to her rescue, Nancy reacts to the primal violence of the setting with horror, covering her eyes at the detective's behest while he brutally castrates her assailant, the senator's son. She is saved by a good male force, just as Lynch was said to have been saved by her brothers in arms.

Figure 3.2. Before growing up to be a femme fatale, Callahan is portrayed as a victim in a subordinated position to seemingly gigantesque male captors. *Sin City*.

Eight years later, however, the once meek girl is in command of a sexuality and a violence that permit her to dominate the male-controlled space that once threatened to destroy her. Nancy dances at the nightclub where she works, hypnotizing the male clientele and completely controlling their attention. In the logic of classic noir, the femme fatale achieves her power via overwhelming sexuality, which she employs as a weapon to achieve her desired ends, and thereby gains a transcendent strength through her body.[9] Framed in a wide shot, Nancy stands at the edge of the dancing stage, positioned high above the men, whose silhouettes jut into the bottom third of the frame (Fig. 3.3). Dressed in western style, she twirls a lasso above those who have flocked to see her, ensnaring nameless men as easily as a cowgirl ensnares cattle. Shots follow that fracture her body; the focus on her curves troubled by guns in their holsters serves as a reminder that her sexuality is intertwined with and complements a violent efficacy. Nancy later reveals that a loaded Magnum revolver is also hidden under the driver's seat of her car, confirming that, as an adult, Nancy resembles a gunslinger from the Wild West able to protect herself with the pull of a trigger. That she derives her last name from a Magnum-toting masculine icon (Harry Callahan, popularly known as Dirty Harry) reinforces her transformation into a woman comfortable with violent force.

Nancy's cooptation of power is at its most surprising the very moment she appears most subjugated: during her second abduction by

Figure 3.3. A femme fatale twirls her lasso on stage, ensnaring men as easily as a cowgirl ensnares cattle. *Sin City*.

the senator's son. Through the process of surgery to restore his genitalia, his skin turned a monstrous yellow, and he came to be known as the Yellow Bastard. Unlike the first scene of entrapment, in which Nancy is diminished against the looming shadows of her captors, this torture sequence relies extensively on close-ups of her face, indifferent to the frenzied whipping by her assailant. Never does the Yellow Bastard break her control over her body, a fact confirmed when the two meet in a culminating mid-shot. She lifts herself up and turns to gaze at her captor, who has leaned in to whisper in her ear. A close-up on Nancy's face shows how she forces him to reckon with the very impotence that his need for a weakened woman denotes. She then spews, "You can't get it up unless I scream. You're pathetic. You're pathetic." Her indictment robs the captor of his strength, and he retreats out of the frame. Her strategy recalls Marcus's assessment: "Verbal self-defense can successfully disrupt the rape script by refusing to concede the rapist's power" (Marcus 1992, 396). Nancy shows a canny awareness of the roles women are meant to play, twisting or shirking them completely in order to gain authority over the patriarchal forces. Following the verbal evisceration of the would-be rapist, the film makes Nancy the master of the torture chamber, suggesting that analogous archetypes, like the transforming images of Jessica Lynch, ultimately highlight a military masculinity completely unsure of itself.

Nancy fulfills the role of the captured woman sexually assaulted by the enemy, serving as a cinematic equivalent to the most grotesque mass media imaginings of the fates of Rathburn-Neely and Lynch. Her critical edge cuts most sharply as her impotent, perverted captor exists disquietingly between the domestic and foreign spheres. The emphasized yellowness of the lecherous Yellow Bastard, at odds with the film's predominantly black-and-white cinematography, and his muteness for much of the film make him a grotesque embodiment of the Yellow Peril. When he is revealed to be Patrick Henry Rourke Jr., the son of a corrupt U.S. senator, the film marks him as more of an American threat than a foreign one. Through his connection with a legislator named after a Founding Father, the Yellow Bastard exposes a malignancy at the heart of American power, revealing it to be both fearful of and enemy to women like Nancy. *Sin City's* Yellow Bastard exposes the enemy within, underlining the deeply ingrained misogyny of state institutions such as the military, which are implicitly indicted. The critique offered by Nancy and those who menace her encompasses the law's role in protecting this insidious enemy while further marginalizing his victims.

A fleeting but pointedly specific reference to the criminal code, Nancy's annotated textbook, *Criminal Law: Case and Manuals*, gestures toward the law in relation to female victims of male abuse. More abstractly, it highlights the fundamental absurdity of the illusion that such strictures can offer justice to victims of abuse (Fig. 3.4). The film presents the textbook after Hartigan has been released from prison. Over the years,

Figure 3.4. Wielding the law as a weapon. A femme fatale finds an "opportunity to fake ignor[ance]" in a legal loophole, uncovering a means to conceal the true depths of her knowledge. *Sin City.*

Hartigan and Nancy have remained pen pals. Her powerful tormentors have had him released so that he might lead them back to Nancy, who has been in hiding. Believing that the now-adult Nancy has once again been abducted, Hartigan rushes into her home, where he discovers the scholarly life that she never mentioned in their past correspondence. Unlike Nancy from the comics, who is said to study literature, the cinematic incarnation focuses on the law. Written in Nancy's careful hand on an interior page of the textbook are citations of basic rights, including due process. This seems laughable given Nancy's childhood experiences with the legal system. After Hartigan saves her as a child, the police proceed to frame him for her abduction. Nancy goes to his hospital bed where he is recuperating from a bullet wound, and she laments that the authorities will not let her testify in his defense. The wizened Hartigan roughly responds, "Sometimes, the truth doesn't matter like it ought," depicting the legal system as a realm of deception and lies. Their exchange follows the monologue of Senator Rourke, who exclaims, in Joseph Goebbels–like fashion, "Power comes from lying. . . . Lying big and gettin' the whole damn world to play along with you." The legislator and his work are separated from truth, separated even from any morality, as shown by Nancy's experience with a law designed to protect the perpetrators. Seen in this context, rights such as due process appear as pitiful deceptions for victims who are ultimately made powerless by the very apparatus said to provide them with recourse.

Nancy's note referencing due process is placed against two cases that appear utterly irrelevant to her plight: one about drug use and the other about fishing rights. The language of the briefly glimpsed text also illustrates the nuance with which the film cites the law to articulate her survival strategies, resting on canny performance. This femme fatale masters the law, the system codified and controlled by men, in order to escape its clutches. The two seemingly disparate cases, along with Nancy's note, provide a coherent legal philosophy aware of the risks involved when the quintessential victim attempts to co-opt the system that frees her victimizers from accountability. On the top portion of the visible page, the drug case includes the note that "lack of knowledge that the possession of controlled dangerous substances is illegal" does not stand as a valid defense. The phrasing crystallizes a general rule often applied by courts: ignorance of the law is not an excuse. The second case depicted, *STATE v OSTROSKY*, establishes an exception to the maxim, known as reasonable reliance. In short, the case is between the state and a fisherman who did not believe in permits; Ostrosky was continually charged with violating the state's hunting and fishing guidelines. However, he was able to mount a reasonable reliance defense, since he based his actions on a judge's concurrent ruling that fishing permits were unconstitutional (*STATE v OSTROSKY*). Nancy's notes under the headline "Reasonable Reliance Issues" indicate that she is aware of the exception, since the phrase "opportunity to fake ignor[ance]" comes briefly into view when Hartigan begins to close the textbook. She has studied the finer points of the law to uncover a defense that permits her to deceive, to conceal the true depths of her knowledge and thereby remain legally blameless for her actions. Legal scholar D. M. Kahan, in an essay on reasonable reliance, writes that in a framework defined by liberal positivism where the law is not intertwined with more general ideas of right and wrong, extensive knowledge of it becomes a danger because, "[t]he more readily individuals can discover the law's content, the more readily they'll be able to discern, and exploit, the gaps between what's immoral and what's illegal" (Kahan 1997, 129). Nancy is finding the means to act for her own benefit, free from the control of unspoken norms. An ability to fake ignorance, to hide her knowledge and, essentially, pass as the stereotypically uninformed woman, gives her the capacity to maintain a superior understanding of the machinations of the powerful without subordinating herself to the law.

Lynndie England Comes to Sin City: The Femme Fatale as Revolutionary Perpetrator and Useful Fall Girl

Expressing the extent of Nancy's transformation from victimized child to would-be Rambo, the vignette culminates with another scene where Hartigan castrates Yellow Bastard. Although Nancy once would have shielded her eyes, now she regards her tormentor's emasculation with a smile. This moment interlinking torture's violence with pleasure reflects the infamous image of Private Lynndie England in Abu Ghraib that saturated the media in the year before the film's release. Commentators remarked that one of the more unsettling features of the photographs was England's ever-present smile while she pointed at naked Iraqi prisoners in various formations. Social critic Barbara Ehrenreich wrote in a *Los Angeles Times* opinion piece that England's grin brought to mind not the banality but "the cuteness of evil," shattering her view of female soldiers as morally blameless and forcing her to confront the idea that women are capable of sexual sadism (Ehrenreich 2004). Nancy's final grin links her less to the increasingly infantilized figure of Lynch than to the joyously cruel England.

According to gender scholars Lindsay Feitz and Joane Nagel, the outwardly malicious England was Lynch's "photographic negative," who fulfilled an important role in the state's propaganda machine by drawing media attention away from the policy behind the uncovered prisoner abuse, thereby sustaining the narrative that the brutality was carried out by only a few deranged soldiers (qtd. in Feitz and Nagel 2008, 208). Nancy's smile hints at one woman's plunge into the sadistic, a shift further explored via England's more direct analogue in the film, Gail (Rosario Dawson), who not only smiles but, according to her former lover Dwight (Clive Owen), also laughs at violence "with the pure, hateful, bloodthirsty joy of the slaughter." Similar to the way the Nancy figure overturns the prevalent antifeminist narrative of Lynch as the quintessentially fragile woman, Gail and her peers challenge feminist readings of England that attempt to rationalize her violence by arguing that the military indoctrinated her to the extent that it made her a proxy for the masculine order. By situating a unique community of femmes fatales within popular cultural and mythic traditions of figures defined by their independence from dominant gender or political confines, the film suggests that such sadism might represent a newly autonomous, bloodthirsty femininity with the potential to break down the masculine identity upon which the military is founded.

Grappling with the violence on display in the Abu Ghraib photos of England, Zillah Eisenstein coined the term *gender decoy* to describe the smiling soldier. She concluded that the torturing woman represented not a new form of femininity, vicious and violently strong, but a stand-in for the male soldier. The strength of the male identity is not shaken by this, as the "gender swapping and switching leaves masculinists/racialized gender in play [so that] just the sex has changed; the uniform remains the same" (qtd. in Feitz and Nagel 2008, 217). While the film links the male law enforcement arm of the police with the prostitutes of Gail's Old Town, suggesting that they perform the same function in their respective territories, Eisenstein's conception is less apt for Gail and the women of Old Town, given their antagonistic relationship with male authority. Rather, a representation of the gender decoy comes in the form of a briefly featured female justice of the peace. Her defeminized presentation, where even her curly hair resembles the wigs of traditional English judges, is consistent with the idea of the decoy whose femininity becomes entirely absorbed by her uniform and by her role in the legal system. Gail, meanwhile, has all the violent potency and sadistic tendencies of her male equivalents but represents a politically separate and independent order that, for a time, exists concurrently with the traditional male one.

To signal absolute control over territory legally emancipated by a "shaky truce" with the police, the film captures the women of Old Town in a monumental fashion while focusing on their uniforms. One woman wears a replica of the superhero Wonder Woman's costume (Fig. 3.5). The reference situates the women in a broader tradition of American (and ancient Greek) myths that provide insight into Old Town's antagonistic relationship with the male establishment. Cultural scholars have articulated the sadomasochistic roots of the Amazonian superheroine, conceptualized by her creator as a dominatrix who would enlighten men by forcing them into submission.[10] A vital piece of the heroine's accoutrement, her metal bracelets, testified to the Amazonians' ultimate servitude to the male hegemony. To remove those would render Wonder Woman "maniacally, insanely destructive" (Stanley 2005, 148).[11] By changing them from metal to leather, Miller plays with the established mythos to emphasize that the women who control Old Town's streets not only remain free of the patriarchy's shackles but also contain within themselves the strength to

Figure 3.5. The Wonder Women of Old Town. The leather bracelets on the Wonder Woman analogue (not metal as typical) metaphorically signify the femmes fatales' power to disrupt and destroy the patriarchy. *Sin City*.

bring about its destruction.[12] Wonder Woman's insignia appears at the very moment when the women unknowingly slay a police officer, an action sure to incite a war. In an overhead shot of the man's dead body surrounded by the Old Town women, as the camera zooms out, the film reveals that the women stand around him in a W formation. The presence in the crowd of the Wonder Woman substitute further ties this assembly of women to the superheroine.

Gail and her peers initially function alongside the police; however, the shaky truce is broken by the murder in a sequence whose imagery exposes how these women warriors exist in conflict with their male peers. Gail leads an alternative law enforcement region, as is confirmed when a police car reaches the edge of Old Town only to silence its sirens and turn around. The voiceover notes that the police officer "knows he's not the law, not in Old Town. The ladies are the law here. Beautiful and merciless." The movement of the women as they lock down Old Town to contain threatening drunken men later revealed to be plainclothes policemen is intercut with shots of Gail calmly looking on. After the narrator makes references to the women's trap, the girls slam shut a wrought-iron gate that resembles prison bars, framing Old Town as the prison, the prostitutes as the jailers of men, and Gail as the warden (Fig. 3.6). Is Old Town this world's Abu Ghraib?

Figure 3.6. Slamming the doors shut when Old Town becomes a prison where, like Abu Ghraib, women are the jailers. A perpetrating femininity emerges that can at once dismantle and obscure patriarchal violence of the military. *Sin City*.

The transformation of these women from a sanctioned part of the legal system to its enemy parallels the discourse around England following the Abu Ghraib scandal that sought to absolve the established military authority of any wrongdoing by framing the female soldier as an exception. Feitz and Nagel argue that the prevailing narrative drew attention away from the broader systemic issues that created the culture of violence on display in Abu Ghraib (2008, 209). Following the release of the photos, an official Department of Defense report concluded that such sexual torture was standard practice in U.S. military prisons (ibid., 211). Male as well as female soldiers regularly took part in activities that touched upon taboos thought to be held by the Arab men that, when breached, might lead to a psychological breakdown. But the documented complicity of the wider military apparatus was largely ignored, and "the torture and abuse of prisoners became an incidental backdrop to the more important media story—the sexual soap opera and the demonization of its bad girl star, Lynndie England" (ibid.). The abuses were labeled by the head of the Department of Defense, Donald Rumsfeld, as the actions of "a few bad apples," and England was defined by the military as a rogue element ("Donald Rumsfeld: What Did He Know?").

Presenting Gail as a hypnotic distraction from the violence taking place around her, the film touches upon how such a violent femininity might conceal systemic issues within the existing military apparatus that may lead to soldiers acting with wanton brutality. Dwight is overwhelmed by Gail's sexual potency when she stops him from intercepting the drunken male intruders by jokingly telling him to "enjoy the show," an ostensible reference not only to the forthcoming execution but also to her own body as transfixing spectacle. Her success is made clear when he notes in voiceover that "all kinds of death is about to hit less than twenty yards ahead of us, and still it's hard to take my eyes off her." The term *show*, linking her physique with the violence, recalls critiques of the War on Terror that found that the female body was rhetorically transformed into a spectacle by the state, one that emblematized the supposed liberating facets of the global conflict.[13] Ideologically, however, such women are less a distraction than an integral part of the process. England, for example, was said to be a "fall girl" for a military system that encouraged inhumane treatment against captured enemy forces (Goodman 2005). By the way its form emulates Dwight's desirous view toward Gail, the film shows that the creation of a fall girl does not absolve the military of blame. Such a sexually potent symbol sustains the violence of the war machine by rendering it palpable, into a spectacle in and of itself.

At the same time, the film illustrates the destructive potency of a militarized femininity free from patriarchal legal structures. When the prostitutes come to understand the consequences of the policeman's death, Dwight describes Old Town's fate: "It'll be war. The streets will run red with blood. Women's blood." The statement of these words over a shot of Gail's posterior suggests a menstrual subtext.[14] A similar valence marks the scene where Dwight and the girls of Old Town trap the Mafiosi in a crevice-like alley, as if in a lethal return to the womb. Luring them on the pretense of exchanging the head of the slain policeman for the captured Gail, Dwight sets the stage for the massacre to come. His voiceover highlights the tactical advantages of the alley, "crooked, dark, and very narrow. They can't surround me. Sometimes you can beat the odds with a careful choice of where to fight." High-angle shots of the heavily armed mobsters expose their presently confined state. At the point where Gail and Dwight are reunited at the end of the passageway, they draw the mobsters' gazes upward to the women of Old Town standing on the rooftops above them. The film presents a shot of a gun-toting prostitute wearing a broad smile, similar to the torturing England, before sweeping down from the rooftop, bringing the stormy red sky into view. From the low-angle position of this shot, which mirrors the vantage point of the mobsters, the alley is further transformed into an imprisoning orifice. The red sky, with the inverted triangle form of the opening, metaphorically demarks this moment where men are confronted and defeated by a uniquely feminine fury. The film then fluctuates between shots of men being punctured by bullets and women firing their guns while laughing hysterically. Dwight, in his narration, describes Gail as a Valkyrie, a warrior woman from Norse myth, underlining that just when she and her kind most violently rebuke their male rivals, they have most completely embraced their inner soldiers. However, her zestful retribution is directed not at some external enemy but at the very law enforcement system with which she was once affiliated.

In conflating Gail and her peers with the mythic Spartans that Frank Miller actually went on to depict in *300* (adapted to the screen in 2007 by Zack Snyder), *Sin City* suggests that a torturing femininity is not a subsuming of the male order but a separate power that might destroy the apparatus that keeps female soldiers subservient and disenfranchised. The fifth issue of "The Big Fat Kill," the *Sin City* comic book saga featuring Gail and Dwight, opens with a full-page image of a Spartan warrior and a description of King Leonidas's stand against the Persian army, where "the whole of civilization [was] kept alive by Spartan courage and a careful choice of where to fight" (Miller 1995, 1). The linkage to antiquity not only places the women as substitutes for those Spartan heroes but also transforms the men they are fighting into the Persians bent on destroying their culture and taking away their freedom.[15] American representatives of male authority are made akin to a Middle Eastern empire that sought to "extinguish the only light of reason in the world" (ibid.). Just as it took but a few Spartans to bring Persia's war machine to a halt, *Sin City* wonders whether (and enacts a fantasy that) only a few sadistically violent women might devastate the entire ideological framework and undermine the ideals of a modern patriarchal empire's army.

Seen in the context of the military's sexual abuse epidemic, the sequence's culminating scene, of Gail and Dwight pointing their weapons at a common enemy, has a utopian air. When describing how women on the battlefield face two fronts, out in the streets and in their barracks, Feitz and Nagel include a telling quote from Specialist Michaela Montoya on why she carries a knife: "The knife wasn't for the Iraqis . . . it was for the guys on my own side" (qtd. in Feitz and Nagel 2008, 214). The weapon designed for close combat heightens the intimate dimensions of the institutional war in which female combatants are embroiled. In *Sin City*'s very moment of feminist victory, when the Old Town women are aided by an understanding male, the film shows an awareness of the impossibility of this framework via Dwight's pessimistic final line. After he embraces Gail, he admits, "There's no place in this world for our kind of fire, my warrior woman, my Valkyrie. You'll always be mine. Always and never." *Sin City* thus recognizes that the destabilizing warring femininity it depicts may remain cinematic fantasy. However, as Janey Place asserts, whenever the classic femme fatale meets her fatal end, "we retain the image of the erotic, strong, unrepressed (if destructive) woman" (Place 1998, 48).

Pop culture ideals in the forms of Wonder Woman and Dirty Harry undergird the representations of the violently empowered women of Sin City, who transcend the legally codified masculine order to assert their independence. As previously discussed, Wonder Woman is directly alluded to via the costuming and staging of some of the Old Town women, while Nancy Callahan shares Dirty Harry's last name and handgun of choice. These militant femmes fatales are aligned with powerful pop culture icons who challenge the existing legal and patriarchal order and linger in the memory of popular culture. Such a connection points to how the women in *Sin City* draw out and strengthen the fleeting impression left by the real-world femmes fatales that they allegorize—Jessica Lynch and

Lynndie England. They encourage viewers to look beyond their ends scripted by the mass media and the state and to instead retain the image of Lynch—not as an object but as a subject of violent power—and of England—not as a "bad apple" but as a blinding smokescreen veiling systemic corrosion. Within such political discourses, as within the noir form, violent femininity at once contains an obliterating force against patriarchal legal struggles (as suggested by how quickly the Rambo-like narrative of Lynch was quashed) and is a useful distracting trope deployed by the state to hide its own deficiencies. David Fincher's 2007 *Zodiac* focuses on the noir convention of the detective to explore the influence that cinematic fantasies of empowered masculinity might have on the worldview of those framing as well as fighting the War on Terror. In contrast to the femme fatale trope, which can function to exculpate the state, *Zodiac* shows how lawless heroes on the silver screen expose the perceived systemic deficiencies within the state's bureaucracy.

Zodiac and the Allegorical Representation of Bureaucratic Failure in the War on Terror

Like the femmes fatales in *Sin City* who wrestle with the sometimes constraining force of genre archetypes, the detectives of *Zodiac* confront mythic representations of themselves that propagate in the media. Most notably, Don Siegel's aforementioned 1971 *Dirty Harry*, a cinematic portrayal of a crime spree inspired by the Zodiac killings starring Clint Eastwood in the titlular role, appears as a film-within-a-film. These larger-than-life onscreen representations of police work make a mockery of the detectives' struggles against legal constraints and day-to-day bureaucratic obstacles. *Zodiac* ultimately shows that genre film holds an influential, indeed determining position in the conceptualization of how crime should be fought, in the minds of both the public and the executive.

Zodiac reconstructs the unsuccessful manhunt for the Zodiac Killer, who haunted the San Francisco Bay area for much of the 1970s, creating a searing portrait of law enforcement impotence. When the director spoke of the model for *Zodiac*, he referenced 1976's *All the President's Men*, about the Watergate scandal and the journalists who broke the story ("Zodiac Production Notes" 2007, 35). Through its opening images, establishing shots of San Francisco at night on July 4, 1969, *Zodiac* situates the isolated murders as significant to broader U.S. history. Although rarely read as a post-9/11 film, *Zodiac* meditates with nuance on systemic failures in the lead-up to the attacks and in the search for Osama bin Laden. It uses the cynicism of noir to reflect upon the nightmarish reality of a law enforcement community unable to effectively combat its chief menace.

Some may doubt that a film about a serial killer that begins in 1969 can be interpreted as a parable for the search for bin Laden during the post-9/11 era. It is worth noting that the film primes the viewer to make such transhistorical connections. A sonic montage in the director's cut, designed to condense four years, merges audio detailing the end of the Vietnam War and the pardoning of President Nixon with audio about the Symbionese Liberation Army and the Son of Sam. This linkage made in the film's soundscape illustrates that, in *Zodiac*, contemporary instances of war and terrorism in America coexist with serial killers. Furthermore, the mention of the executive and the Vietnam War encourages reflection on the twenty-first-century wars over which members of the Nixon administration (Donald Rumsfeld and Dick Cheney) would also preside. The jihadist tenor of the Zodiac's messages to the media, which I will discuss in more detail shortly, further connects him with bin Laden. Even if the reader remains unconvinced that the Zodiac Killer is an analogue for bin Laden, the film productively visualizes the bureaucratic obstacles facing a state seeking out a wanted man. These obstacles would be at the root of the intelligence community's failure to prevent 9/11 and of its then unsuccessful attempt to capture bin Laden.

On September 10, 2001, Donald Rumsfeld, secretary of defense under both Nixon and Bush, delivered a prescient speech concerning an "internal threat" to American society. He described this enemy as not some far-flung, despotic nation-state but an "adversary closer to home. It's the Pentagon bureaucracy. Not the people, but the process. Not the civilians, but the systems" (Rumsfeld 2012, 333). Rumsfeld's conceptualization was confirmed the following day when Al Qaeda's terrorist attacks took the U.S. security system by surprise. The 9/11 Commission later concluded that the attacks succeeded largely because the sprawling intelligence community was unable to gather or process information about the terrorist threat. Many studies identify legislation of the 1970s, such as the Foreign Intelligence Surveillance Act, as a root cause of the inability to coordinate to the degree necessary to prevent 9/11 (Burch 2008). *Zodiac* invites a multidirectional or transtemporal engagement with recent history to suggest how the paranoid thinking and executive excesses of the Nixon presidency shaped the worldview of the Bush administration and led to protocols that stifled intelligence agencies.

The film employs generic tropes to perform an institutional critique in an early montage where the nation's premier law enforcement and intelligence agencies attempt to decipher a code that the killer sends to

The San Francisco Chronicle. From a tight cut-in on a copy of the cipher left on the wall of a suburban home, the film cuts to brief shots of the Naval Intelligence Center, the Federal Bureau of Investigation, and the Central Intelligence Agency. These disparate settings appear systematic and organized, in stark contrast to the quiet domestic locale that opens the sequence. Undercutting the presumed strength of these security institutions, however, the sequence culminates with a return to suburbia, specifically to the breakfast nook of Donald and Bettye Harden. These ordinary citizens solve the cipher, shattering the security state's façade of competence.

This early comic sequence establishes the focus of *Zodiac* on a hunt for a killer who, like bin Laden, cannily transforms the media into a platform for his violent antiestablishment rhetoric. The film draws such a parallel with a crucial excerpt from the Zodiac Killer's letters that echoes bin Laden's jihadist philosophy, centered upon a desire for martyrdom and a blissful eternal life. A translation of the killer's ciphers is read aloud in the film: "the best part of it is that when I die, I will be reborn in paradise. And all that I have killed will become my slaves." The mass murderer's violent actions are driven by a spiritual fervor resembling that which drove Al Qaeda's crusade. This particular passage recalls a popularly known reward for a soldier's death in holy war that bin Laden cited in his 1996 Declaration of Jihad: any martyr will live in paradise married to seventy-two virgins (bin Laden 2005, 29). Using this excerpt, the film positions the Zodiac Killer in equivalent terms to a modern-day jihadist—both seek eternal glory.

Examining this politically resonant production, released when the search for bin Laden was ongoing, through the lens of *The 9/11 Commission Report* as well as sociological studies of the intelligence community's failures, crystallizes the scathing indictment at the heart of the procedural noir—that the bureaucratic structures of the institutions designed to promote security actually left the nation vulnerable. *Zodiac* offers an empathetic but skeptical portrait of the individuals responsible for maintaining national security, who are burdened by the grand visions of unencumbered law enforcement found in popular culture. The film's eventual shift in focus from agents of the state to an amateur detective equated with a disgraced president mirrors the mythic framework of the War on Terror. *Zodiac* illustrates the dangerously myopic quality of an executive worldview built on models from popular culture, one devoid of restraint that sees the law as a surmountable hindrance.

In her study *Spying Blind*, which examines the structural reasons for the intelligence community's failure to prevent 9/11, Amy Zegart argues that a fragmented organizational structure ensured that the intelligence agencies would be unable to utilize the information they had acquired on Al Qaeda and its plans to launch a domestic attack (2007, 48). The lack of formal mechanisms promoting integration made sharing information within and across agencies exceedingly difficult. Furthermore, fear of prosecution for breaking the strict legal protocols that governed interagency coordination made intelligence institutions averse to sharing (ibid., 93). Yet at the time, terrorists could easily cross jurisdictional lines in their moves between the foreign and domestic spheres (ibid., 65). Indeed, transnational terrorism necessitates an agile and cohesive security community antithetical to the pre-9/11 system, where "trails would run cold, information would not be shared, and dots would not be connected" (ibid., 113).

The fate of a 1998 directive on bin Laden written by then director of central intelligence George Tenet, illustrates the extent of the structural fragmentation. The letter stated that the United States was "at war" with bin Laden and called for a community-wide shift in focus to combat terrorism, but then-NSA director Lieutenant General Kenneth Minihan bluntly told the 9/11 Commission that he assumed the letter applied only to the CIA (National Commission 2004, 357). Those in the CIA, however, believed Tenet's message solely targeted the other intelligence agencies; hence, Tenet's call for wider focus on bin Laden was completely ignored. A similarly fractured reality plagues the police force in *Zodiac*, amid what one former police officer describes in the film's press kit as "the first multi-jurisdictional police investigation in California. Before [the Zodiac] case, there was no organized effort between departments as a rule" ("Zodiac Production Notes" 2007, 20).

Zodiac subtly articulates the disjunctures within and between law enforcement agencies by the sonic motif of the ringing phone. The film lays this sound over every exchange between officers from different police departments. The rings often punctuate the moments when jurisdictional challenges emerge in the case. The sound's discordant quality emphasizes the frustration due to the case's expansive complexity, which muddles the macrolevel view of the information available to the police. This complements the aggressive tone of the phone conversations between departments, as when the San Francisco detective defensively asserts, "I don't want to get into a jurisdictional thing here." A later ring from Vallejo County informs San Francisco officers that a prime suspect has been disqualified because of a handwriting sample.

The film adds another partly contradictory layer of meaning to the sound, linking it to the Zodiac Killer's invasions of the lives of those attempting to find him. A political cartoonist, Robert Graysmith (Jake Gyllenhaal), takes up the investigation in an amateur fashion and is menaced by a mysterious caller once his role in the case becomes public. The first instance of the frightening anonymous communication laces the mechanical sound with an element of terror. This scene begins with Graysmith numbly brushing his teeth, only to be startled by the phone's piercing call. Over the course of two shots, the film settles in on a close-up of Graysmith's scared face as he picks up the phone and hears labored breathing on the other end. An aggregation of factors—from Graysmith's shaken appearance and wide-eyed expression to the corridor setting shrouded in shadows—briefly thrusts the noir into the domain of the traditional horror film, establishing the sound of the phone as a herald for the film's terrorizing force. Via the mirrored sound design, the film creates a startling parallel between bureaucracy and the killer, state security forces and the terrorist. For the Zodiac Killer, the rings stand as a testament to his reach; but for the state's fractured bureaucracy, these rings metaphorically serve as a warning alarm that futilely calls attention to its blinding sprawl.

In her study of the intelligence community's struggle with bureaucracy, Zegart elaborates upon the burden that mythic ideals of intelligence agents placed on their real-world counterparts. From its inception, the FBI's culture idealized agents, or G-Men, who were often depicted in films and who showed distaste toward the analysts who composed the bulk of the organization. In its early days, the handsome J. Edgar Hoover posed for publicity shots holding a machine gun with a Hollywood leading lady by his side (Weiner 2013, 70). His cinematic ideal was ingrained not only in the minds of the public but also in the minds of the FBI operatives. A veteran agent summed up the prevailing attitude: "Real men don't type. The only thing a real agent needs is a notebook, a pen, and a gun" (qtd. in Zegart 2007, 4).[16] Although this worldview served the FBI well when it was a reactive entity solving crimes, Zegart argues that it led to ineffectiveness when the bureau had to take on a more preventive role after the emergence of transnational terrorism (ibid., 129). Terrorism made the arrest-and-conviction mindset of the G-Man obsolete.

Like the real-world FBI operatives who struggled against the model of what a "real agent" should be, the investigators in *Zodiac* continually confront their mythic analogues projected on the silver screen. They are even shown at the movies watching a character like Dirty Harry who ignores policy and legal guidelines in his violent pursuit of justice. At one point in the 1971 film named for its protagonist and marked Hollywood's response to the Zodiac case, Dirty Harry declares, "The law is crazy." This contrast between the featured hero from a contemporary Hollywood film and the investigators portrayed in *Zodiac* frames the chasm between the romantic model of law enforcement found in popular culture, where officers can freely write the law off as "crazy," and the less glamorous reality of a profession beholden to legal protocol. In *Zodiac*, lead SFPD detective Dave Toschi (Mark Ruffalo), the real-life inspiration for movie icons such as Steve McQueen's police lieutenant Frank Bullitt and Clint Eastwood's Dirty Harry, typifies what a policeman should be for the citizens who work with him on the case ("Zodiac Production Notes" 2007, 17). Upon seeing Toschi for the first time, Graysmith remarks, "Dude, he wears his gun like Bullitt." A wizened colleague corrects him, "No, McQueen got that from Toschi." With his attitude and even in the particular way he holsters his sidearm, the real-world detective inspired Hollywood's most famously suave representation of the police. In the world of *Zodiac*, as in the world of law enforcement outside the film, the line between fiction and reality can become dangerously confused.

The film goes on to emphasize that Toschi's analogues in cinema ultimately stand in mocking counterpoint to him and to the legal strictures he operates within during a scene where the detective goes to the movies. Troubled by *Dirty Harry*'s sensationalist representation of a Zodiac-like series of killings, Toschi leaves a police screening of the Clint Eastwood picture in disgust. Walking through the theater lobby, he walks under a giant cardboard cutout of Dirty Harry (Fig. 3.7). Compositionally,

Figure 3.7. A real-world detective walks under the gun of his cinematic analogue, Dirty Harry. The legally unbounded cinematic hero may obliterate the public's acceptance of bounded law enforcement. *Zodiac*.

the character points his Magnum directly at Toschi, creating a visual metaphor for how such larger-than-life heroes effectively diminish the standing of law-abiding police in the eye of the public. This is apparent when one elated moviegoer mocks Toschi on his way out, "Dave, that Harry Callahan did a hell of a job with your case!"

Of the very few critics to consider how the film relates to post-9/11 political concerns, Elbert Ventura characterized this sequence as a "rebuke to the shoot-from-the-hip heroics of a show like *24*," a television program starring a Dirty Harry–like antihero who gladly tortures in his quest for justice in an America fighting the War on Terror (Ventura 2008). By situating Dirty Harry—both his projected self on the theater screen and his giant cardboard image in the theater lobby—in a superior visual position to the real-life detective, the film seduces the viewer with the perceived superiority of extralegal executive power. The intelligence community was faced with a similar temptation around the time of the film's release, when the search for bin Laden was being "hindered" less by gaps in intelligence than by legal constraints over the issue of national sovereignty. By 2006, there was a consensus that the Al Qaeda leadership had taken up residence in Pakistan. Fear of damaging an already fragile relationship with Pakistan left U.S. executive agencies at a standstill (Bergen 2012, 160). An FBI agent stated that "the biggest threat to us now, [Osama bin Laden], is getting the most 'protection'" (qtd. in National Commission 2004, 271). At the moment when Toschi confronts his own ineffectuality through viewing the onscreen exploits of Dirty Harry, the film evokes the frustrations of those in law enforcement and the intelligence community that the laws do more to protect the terrorists than their victims.

Zodiac's narrative, concerned with how the media propagates the killer's message at the risk of jeopardizing the investigation, reflects an intelligence community at odds not only with limiting laws and regulations but also with the press, especially in the aftermath of the Cold War. Zegart describes how the rise of twenty-four-hour news networks eroded the quality of the CIA's strategic analysis so that it had to forgo a long-term understanding of developing terrorist networks (Zegart 2007, 100). This conflict is visually expressed in a sequence where the Zodiac letters published by *The San Francisco Chronicle* are layered over the film frame, appearing to overtake the police officers as they walk into the newsroom. Multiple exposures, superimposing one image on top of another, create the sense that the officers are deluged by the Zodiac's taunts broadcasted by the media. A sign for *The San Francisco Chronicle* breaches the top of the frame, cynically establishing the importance of the media in driving forward the enemy's terror mission. The battleground between the state and the film's terrorizing force is on the front page.

Within this montage sequence, the placement in the frame of the gunsight-like symbol that the Zodiac killer uses to sign his letters to the news media points to the inability of those caught inside the bureaucracy to succeed in their mission. The Zodiac symbol falls on Toschi's upper back, indicating his present obsession with the case (Fig. 3.8). The film then cuts to a mid-shot of the cartoonist Robert Graysmith in which his face is encompassed by the symbol (Fig. 3.9). It expands out of the frame, keeping its crosshairs dead center on his face, foreshadowing how he too will eventually be consumed by the murderer's puzzle. The film then hints at the result of the organization's inability to mobilize when the symbol moves offscreen and a scrawled phrase, "The police shall never catch me," appears (Fig. 3.10). The cartoonist seems to come closest to uncovering the identity of the killer, which suggests that only someone outside the police system could, to use Graysmith's words, "put all the information together . . . [and] could jog something loose."

Graysmith's blessing appears to be his relative naïveté about the legal realities of bureaucracy and the distorting force of sensationalizing myths in popular culture. An understanding of both implicitly looms over his *San Francisco Chronicle* colleague, crime reporter Paul Avery (Robert Downey Jr.), who falls into the fate of the classic noir male, becoming "a broken image of modern urban man" (Dickos 2002, 66). Similar to Toschi's own disgust with Dirty Harry, Avery lashes out against the very mythologized nature of the enemy his reporting helped to construct. Avery's ire reflects

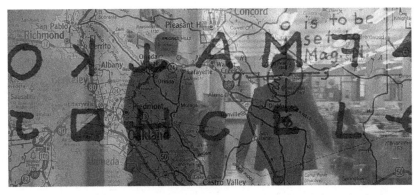

Figure 3.8. A hint toward the detective's destructive obsession with catching a mass-mediated killer. He comes into the Zodiac Killer's crosshairs. *Zodiac.*

Figure 3.9 (Above) Figure 3.10 (Below). The Zodiac Killer's aim falls upon a cartoonist, foreshadowing the civilian's own obsession with the case. *Zodiac*.

the statements of Bush administration officials in the year prior to the film's release who complained about bin Laden's identification as public enemy number one. In July 2006, the CIA reportedly disbanded its Osama bin Laden unit to improve focus, but many perceived the shift in resources as suggesting the state's inability to achieve any quantifiable successes in its global manhunt ("CIA Reportedly Disbands" 2006). Former White House spokesman Tony Snow asserted that the War on Terror was not "a war against one guy, Osama bin Laden. It [was] against a network" ("US Remembers 9/11" 2007). The hidden bin Laden not only proved distracting but also remained a failure that tainted any ostensible success in the fight against a transnational threat. The genre framework that gave the wartime actions such unassailable logic—situating Osama bin Laden as targeted outlaw—had become a burden.

In the film, when Graysmith asks Avery why he does not write a book on the Zodiac murders, the former crime reporter responds with the same logic that Tony Snow used when contemplating the hunt for bin Laden: "Do you know that more people die in the East Bay commute every three months than that idiot ever killed?" Becoming a myth only further imbues the Zodiac with power, and his elevated status in the public discourse turns a lone idiot into a mysterious killer. Avery's lucid argument is undermined by the staging of the scene. A harsh ray of white light falls upon him, making the former journalist into an almost spectral presence and indicating the psychic cost of this mass media creation. While Avery appears broken by the knowledge of the Zodiac's hold on his and the wider public's imaginations, Graysmith is unmoved. An outsider's perspective and a cinephilic vision permit him to perceive himself in mythic terms—he can be the Dirty Harry icon that neither Toschi nor Avery can fully emulate. Ironically, the milquetoast Graysmith functions as the film's closest proxy for Dirty Harry by eliding the standard operating procedure. He can imagine himself beyond such concerns.

In contrast to Toschi, who loathes the mythic visions of himself, Graysmith is presented as a man who sees himself as the heroic alternative to the Zodiac villain. A cult of personality propels him forward, past the obstacles that cause his contemporaries to stumble in their respective investigations. In his home, he surrounds himself with posters of classic films noirs, such as 1950's *The Asphalt Jungle* and 1955's *I Died a Thousand Times*. The latter film, about a successful police manhunt, is an ideal counterpoint to Graysmith's stymied reality as well as a model to emulate. These posters reinforce how Graysmith constructs an identity via a framework of genre cinema. Suggesting that he finds encouragement rather than reflections of any existential angst in these noir texts, he stands next to a poster for Alfred Hitchcock's 1956 *The Wrong Man*. The only Hitchcock film based directly on a real-life occurrence details the plight of a man wrongly accused of a crime. Like the puzzle-loving Graysmith, Henry Fonda's character in the film likes playing the odds on horse races with nothing at stake. Both men create a position as outside observer and never lose their innocence or their faith that they will succeed against malevolent forces. When Police Captain Narlowe asks Graysmith if he's "some kind of Boy Scout," the cartoonist seriously replies, "Eagle Scout, actually. First class." Graysmith may not carry a gun, but his ingenuity and pop frame of reference allow him to see beyond the limited visions of his more jaded peers.

In addition to being fundamental to his self-envisioning as a hero, the cinema spiritually connects the cartoonist with the Zodiac: they both perceive their endeavors through the framework of popular culture. They also echo George W. Bush's narrative pitting himself against bin Laden, rather than the U.S. law enforcement and intelligence agencies' battle against a network of transnational terrorists. Early on, Graysmith responds to one of the Zodiac's ciphers that "man is the most dangerous animal of all." Apparently meaningless to the other journalists and police officers, this phrase immediately rattles the cartoonist's pop culture-saturated mind, before he realizes that it comes from the 1932 film *The Most Dangerous Game*. The Zodiac's letters presented throughout the film are full of other pop cultural references, at one point linking the police to the Blue Meanies, the antagonists in the Beatles' 1968 animated film *Yellow Submarine*. The conflation of law enforcement officers with a race that stands against love and happiness implies that the Zodiac perceives his enemies to be on a different spiritual plane. He thus resembles a juvenile rendering of bin Laden, who often described his battles against the United States as a conflict not against a nation but against the Great Satan. *Zodiac* depicts ever more narrowly a mythic conflict that exists outside the realm of bureaucratic reality—an American Eagle Scout who associates himself with an actor most famous for his portrayal of a kind-hearted Abraham Lincoln against a terrorizing force that views American power as entirely antithetical to his principles. *Zodiac* thus frames the War on Terror in absurd terms, uncovering how this simplistic rendering of a moral universe encourages letting any constraints on executive power fall by the wayside.

Undercutting this classic hero-versus-villain narrative, the film views the outlaw-cartoonist with suspicion, connecting him with the vilified embodiment of executive excess, Richard Nixon. In one shot, the film frames Graysmith leaning on a desk that is prominently decorated with a Nixon presidential pin. The placement of the white pin with all-caps red lettering of the name NIXON almost makes the shot appear like a political cartoon that labels Graysmith as a proxy for the controversial president. Graysmith also never appears to have any qualms about following the advice of policemen who encourage him to overstep his bounds as a private citizen, becoming in effect their extralegal proxy. The Nixon presidency has been conceptualized as an administration where paranoia dictated all aspects of executive thinking, thrusting Nixon toward an unconstitutional mode of action that culminated with the Watergate scandal. Afterward, Nixon himself noted, "I was a paranoiac, or almost a basket case, with regard to secrecy" (qtd. in Wheen 2009, 98). Like Graysmith, he was also enamored of the movies; Nixon screened more than five hundred films during his presidency (ibid., 31).[17] The president and the cartoonist both find on the silver screen not just their heroes but their role models.

Genre cinema is a dangerous influence when negotiating a complex reality antithetical to the simplicity of archetypes. By comparing the ostensible hero of *Zodiac* with Nixon, the film critiques Graysmith's investigative practices while unveiling the corrupt nature of a worldview dependent on larger-than-life heroes. At the same time, the film acknowledges that the skewed ideals saturating public discourse have disquietingly real impact on both citizens' and the state's conceptions of how to fight crime. Employing the Nixon era as a prism to consider the post-9/11 era illustrates how genre films continue to exert a strong influence on the public discourses on terror. *Zodiac* makes explicit how the antiestablishment noir occupies a privileged position. Silver screen heroes encourage a perpetuation of Dirty Harry's dangerous attitude that the law, a vital check on executive power, "is crazy." Self-critical noir films like *Zodiac* reflect on the risks of this perception within both cinema and public discourse across different moments of American history.

A key quotation in the DVD commentary of the film's director's cut further elucidates the noir's discursive complexity. During the scene where Toschi and Graysmith attend a screening of *Dirty Harry*, David Fincher not only stresses the Clint Eastwood–starring film's centrality to the plot, underlining the inefficient reality of the very investigation that inspired it, but also identifies the scene as the moment when the audience is meant to feel "despair." This mirrors the real Toschi's true feelings toward *Dirty Harry*; he told Fincher that he was "a little sickened by how easy it was all concluded in the movie." *Zodiac*, in this meta-moment, engenders repulsion toward Harry and his analogue Graysmith, whose outfit in the scene echoes the screen icon's.[18] If the film, in its very construction, heightens frustration with the law, it also creates sympathy with those who follow its constraints. Graysmith and Toschi again refer to *Dirty Harry* in their last scene together, when the cartoonist manically declares that he has solved the Zodiac case. Frustrated that the policeman dubs all the evidence circumstantial and therefore legally invalid, Graysmith asks for Toschi's nonprofessional opinion. Toschi cautions, "Easy, Dirty Harry." In this call for restraint, *Zodiac* offers a salient example of a genre film looking back on itself to show that the promise of an easy answer to crime stands apart from the ethical pursuit of justice.

Conclusion

Both *Sin City* and *Zodiac* include law-abiding characters; however, such allegiance cannot fit within the mythic narrative created in genre films and espoused by the executive. Nancy Callahan never fires the Magnum gun she shares with her namesake Dirty Harry Callahan, suggesting that she has been liberated by her legal savvy, which, like her firearm that "kicks like a mule," had to be mastered. The film leaves the viewer to infer her fate, seemingly unwilling or perhaps unable to present her expertise of and commitment to the law beyond a few seconds of screen time. *Zodiac* offers an epilogue wherein one of the killer's targets who survived points out the Zodiac's photo from a lineup of portraits. The scene's bespectacled policeman speaks with none of the conviction of Graysmith or Toschi before him, even cautioning the interview subject to resist jumping to conclusions. That the "Eureka!" moment exists in an epilogue, sheared from the central action of the plot by a decade and a fade to black, speaks to the laboriousness of due process. With what both productions leave unseen, they highlight a cinematic dilemma—operating within the confines of the law simply fails as spectacle.

Executive actors, allegorically presented within these films, articulated the shock of such a disjuncture. If, as Rabinowitz describes, "American fiction has performed political theory through sensational narratives," executive actors directly evoke and are keenly aware of such narratives in their exercise of political power (Rabinowitz 2002, 18). In making themselves into mythic heroes fighting similarly monumental villains, however, they have to confront the disquieting reality of their own limitations. As the search for bin Laden wore on, President Bush spoke of the terrorist less and less; however, in private, bin Laden remained a focal point of his concerns. Former CIA director Michael Hayden said that the first question Bush asked him during their daily meetings was the status of the manhunt (Bergen 2012, 103). The administration's frustration manifested outwardly during a routine press conference in Bush's second term. Discussing the inability to capture bin Laden, Press Secretary Dana Perino brusquely responded, "This is not the movies, we don't have superpowers" (qtd. in Stolberg 2008). The spokeswoman for the president lost the ability to speak in hyperbolic terms in the face of bureaucratic reality, and an executive who so often invoked a despairing noir rhetoric reached a moment where such discourses failed. Ironically, in that very failure Perino enacted another noir convention, what Borde and Chaumeton refer to as "the disappearance of psychological bearings or guideposts" (qtd. in Naremore 1995–96, 19). Perino's moment of public vulnerability where she seemed overcome by her own rhetoric shows the noir genre's potency to challenge the very actors who seek to use its trappings of paranoia as a mechanism of control.

In contrast, then presidential candidate Barack Obama did not shirk from but rhetorically embraced the figure of the superhero. Prior to his first presidential campaign, the self-professed comics fan struck a pose in front of a Superman statue in Metropolis, Illinois (Nel 340). Later, he even joked during a fundraising dinner that he was the Man of Steel, coming down to earth from Krypton to act as Earth's salvation ("US Elections" 2008). Obama thus positioned himself as a superpowered alternative to the seemingly powerless Bush, a savior for a nation mired in the moral ambiguity of the War on Terror. As the years passed and Obama continued and even expanded many Bush-era policies, the self-valorizing myth broke down. Much as the noir genre commented with skepticism on executive actors who perceive their reality through archetypal lenses, the superhero films of the past two decades, in particular Christopher Nolan's *The Dark Knight* trilogy, showed that *übermenschen* flying above the law lose sight of the human consequences of their actions.

4

Soaring Above the Law

The Post-9/11 Superhero

The Damsel's Troubled Gaze:
Loving the Superhero in Times of Mass Violence

WHILE MY FAMILY LARGELY supported my passion for all things Batman, even creating running jokes lifted from the dialogue of superhero movies, my maternal uncle was the first to express suspicion about my fanboy ardor. During the summers of my adolescence, I visited my mother's family in the French Alps. Although the ostensible goal was for me to learn French grammar from my uncle, we would spend hours discussing popular culture, including comic books and films. I tried to engage in such enthusiastic conversations using my budding French, though sometimes English hyperbole would spill out of my mouth. With great pride, I filled my suitcase with my most prized comics, as I was eager to get my uncle's refined opinion. One year, I brought him Frank Miller's 1986 *The Dark Knight Returns*, about an aging and disillusioned Batman. To my shock, my uncle lacerated Miller's inhumane Batman. He questioned the portrayal of the character as a masked fascist and asked why we never saw the hero helping others without using violent force. Why, he mused, do we never see Batman at a hospice taking care of the sick? This incongruous image of Batman, in full costume, acting as a compassionate caretaker for the vulnerable both charmed me and made me realize that the hero's representations were built on the bruises and the broken bones of his enemies. In such a spectacle, there seemed to be very little room for compassion. My uncle forced me to reconsider the superhero's stranglehold on my imagination and my desire to always be close to him. Years later, watching Christopher Nolan's *The Dark Knight Rises*, which was heavily influenced by the Miller story, I again confronted how the superhero corroded my empathy.

On July 20, 2012, at 12:30 a.m., James Holmes attacked moviegoers during a midnight screening of *The Dark Knight Rises* in Aurora, Colorado, killing twelve and injuring seventy. As described in chapter 1, some of the Aurora survivors initially could not separate the overwhelming violence occurring in the auditorium from the violent spectacle depicted onscreen (Breznican 2012). Blurring the lines further, the bright-haired Holmes was described by law enforcement as a figure who resembled the Joker (Desta 2019). That night, the police recounted a horrifying story of a supervillain who had manifested in the aisle of the cinema, breaking through the fourth wall with guns blazing. Such terrors demand heroes. By comparing the mass shooter to the Joker, the police in Colorado implied that citizens need the protection of a hero, a real-life Batman. And just as President Obama had done with his own references to the Joker (as I will discuss), the police positioned themselves as the superhero. Who are the powerless citizens in all these analogies to the Joker and the superhero? They are the denizens of Gotham City, perhaps most resembling damsels in distress waiting to be attacked and waiting to be saved.

On July 21, 2012, I stood in line at 7:30 a.m. for the 8 o'clock matinee of *The Dark Knight Rises* at the IMAX theater of the San Francisco Metreon. The Aurora shooting cast an atmosphere of dread over the screening. As I waited outside, my then-partner gifted me with a black scarf she had knitted, emblazoned with the yellow Batman symbol. Taking photos of me wearing the stylish accessory somewhat tempered the gloom that had settled over the sunny morning. As I literally preened for the camera, I realized a ghoulish dimension to my fandom, knowing full well that just the day before, people had died in front of the film I was about to consume with relish.

Once inside, I (perhaps antisocially) left my group on the edges of the auditorium to find myself a seat at the center. I glanced at the nearest exit, briefly wondering if I would also leave my loved ones to fend for themselves should a shooter appear. Wearing my new jaunty scarf while feeling scared, I certainly did not feel myself to be a superhero. If anything, I felt an affinity for the stereotypically passive damsel in distress who waits for salvation to come. The cruel calculation I made as I imagined a hypothetical shooting in the Metreon, where only I was somehow saved, suggests how such psychic investment in the superhero as savior could dull my empathy for others and even for myself.

Since 9/11, more often than not, superhero films have framed those with an Arab or Near Eastern identity as little more than terrorists or Islamic fundamentalists. Most egregiously, as described in the introduction, in 2008's *Iron Man* the hero flies to a town square in Afghanistan and faces a group of Taliban-like fighters who hold several civilians hostage. The hero uses facial recognition technology to label the civilians, then proceeds to kill their captors. Whereas the scene was previously filled with their un-subtitled threats, presented as incomprehensible babble, their execution brings a momentary silence. Iron Man stands in the foreground, removed from the pile of brown corpses. The hostages, meanwhile, are momentarily frozen amid the bodies—they look in horror at the American source of their salvation. Seconds later, the hero throws a hiding fighter out of a hotel lobby. As he does so, a hotel sign briefly appears in the shot that features the English misspelling "BADROWN." While this is ostensibly a misspelling of "bedroom," given the abundant Middle Eastern stereotypes on display, I view it as a portmanteau of "BAD BROWN." The scene acknowledges its own stereotyping logic and reveals, just for a moment, the human devastation of America's War on Terror fought through the machine eye of the drone.

Even as such superhero films traffic in racist tropes, I feel refreshed by the candor. Here lies a genre that readily admits that someone brown like me is dehumanized and targeted within the post-9/11 American imaginary. At the same time it somehow proves that such rhetoric is as artificial as a CGI-filled set piece. The "bad brown" scene in *Iron Man* seemed to wink toward a broader formula within the neoconservative rhetoric of the Bush administration during the War on Terror. It playfully drew out the macabre harmony underlying the nationalistic melody sung by many politicians and media during post-9/11 wars: brown people are bad and ideally should be removed in a surgical strike, if not by Iron Man, then by a weaponized drone. This is how such genre films exhilarated me in the past few decades—they have the gall to openly frame me as a stain in America to be blotted out. At the same time, as revealed on the faces of the terrorized civilians in the scene, they encourage me to stand among the corpses that fall under the nation's military might. These spectacular films allude to the horror of an American brand of global policing from the perspective of targeted groups. Often contradictory, at times both critical and valorizing of extralegal lethal force, they invite me to stand beside the death-dealing hero and consider my fraught sympathy with him as he defeats those who may well be my cousins with a well-timed punch or a pull of the trigger.

Being so close to great power but ultimately knowing that I am not imbued with it, I am able to linger on the vexed nature of my disenfranchisement, which is felt even within my privilege. Together with the damsels in distress in certain post-9/11 superhero films, I critically contemplate our beloved protectors. Sam Raimi's 2004 *Spider-Man 2* ends with a shot of Mary Jane Watson (Kirsten Dunst) watching her love swing away to fight crime. She had just left her fiancé at the altar and rushed to the superhero's apartment in time to tell him, "I can't survive without you." Through her wedding dress and unsettled expression, Raimi alludes to the final image of Mike Nichols's 1967 *The Graduate*, wherein a bride leaves her fiancé for another lover, only for the couple to look out toward their future with uncertainty. Raimi's homage to the sequence presents only the bride staring off into the middle distance—Spider-Man seems to have no introspective capacity. Mary Jane looks out the window, following the path of her superheroic lover. Reflected on the glass, the U.S. flag appears small and fuzzy, like a mirage. This final scene differs greatly from the 2002 *Spider-Man*, which ends with the hero leaping off a giant American flag toward the camera. In the 2004 sequel, produced during the U.S.'s initial invasion of Iraq, Raimi introduces the unsettled gaze of the damsel. Before her, the American flag seems diminished. It is as though her look of skepticism toward the superhero also begins to efface the icons of the very nation the superhero protects.

Even as she watches with a critical gaze, Mary Jane stands by the superhero's bed. Her placement in such an intimate space is worth lingering on if we are to sense her disruptive power. As the damsel, she sees the superhero at his most unguarded and catches his frail humanity. With such proximity to him, she can also sense his distance from the ideals of responsibility and altruism that he espouses. Moreover, the damsel is the object of the hero's obsession: she reveals that such figures, stand-ins for American institutions of power, are self-interested actors doing their good deeds for the prospect of a valedictory kiss. The most personal of thrills motivate their heroics. The damsel might seem to occupy a position of pure powerlessness, but seeing the world through her eyes gives me a chance to sense the façade of a dominating power, tearing off its mask as I go to embrace it. Being so close to yet so far from the American superhero, I can appreciate how he crosses moral and ethical boundaries as he courts me and fellow audience members with his undeniably thrilling feats.

Presenting a damsel who does not survive, Nolan's 2008 *The Dark Knight* more brutally stages how such archetypal characters look upon themselves and their vulnerability. Rachel Dawes (Maggie Gyllenhaal) is the love interest of Bruce Wayne (Christian Bale), whose vigilante alias is Batman. The Joker ties her up against oil drums timed to explode. Her boyfriend and Batman's romantic rival, Harvey Dent (Aaron Eckhart), is also strapped to explosives in a second location. Over the speaker phone, Rachel describes Joker's plot to Harvey: "They told me only one of us was gonna make it and that they were going to let our friends choose." Their conversation is crosscut with images of Batman and the police speeding toward the two locations. When the frantic Harvey assures the calm Rachel that their friends are coming to save her, she replies, "I know they are but I don't want them to." Expecting to be consigned to a world without Harvey, Rachel shifts her allegiance away from Batman and accepts Harvey's earlier marriage proposal. She cries out, "I do have an answer for you, and my answer is yes!"

Just as the damsel shows that she fully trusts her own security and can thus take the protection of the superhero for granted, the film shatters expectations. Batman bursts onto the scene, kicking down the warehouse door. A point-of-view shot shows that the hero unexpectedly comes upon Harvey, not Rachel. Harvey, lying in a pool of gasoline, screams, "No, not me! Why are you coming for me?" His question is overlaid against a mid-shot of a terrified Rachel—she realizes then that Batman is not coming to save her. As Batman drags Harvey out of the warehouse, he hysterically screams Rachel's name. The camera then cuts back to the damsel, who listens to Harvey being rescued. She tries to steady herself as his voice fades away, "Harvey, it's okay. It's alright. Listen, someone will—" The blast interrupts her speech, and her hair flutters from its reverberating current as the camera cuts away. Half of Harvey's face is burned in the timed explosion, beginning his transformation. While the damsel dies, a new supervillain, Two Face, emerges.

Through this damsel forced to face her own obliteration alone, Nolan illustrates that a superhero cannot offer us salvation. Instead, representations of heroes can force viewers like me to glimpse the impotence of the structures meant to protect us. The plot overtly notes that Batman intended to save Rachel and that the Joker tricked him into saving his rival Harvey. Still, in so reversing expectations and leaving the damsel to die, the film prompts us to take Harvey's question seriously:

Why *does* Batman save him? By having Batman rescue his rival at the moment he physically morphs into Two Face, the film suggests the only character necessary to maintain the superhero is the enemy. Batman can survive without his damsel, without those he loves and who (at least, he believes) love him. Antagonism, the specter of an ever-present threat, is what sustains and justifies the superhero, and all his antics of power.

In 2008, I stumbled out of *The Dark Knight* moved yet strangely elated by what I had seen: Rachel Dawes recognized the superhero as an illusion from which she needed to break free. When that illusion was broken, however, she had to face the desolation of her expendable status. I wandered to my favorite pub and ordered a blue cheeseburger, medium rare, with onion rings and a side of ranch. While I waited for the thousands of calories to arrive, I wrote, and wrote, and wrote. In my trusty sketchpad, I detailed how 9/11 and War on Terror policy shaped *The Dark Knight*. I frantically scribbled notes about the film's underlying critique: in states of emergency defined by the threat of terrorism, which generate security apparatuses unbounded by law, the citizen becomes disposable. Between bites, each rich with grease, I relished how the film gave me a seam ripper to tear at the stiches of the myth of unity and solidarity that defined our post-9/11 culture.

Still I wonder: Is the damsel really innocent? Perhaps we comfort ourselves with such a label. Rachel, after all, is a defense attorney who tacitly supports Batman's vigilantism; the ostensibly critical Mary Jane allows Spider-Man to continue his fight, never questioning the violence of his crusade. Affirming my uncle's suspicion about my blinding love of the hero, I myself have hidden these facts away from you, the reader. Am I so desperate to preserve the sanctity of the hero, or at least those who love him, that I am willing to conceal his true and troubling nature? Whereas westerns and noirs encouraged generative reflection about my own weakness and self-loathing, superhero films have a more toxic allure. The superhero, especially its post-9/11 variant, invites me to seek out and take pleasure in images of my own destruction. He reveals that there is no innocent observer: I am not unsullied by the violence and suffering he inflicts on others. And despite it all, I love him.

Introducing the Conflicted Post-9/11 Superhero and Christopher Nolan's Batman

On the campaign trail, the future president Barack Obama often jokingly positioned himself as a superhero alternative to the disappointingly mortal

George W. Bush—as a moral agent who would return the nation to the role of principled superpower on the world stage. He joked that he was the Man of Steel, coming down from Krypton to save Earth ("US Elections" 2008). Crossing the line from DC Comics to Marvel, Obama was also visualized as a peer of Spider-Man on a January 2009 comic-book cover; however, late in his first term, the White House released a photo of the president caught in the hero's web (Bicker 2012). Though delivered with humor, the photo suggests that the Obama administration grew to understand the stifling possibility of a mythic discourse and how it can trap a leader within an impossible ideal. At the same time, the official photograph actually posits Obama as a villain in relation to the webslinger, signaling how his realpolitik wartime policies transformed him from a Bush alternative to a mere continuation. A variety of perceived cultural traumas beyond 9/11, from the conflicts stemming from the War on Terror to even the Obama presidency itself, were narrativized using the superhero.

Even as they served to implicitly critique his policies, figures from post-9/11 superhero films were internally deployed within the Obama administration. In the public sphere, political opponents compared Obama to the Batman supervillain the Joker; however, in private, he deployed the example of the supervillain to clarify complex geopolitical realities in the Middle East for his security team. When detailing the protests of the Tea Party movement against his health care reforms, Obama described seeing posters linking him to the Joker: "Some waved doctored pictures of me looking like Heath Ledger's Joker, in *The Dark Knight*, with blackened eyes and thickly caked makeup, appearing almost demonic" (Obama 2020). Obama saw his image being conflated with that of a supervillain, becoming something demonic in the process.

Behind closed doors, Obama spoke about the very scene that inspired this book's title, wherein the Joker claims Batman has "no jurisdiction." Notably, we draw quite different lessons from the scene. I read it as a critique of boundless power; however, Obama read it more as a useful articulation of contemporary geopolitical realities. One advisor described:

> "There's a scene in the beginning in which the gang leaders of Gotham are meeting," the president would say. "These are men who had the city divided up. They were thugs, but there was a kind of order. Everyone had his turf. And then the Joker comes in and lights the whole city on fire. ISIL [the Islamic State of Iraq and the Levant] is the Joker. It has the capacity to set the whole region on fire. That's why we have to fight it." (qtd. in Goldberg 2016)

If we follow the president's own analogy, he considers himself akin to Batman. His comparison troubles in part because of Batman's status as a vigilante outside the law—Obama sees himself as and claims the mantle of the figure who is explicitly said to operate with no jurisdiction. The way *The Dark Knight* seeped into rhetoric around and within the Obama presidency illustrated how the post-9/11 superhero served as a useful metaphor for both the executive and his critics.

Obama's vexed relationship with the superhero presaged that of President Trump, whose inaugural address played off a speech from a Batman supervillain (Tilo Jung 2017). Across the country in the summer of 2020, while violently quashing the Black Lives Matter protests that erupted in response to George Floyd's murder, armed police officers wore the logo of the Punisher, a vigilante superhero (Cascone 2020). For some law enforcement personnel and recent heads of state, this figure had come to glamorize the idea of a post-9/11 executive operating outside the law. This chapter focuses on superhero films made before the Trump presidency that first proposed that model and explored the stakes of that conflation.

The superhero films of the 2000s and 2010s, in particular Christopher Nolan's *The Dark Knight* trilogy, offer an implicit critique of a wartime policy marked by enhanced interrogation techniques under Bush, drone warfare under his successor, and domestic surveillance under both. Here I examine Batman across the Bush and Obama administrations to uncover a conflicted figure acting out the very policies that expose the chasm between the nation's actions and its stated ideals. Such depictions speak to the critical force of the post-9/11 superhero more generally, as Nolan's films express the thrill of unbounded power while simultaneously exposing its sometimes devastating ethical costs.

To combat terrorist threats, Nolan's Batman adopts many of the controversial policies that have underpinned the War on Terror, from torture, both physical and psychological, to pervasive foreign and domestic surveillance. The state with which Batman works—by day as a government contractor and by night as an often-helpful vigilante—perceives its citizens with skepticism, if it sees them at all. For example, in an oblique allusion to the Bush administration's failure during and after Hurricane Katrina to provide support for the impoverished majority Black population of New Orleans, the state abandons the poor of the city in 2012's *The Dark Knight Rises*. The superhero genre can illustrate the dangerous allure of ethically fraught policies when America's military and intelligence agencies are reframed and narratively configured as invulnerable, all-seeing entities. Genre spectacle can then be used to normalize or to critique increasingly intense state violence.

The first film in Nolan's trilogy, 2005's *Batman Begins*, shows the grief-stricken Bruce Wayne obsessed with avenging his parents' death. He trains with the terrorist organization the League of Shadows before eventually adopting the persona of Batman to commence his war on crime in Gotham City. The threat escalates in the 2008 sequel, *The Dark Knight*, as the terrorist Joker (Heath Ledger) emerges on the scene. To combat the clownlike supervillain, Batman surveys the entire city with his fantastic technology. Following his victory over the Joker, Batman exiles himself, taking the blame for a series of murders committed by the deranged District Attorney Harvey Dent. Such self-incrimination allows the city to pass repressive laws, called The Dent Act, in its efforts to preserve law and order. In the third film, 2012's *The Dark Knight Rises*, Batman returns from exile eight years later to battle the masked terrorist Bane (Tom Hardy), who coerces the state to abandon Gotham City. Bane, while promising to deliver the city back to the disenfranchised citizens, aims to destroy it with a nuclear bomb. Although the supervillain sends the superhero to a foreign prison so that he might witness his city's destruction from afar, Batman ultimately triumphs and is memorialized in a statue at City Hall. Bruce Wayne, having faked his own death, passes the cape on to an apprentice. The symbol of Batman endures.

The series embodies a crucial trope of post-9/11 superhero film: the redefinition of superhero as super soldier. The company owned by Bruce Wayne, Batman's billionaire alter ego, acts (at least initially) as an arms manufacturer for the U.S. government. Undermining Wayne's valiant repudiation of the death-dealing technology, his Batman suit and gadgets are all reappropriated military equipment. He is a super soldier in the guise of a cape-wearing vigilante. Although Batman is a DC Comics hero, this trope is also present in many Marvel films made since 2000, culminating with Joss Whedon's 2012 superhero team-up film *The Avengers*, which features a group that operates under the jurisdiction of the covert military agency known as S.H.I.E.L.D.[1] That most superheroes have been linked to the military places many of these films in a vexed position in relation to government authority.

Nolan's films reveal a deep suspicion toward such institutions and evoke a host of complex and related legal concerns; the filmmaker has stated that his Batman movies seek both to enjoy and to question vigilan-tism (Holleran 2005). Narratively and formally, *The Dark Knight* trilogy relishes the superhuman capacity of its hero while continually linking state power, represented by Batman, to varying forms of terrorism. The films subtly frame these connections via a briefly shifting musical score or a fleeting metaphoric staging. The finessed touch of these linkages, their blink-and-you'll-miss-it quality, gestures toward the public's myopia about (or, more starkly, its urge to ignore) the harm caused by building a post-9/11 legal order upon a foundation of fear.

The films are narratively concerned with shifting legal frameworks in the face of terrorism. *The Dark Knight Rises*, released at the end of the Obama era, plays upon disillusionment with the administration that in many ways continued within the same conceptual frameworks of the Bush era.[2] In the film, the civic leadership of Gotham City has adopted sweeping policies that arbitrarily detain criminals, like the spongy "enemy combatant" concept developed following 9/11. *The Dark Knight* directly cites the RICO (Racketeer Influenced and Corrupt Organizations) laws developed in the 1970s to quell organized crime, policies that in the film seem impotent in the terrorizing presence of the Joker, who so easily breaks free from the custody of traditional law enforcement. In response, Batman progressively transforms into a paranoid surveyor, and his city becomes an urban panopticon. *The Dark Knight* formally expresses a marked ambivalence toward Batman's metamorphosis into an Orwellian Big Brother who deploys warrantless domestic surveillance techniques to stop the terrorist threat.

The Nolan Batman films, so concerned with the law's impotence, reveal a power-valorizing genre well positioned to reveal the cracks in façades of power. Alejandro González Iñárritu's 2014 *Birdman: Or (The Unexpected Virtue of Ignorance)* meditates on why the superhero film now is what one critic describes as the nation's new ur-text, replacing the western, in the post-9/11 era (Baron 2012). Directly citing the attacks with the nightmarish image of a burning bird, or man (or is it a plane?) streaking above New York City, Iñárritu uncovers a strand of weakness woven into the genre's fabric. The satirical film thus posits that our current infatuation with this genre does not signal a collective desire for escape. Instead, it is through a genre obsessed with super strength that American weakness can be confronted, if only momentarily. In one of the film's closing images, the mad protagonist, the former onscreen superhero Reegan Thomson (played by the former Batman Michael Keaton), stares through bandages on his face. His bruises resemble the black makeup beneath the eyelets of the cinematic superhero's mask. *Birdman* shows that a wound underlies the iconic myth of the superhero and lends it a transfixing vitality.

Testimonies of comic book creators and various comic book materials produced in the aftermath of 9/11 demonstrate the sizable impact the attacks had on the representation of superheroes. Speaking about his 2004 series *Identity Crisis*, where DC superheroes are attacked and brutalized in their homes, author Brad Meltzer notes, "Without question, *Identity Crisis* was a reaction to 9/11. The Norman Rockwell picture of America and firemen and policemen was shattered. And so the popular culture goes too. It was weeks after that I began the series, determined to remind people of that humanity in heroes" (qtd. in Marano 2008, 82). Batman artist Paul Pope similarly noted, "After 9/11, there was a lot of weltschmerz among professional cartoonists regarding the purpose of why we make comics. My answer was to read *Beowulf*. We literally *need* heroic projections" (Pope 2017; emphasis his).

Shortly after the attacks, both DC Comics and Marvel released anthologies for 9/11 charities wherein their various superheroes reacted to the attacks, offering readers heroic projections linked to a moment of crisis. Many of the vignettes evoke a sense of total shock that suggests the inability of the superhero form to fully encompass a traumatic event of such magnitude. One portrait by artist Phil Noto shows the *Daily Planet* photographer, Superman's colleague Jimmy Olsen, looking up at what is presumably the World Trade Center (Noto 2002, 173). Holding his trademark camera at his midsection, the reporter who has enthusiastically framed the many exploits of Superman seems unable to capture the attack on American soil. The image knowingly plays with the catchphrase, "Look up in the sky! It's a bird! It's a plane! It's Superman!" In a post-9/11 world, the sky, the wondrous domain of the quintessential American superhero, has been desecrated by horror.

To more broadly contextualize why the superhero genre seems so engaged with changing contemporary political concerns, it is helpful to consider the evolution of Superman's mantra from the comic books and cartoons of World War II to post-9/11 film. The superhero comic reached its initial apex during the trauma of World War II.[3] Early incarnations of Superman offered readers a reassuringly nationalistic message: "For Truth, Justice, and the American Way." Following 9/11, with some earlier key exceptions, the superhero film emerged as a prominent cinematic genre. The effects of the attacks and the wars that followed are perhaps best expressed in Bryan Singer's 2006 *Superman Returns*. Denoting a marked ambivalence toward the present American way, the incredulous newspaper editor Perry White (Frank Langella) questions the superhero's motto: "Does he still stand for truth, justice, all that stuff?" In the context of

9/11 and the United States embarking on an internationally criticized global war, Superman's American Way seems dubious, even inexpressible.

Moreover, Superman of the post-9/11 era appears to have grown strangely passive. Reading animated Superman cartoons from World War II, media scholar Aldo J. Regalado notes that the jingoist short films underlined how the hero mirrored the American flag—red cape, white skin, and blue leotard (Regalado, 139). Superman and the other superheroes of the day were "[u]nequivocally supportive of the war effort, [and] comics continued to serve as propaganda pieces" (ibid., 140). In another scene from *Superman Returns*, quite unlike his aggressive forties-era equivalent who fought the Axis powers with his bare hands, the superhero (Brandon Roth) confronts the Iraq War while sitting on his sofa.[4] Seeing the carnage in the Middle East broadcast on the evening news, with a veiled Arab woman lamenting her loss, the so-called Man of Steel does not move, unable or unwilling to aid America with its wars abroad. The televisual mediation of seemingly endless conflict does not spur action.

That scene raises key theoretical questions about the televisual representation of catastrophe, genre's mediating potential, and the spectacular envisioning of state violence. Mary Ann Doane's essay "Information, Crisis, Catastrophe" examines the curious temporality of the hypermediated medium of television. When tracing the etymological roots of the word "catastrophe," Doane finds that the dictionary definition—"the final event of the dramatic action, esp. of a tragedy"—"contaminates [catastrophe] with fictionality" (Doane 2005, 255). Framing catastrophes as inherently dramatic events, she encourages us to turn to fictional mediations to more fully understand the wider political context.

Doane later argues that in television "crisis is produced and assimilated as part of the ongoing spectacle," presented in such a way as to deflect attention from the catastrophe's systemic roots (2005, 261). Although she explicitly cites world economic crisis, her conception relates well to the televisual and cinematic mediation of war and other political turmoil. At first glance, Superman's TV-watching pose suggests that the superhero icon is impotent against real-world crisis. When perceived through Doane's framework, however, the scene functions as a potent metacommentary on the inability of the televisual to render such crises viscerally palpable and comprehensible. Television, although transfixing, "thrives on its own forgettability" (ibid., 253–54). In the very ephemerality of its hero's confrontation with the geopolitical reality on his TV screen, *Superman Returns* underlines that this medium places an insurmountable distance between spectator and victim. Does mythic storytelling stand as an antidote, capable of providing decontextualized catastrophe with sufficient background to permit greater or more meaningful engagement?

In Doane's estimation, television's ability to color the catastrophic with the hue of the spectacular strips individual events of context and meaning. Spectacle, she reminds us, can blind. Many Obama administration officials perceived the execution of Osama bin Laden through a televisual lens. The U.S. soldiers at bin Laden's Pakistani compound wore cameras that broadcast the operation back to the White House. Yet they also invoked cinematic discourses: remembering the explosion of a downed helicopter, one Obama official declared, "[It was] like a Jerry Bruckheimer movie!" (qtd. in Bergen 2012, 228). Secretary of State Hillary Clinton blurred TV and cinematic figures: "This was like any episode of *24* or any movie you could ever imagine" (qtd. in ibid., 220). The officials either made sense of or distanced themselves from the corporeal reality of the assassination by perceiving it as a particularly kinetic televisual or cinematic set piece. Their testimonies underline how state violence on such a scale is both inherently spectacular and potentially choreographed in ways that refer to cinematic tropes.

The challenge that a subset of these superhero films take up is to reframe our perception, to "*displace and redirect* (as well as simply expand) [the] aperture of visibility" upon spectacular, hypervisible state violence (Sedgwick 2003, 140). Besides showing how cinematic presentation of inherently spectacular violence can alter our perspective on state practices, this chapter also explores whether spectacle can delineate the complex discourses of victim and perpetrator, state-sponsored and terrorist violence, perhaps even allowing for empathy toward the victims. How do the immersiveness and exhilaration of genre cinema's reflections on state violence at times collude with and at other times counter the "live" yet distancing televised catastrophe?

"The Power of Fear" and Psychological Torture in *Batman Begins*

In a meeting with a Gotham City crime boss (Tom Wilkinson), young Bruce Wayne learns a formative lesson that shapes his ethos as a crime fighter and gestures toward the trilogy's thematic linking of justice with terrorism. The mobster pulls a gun on Wayne and, after listing the various officials and judges surrounding him in the bar, notes, "Now, I wouldn't have a second's hesitation of blowing your head off right here and right now in front of 'em. Now, that's power you can't buy. That's the power of fear." As a vigilante, without any compunction, Wayne co-opts the criminal's mantra as he adopts his superhero alter ego. Moreover, he learns his spectacular "theatricality" in the mountains of central Asia, from the League of Shadows, his world's Al Qaeda.[5] Yet he practices a state-sanctioned form of terror whose mode of psychological domination echoes not bin Laden's organization but the Bush administration. The executive's enhanced interrogation techniques made headlines the year before *Batman Begins* was released with the leak of Assistant Attorney General Jay S. Bybee's 2002 memo on the standard conduct for interrogation, aka the Torture Memo.

Batman's rules of engagement in his "war on crime" resemble the Bush administration's notoriously limited definition of torture in the memo: "Physical pain amounting to torture must be equivalent in intensity to the pain accompanying serious physical injury, such as organ failure, impairment of bodily function, or even death" (Bybee and Gonzalez 2006, 317). Just as Batman enacts all manner of nonlethal violence, Bybee argues for the narrowest definition of torture (which is absolutely forbidden under international law) where extreme physical violence is acceptable. He reads the Convention Against Torture, to which the United States is a signatory, as defining torture at "the farthest end of impermissible actions, and that it is distinct and separate from the lower level of 'cruel, inhuman, or degrading treatment or punishment'" (ibid., 330). The latter does not carry "criminal penalties and the stigma of torture" (ibid.). To Bybee, in order to count as forms of psychological torture, instigating "prolonged mental harm," the actions "must disrupt profoundly the senses or the personality" of the subject under interrogation (ibid., 322).

Even under the Bybee formula that offers the interrogator very wide and unprosecutable latitude, Nolan's Batman tortures (Bybee and Gonzalez 2006, 334). He reveals his intent to psychologically damage his victims when answering his butler Alfred's (Michael Caine) question: "Why bats, Master Wayne?" Wayne replies flatly, "Bats frighten me. It's time my enemies share my dread." He seeks not merely to control the criminal class but to terrorize it. To this point, the mobster who instructed Bruce Wayne about the power of fear is sent to an asylum following his first meeting with Batman. During the confrontation, the hero straps the criminal up to a fog light in an oddly corporeal, victim-centric staging of the Bat Signal. This recalls the cross-armed pose of a black-hooded prisoner in a much-broadcasted Abu Ghraib photograph. The shadow of the U.S. interrogation practices in the Middle East is thus projected into the sky of an American city, like a warning to Batman's foes.

Accentuating the grotesque quality of its hero and his practices designed to mentally destroy his enemies, Nolan presents Gotham City as a noir labyrinth where Batman has an almost supernatural command of the shadows. This staging, particular to the series' first film, makes the Caped Crusader appear truly horrifying, more monster than man. His tactics resemble a nightmarish iteration of the controversial techniques employed by the CIA in Iraq. An influential text, the 1963 *KUBARK CIA Counterintelligence Interrogation Manual*, states that detention must make the prisoner feel as though he were "being plunged into the strange" (qtd. in Danner 2004, 17). *Batman Begins* often adopts the point of view of the horrified criminals so as to present an estranging image of the iconic hero.[6] Rather than creating a sense of exhilaration and admiration, the film's horror-inspired aesthetic provokes fear toward its own hero. This approach seems to embody Christopher Nolan's unsettled feelings about Batman and his vigilante ways.

Nolan's ambivalence, woven into the entire trilogy, is made visible within the first film's superheroic rendition of the practice of enhanced interrogation. Creating a metaphorical linkage between the interrogation in an alleyway and the intelligence-gathering methods of America's soldiers in the Middle East, the victim, a corrupt police detective, grabs a falafel from a stand and then encounters the hero. He is caught in a trap that sweeps him many stories up the side of a building to face Batman upside down. The rainswept setting contains certain metaphoric resonances with the method where American interrogators "forced fluids down the victim's throat to simulate the sense of drowning" (McCoy 2006, 59). As in waterboarding, the victim is positioned upside down as water rushes down his face, and the threat of death is present as Batman grabs and proceeds to hurl his suspended victim down toward the pavement, stopping just before the moment of impact.

The degree to which Batman works to break the interrogated cop's worldview and assert his total dominance is suggested in their dialogue. After the man cries out, "I don't know, I swear to God," Batman barks back, "Swear to *me!*" The thundering storm matches the movement of the hero's trap—it rumbles whenever the Dark Knight drops his victim down to what seems to be his demise. Coupled with their verbal exchange, the staging reconstitutes the hero into an awe-inspiring divine entity. The discomfiting echo of techniques that have been described as torture, however, provokes profound questions about the righteousness of actions by this god whose creed is the power of fear.[7]

In his essay about the contradictory role of fear in three recent Hollywood films, film scholar Andrew Schopp offers a salient distillation of the post-9/11 anxieties within *Batman Begins* while critiquing what he finds to be the film's ambivalent portrait of the eponymous superhero. Pinpointing the core theme of Nolan's trilogy, the imbrication between villain and hero, he sees the ironies in Bruce Wayne as a defense contractor and notes the resonances between Batman's activities and the U.S. military's actions in Iraq (Schopp 2009, 275). Moreover, Schopp frames Gotham City as a space that embodies America's present front line and home front (ibid.). Nolan employs this multivalent allegorical framework throughout his trilogy: in *Batman Begins*, the torture of Abu Ghraib finds its way to our streets; in *The Dark Knight*, domestic surveillance and drone warfare merge; in *The Dark Knight Rises*, echoing the more blistering critiques of the Bush administration's failed response to Hurricane Katrina, the foreign wars come home and the lower classes become the enemy.

Schopp, however, worries that *Batman Begins*' "vexed and even contradictory messages threaten to mitigate the impact of that interrogation" of the present culture of fear. He concludes that "despite these allusions [to a blurring of enemy and villain], the comic book and Hollywood formulas ultimately demand that we note the distinction between the Batman, who uses fear tactics for 'Good' and who learns to conquer and control his fear, and the other figures who use fear purely for 'Evil' " (Schopp 2009, 280). While I agree that the third Nolan film is intentionally muddled, I find that these core fluctuations are vital to the critical work of the film and similar genre spectacles. Schopp says that the films are constrained "by offering of either a distracting visual spectacle . . . or a melting pot of allusions that are plentiful, yet conflicted" (ibid.). To me, the very distraction and obscuring excitement of the spectacle disrupt overriding Manichean frameworks, breaking down conceptions of absolute "good" and "evil" and thereby encouraging the spectator to acknowledge their own potential collusion with state violence as well as the possibility of being its victim. Nowhere is this breakdown more apparent than in *The Dark Knight*'s presentation of the terrorist, the Joker, who exudes a palpable charisma and with carnivalesque glee reveals the very emptiness of the hero's power.

"It's not about money, it's about sending a message!": The Transformation of a Clown into a Terrorist

With a scene of the Joker standing in a destroyed police station, *The Dark Knight* metaphorically implies that, in a post-9/11 world, established legal practices have been all but obliterated by transnational terrorists. After the Joker is temporarily put into custody, he escapes, using an explosive device. Following the blast, he stands tall among floating shreds of paperwork. Given the setting at the center of law enforcement, the metaphor is clear: in fighting terrorists, established rules of law have been ripped apart. This imagery echoes the discourse of terrorism and legal experts after 9/11.[8]

The villain most potently frames the legal transformation. As he so succinctly puts it, "Batman has no jurisdiction. He'll find [the wanted man] and make him squeal!" Employing legal language, Nolan cannily transforms the superhero convention of omnipresence into an example of the hero's disavowal of the law as a check on his power. The Joker's discourse evokes the oft-criticized framework used by the Bush and Obama administrations of a boundless, global War on Terror. In an article on Obama's secret Kill List, *New York Times* journalists Jo Becker and Scott Shane note, "Justly or not, drones have become a provocative symbol of American power, running roughshod over national sovereignty and killing innocents" (Becker and Shane 2012). The Nolan films often push for a reevaluation of unrestrained American power; however, that it is the villainous Joker who delivers the most salient indictment of Batman's rules of engagement points to the limits of critique within a genre film. Can post-9/11 superhero cinema, often toeing the line between skepticism and wide-eyed wonder toward its heroes' abilities, provoke sympathy with or at least an intellectual understanding of the figure marked as a supervillain, troubling the Manichean construction that has defined and justified the War on Terror?

The amorphous Joker speaks to how inextricably post-9/11 law has become immersed in a muddle of meaning. His own fluid identity echoes a certain flexibility in how the state currently defines terrorists as well as the term *enemy combatant*.[9] As President Obama's adviser Bruce Riedel described it, the terrorist threat is an "existential" one for Americans (qtd. in Mueller and Stewart 2012, 81). The eerily fluctuating Joker mirrors the establishment image of the terrorist as an unknowable and haunting Other, while also illuminating deficiencies in the legal system's ability to define the enemy. Even the way the Joker perverts his legally permitted single phone call while in police custody to detonate an improvised explosive device further positions this supervillain as a terrorist ready to expose how the law can be twisted.

Unlike previous renditions of the character, Nolan's Joker is not a crime-loving anarchist but a calculating political agent, determined to use his spectacular crimes as a way of "sending a message." Nolan visually and narratively pays homage to earlier portrayals of the character across media, crystallizing the most salient features of his post-9/11 iteration. Shots of the Joker staring through the wide-spaced iron bars of his holding cell recall his first comic book appearance in *Batman #1*, released in 1940, particularly the final panel (Kane 1940, 13). In it, the Joker clutches the bars, looks directly at the reader, and exclaims, "They can't keep me here! I know of a way out—the Joker will yet have the last laugh!" The lack of depth within the image makes it seem as though the villain pushes outward. The Joker has always exposed the vulnerability of law enforcement and revealed the tenuous hold of its institutions. Nolan brings this facet of the villain to the forefront of his film, made during a cultural moment when the public was deeply concerned about terrorism and the righteousness of the laws crafted to govern a state of exception.

The film reinforces Joker's ties to contemporary conceptualizations of terrorism through its depiction of his relationship to the media, which again plays with past iterations of the character. In *The Dark Knight* the Joker sends an execution video to the media in which he kills a Batman copycat. The video replicates the visual iconography of the Islamist terrorists' beheading video, particularly prevalent during the War on Terror, which features shaky camera work and noticeable digital pixilation. Beyond its visuals, the Joker's dialogue with his victim mirrors the typical dialogue of the executioner with the victim in such beheading videos, including: "the reading of offenses (transgressions), confession, judgment, last words, execution . . . written or verbal statement of demands" (Perlmutter 2005). The Joker claims that the copycat has transgressed by acting as Batman, forces a confession from him, judges his crime, then executes the victim offscreen after verbally demanding that the true Batman take off his mask. Its creation and broadcast also mirror the work of the Joker in Tim Burton's 1989 *Batman*, who inserted a homemade advertisement into a news program after his deadly makeup had just killed an anchor on air. Such allusions suggest that the Joker has previously exposed systemic failures in the security apparatus and wielded the media as a weapon. Whereas in the Burton film he seems focused on making artistic or aesthetic critiques of fashion-obsessed culture through his terrorizing plot, labeling himself the "world's first fully functioning homicidal artist," Nolan's terrorist Joker espouses a more politically oriented philosophy. The particulars of his worldview are kept vague, but the "agent of chaos" appears dedicated to exposing both the moral emptiness within the established order upheld by Batman and the susceptibility of a security system built on fear.

Like Malkina in *The Counselor*, the Joker of *The Dark Knight* represents genre spectacle's disruptive potential, a quality most apparent during a scene with Batman in the police interrogation room. While Batman is conducting the enhanced interrogation, the very mise-en-scène demonstrates that the Joker holds the power in their encounter. The bright fluorescent lighting of the chamber lends a glow to his makeup while making the Caped Crusader appear faintly ridiculous and drawing attention to the permanent scowl on his face, the "man" behind Batman. Unlike the hero, who speaks in grunts and short phrases, the supervillain waxes poetic on their shared position as "freaks" and on the faux morality of civilization. Further accentuating the conflation of supervillain and superhero, terrorist and state, when Batman begins to physically torture the Joker, punching him, the latter quips, "Never start with the head, the victim gets all fuzzy, he can't feel the next [hit]."[10] The Joker's line of polite professional advice establishes both as victimizers. More disquietingly, the film simultaneously links the violence by the superhero to torture and suggests that his actions are a sign of underlying impotence. With each blow, the Joker laughs ever more exuberantly, chortling, "You have nothing, nothing to threaten me with, nothing to do with all your strength!" Even the very generic framing, a low-angle shot of the hero cut against a high-angle shot of the villain, is undermined as the Joker continues to push himself off the floor, rising in the frame. The Joker unveils here the possibility that the traditional American ideal of the superhero, linked to the military might of the executive in his many post-9/11 iterations, cannot mask a profound ineffectuality that borders on weakness.

Nolan highlights the strong pull of Joker's ideas by the way he continually transfixes the film camera. Seen from behind in the opening sequence, he stages an elaborate bank robbery, and the camera tracks down onto the clown mask that he holds in his hand. The mask resembles one worn by Cesar Romero's sprightlier rendition of the supervillain during the *Batman* television series from the 1960s—an allusion that underlines just how long the brightly colored antagonist has endured. He, and his anarchic ideology antithetical to both the Batman as well as the establishment, can never be shut out. Notably, Romero's Joker deploys a moving van-turned-deathtrap that his U.S.-based corporation, One-Armed Bandit Novelty Company, "built for a whimsical Caribbean dictator . . . [who was] deposed before delivery." The Joker, even in his most outlandish and camp forms, highlights the human rights abuses that spring from the military-industrial complex wherein American enterprises supply authoritarian regimes. With a quick wink to Romero's Joker, Nolan establishes in the opening scene of *The Dark Knight* that his variant of the character fits within an established tradition of a supervillain who brings unsettling systemic corrosion to light. His camera cannot help but be drawn to the Joker and, implicitly, to his opposing ideology that works to expose the core hypocrisies of the hero and the order he defends.

The film showcases the terrorist's motivation not as an unknowable evil but as careful reason, suggesting how genre spectacle might contribute to the richness of the discourses within the public sphere. Replying to a gangster who calls him crazy, the Joker says in a measured tone, "I'm not [crazy]. No. I'm. Not." The director crystallized a key tension in the film:

> Our Joker's—[actor Heath Ledger's] interpretation of The Joker has always been the absolute extreme of anarchy and chaos, effectively. . . . And what makes him terrifying is to not humanise him in narrative terms. Heath found all kinds of fantastic ways to humanise him in terms of simply being real and being a real person, but in narrative terms we didn't want to humanise him, we didn't want to show his origins, show what made him do the things he's doing because then he becomes less threatening (qtd. in Jolin)

Batman's code is, by contrast, crystal clear, like Bush's "with us/against us" dichotomy that opened the War on Terror. The villain indicts the underlying simplicity of the hero's code when he tells him, "You have all these rules, and you think they'll save you!" He taunts Batman with the possibility that the morals founding the system under his protection are nothing but "a bad joke" while his own brand of anarchy bristles with possibility.

The comic book enemies represent order against chaos, an opposition as stark as Bush against bin Laden. Each side perceives rot in the other. *The Dark Knight*'s representation of the terrorist points toward an underlying logic, suggesting that the enemy's viewpoint not only might be valid but also captures the hypocrisy and the perpetration of violence by the state. Still, though made more human and reasonable in character, the enemy is not entirely recognizable. He presents the origin of his facial scars differently over the course of the film, which signals that the audience cannot fully know him. Batman and Bush are so vulnerable with their comprehensive moral codes that they border on self-fashioned caricature. The terrorist Joker takes an antithetical position to the American superpower but is fascinating due to his complexity and charisma. In refashioning an archetypical national enemy into a hypnotic, if inscrutable force, the film testifies to genre's power to humanize, to render the state's opponents newly complex and vivid, unsettling popular conceptions. In *The Dark Knight*, the representative of the state can only grunt, whereas a terrorist might provoke the audience with his lucid speech worthy of Shakespeare's fools.

In his study *Bending Steel*, which analyzes superheroes as well as biographies of their creators to frame such figures as key and ever-changing "cultural responses to American modernity," Aldo J. Regalado notes that the superhero film has become the preeminent forum for these stories, surpassing comics by a wide margin (Regalado, 11). While he describes the stew of contemporary anxieties found in the Nolan films, gesturing to "the postmodern anarchy" represented by enemies such as the Joker, he worries that the corporate scale of film production will dull the critical bite of these pictures to gain mass appeal. In his criticism of the Superman film, Zack Snyder's 2012 *Man of Steel*, Regalado, like Schopp, takes issue with the multiple and opposing sentiments expressed, though he identifies the superhero film's muddled stance as a symptom of producers trying to "maximize profits" (ibid., 227). Even if there is some truth to this, the "postmodern anarchy" of the Joker, perhaps the sharpest expression of the transgressive possibility of this mass art, shows that the oppositional elements bristle because of, not in spite of, the innocuous nature of the commercial vehicle in which they are couched. Testifying to this tension between the ethically ambiguous content and the highly commodified context, the most tonally despairing trailer for *The Dark Knight* was released exclusively for the Domino's Pizza chain. It ends with a series of deleted shots from the film in which the Joker tells a gangster, "This town is mine now." A wider shot then shows the two men standing in front of a pile of money that the Joker burns. Whereas the rest of the trailer contains rapid-style editing, here, the camera lingers upon the criminals staring at each other in silence. The crackle of the burning money while the scene fades to black signals that the terrorist antagonist will make the film his own. As the Joker tells the gangster, who looks upset that the Joker has burned the funds acquired, "It's not about money, it's about sending a message." The Joker's message gains force as it emerges within a mode of mass art designed for maximum profit, ostensibly all about money.

In this way, *The Dark Knight* encapsulates the multiple valences that some film scholars have found possible within the sprawling blockbuster form, which contains critical potential because it is a product designed for mass appeal. As argued by Miriam Hansen in her essay "Early Cinema, Late Cinema: Permutations of the Public Sphere,"

> Blockbuster films are catering to as many diverse constituencies as possible, confronting the problem of, as Timothy Corrigan puts it, "an audience fragmented beyond any controllable identity." These films . . . no longer attempt to homogenize empirically diverse viewers by way of unifying strategies of spectator positioning. . . . Rather, the blockbuster gamble consists of offering something to everyone, of appealing to diverse interests with a diversity of attractions and multiple levels of textuality. (Hansen 1993, 199)

Although Hansen is focused on how such films fracture audience identities, her framework encourages us to see the blockbuster as a form full of ideological fissures and to examine these gaps. No antagonist embodies such fracturing as fully as the Joker. Emerging out of a film designed to sell products as mundane as pizza, Joker frames the interests of the "blockbuster gamble," wherein a cutting message might burn through the piles of money the film both garners and seeks. To signal just how completely his message may dictate the blockbuster, *The Dark Knight* restages the *Batman Begins* scene of psychological torture where Batman hangs a cop in the rain. The restaging, featuring Batman catching the Joker with his grappling hook as the villain falls off a building, contains one striking difference. Whereas in the first iteration the camera frames the corrupt cop upside down, delineating its distance from the character, in the next iteration the camera slowly turns, so that the Joker is framed right side up. The camera turn signifies how the film identifies with the trickster. That the Joker has such influence on the film's formal construction lends weight to his opposing ideology that works to expose the core hypocrisies of the hero and the order he upholds—exemplified by the hypercapitalistic form of the superhero blockbuster itself.

"Beautiful, isn't it?": The Allure and Trap of State Surveillance in *The Dark Knight*

When the Joker passes through public space, the state's existing surveillance apparatus seems unable to control him, even when he allows himself to be fully seen. During the film's opening bank heist, he pointedly stares at a surveillance camera. While holding up a still of the Joker caught on, or rather posing for, the camera, Commissioner Jim Gordon tells the superhero, "He can't resist showing us his face." In response, Batman introduces an all-encompassing surveillance apparatus that transforms Gotham City into a figurative panopticon. *The Dark Knight*, juxtaposing a business mogul/superhero against an unknowable terrorist enemy, highlights the threat of an amorphous identity to the post-9/11 order, as well as its utility in helping transform a domestic space into a surveillance state under the executive's total control.

In its broader portrayal of a hyper-surveyed Gotham City and its representation of the superhero's technology, notably his motorcycle, *The Dark Knight* pays homage to Paul Pope's acclaimed 2006 comic miniseries, *Batman: Year 100*. Set in 2039 in a Gotham City reeling from the emergence of an old urban legend, the titular Caped Crusader, Pope's series positions Batman as an enemy of the surveillance state, bucking against the representations of the superhero as a privileged overseer that *The Dark Knight* fully embraces. Pope frames the vigilante as an object of and challenge to the state's gaze—the one boundary it cannot cross. In a personal interview discussing both the comic series and the Nolan film, the artist spoke about his goals for *Year 100*, noting, "I tried to toss out all that earlier Batman legend and just look at the idea of a surveillance state dealing with a masked man. My Batman is essentially an accidental home-grown terrorist against the state" (Pope 2017). He continued, "The state apparatus requires a rational, knowable and categorizable antagonist. My Batman is a mystical or irrational figure" (ibid.).

Illustrating this disruptive irrationality, in one frame where Batman stares into body cameras, he appears as a glowing and monstrous form on the government's security monitors (Pope 2006, 18). The digital grain distorts him so that his eyes glow like lightning, creating a hazy, ill-defined image in sharp contrast to Pope's normal bold and clean art style. In their essay detailing their concept of a "landscape of fear," sites where states enact the spectacle of security, John R. Gold and George Revill suggest that such a confrontation is destabilizing (Gold and Revill 2003, 42) because "particular rationalities, for example those linked to capitalism or racism [we could add security], produce fears through the processes of ordering and marginalizing" (ibid., 45). Through his blurred gaze, Pope's Batman shows bureaucrats the fear that their cameras maintain and cultivate. Moreover, his Batman submerges these "rational actors" in the very fear sparked by their oppressive mechanisms of surveillance.

Troubling sympathies toward the archrivals depicted in the film, *The Dark Knight* tweaks Pope's formulations—the Joker functions as the home-grown terrorist and remains a "mystical or irrational" figure. He is the one mockingly staring at impotent security cameras, marking himself as the one individual they cannot fully know. In so doing, he transforms Batman into a proponent of a total surveillance state, desperate to extend his grasp over the "landscape of fear" that is Gotham City.

Intercut with the unveiling of Batman's fantastic technology, the film shows that the military is now involved in the city's political crisis, presenting images of armed soldiers on the ground and military helicopters in the sky. The film thus primes the viewer for a vision of its hero's surveillance practices and links it with a government operating in a state of emergency. This too is in keeping with the imagery in Pope's comics series, where the Capitol Building can be seen beyond barbed wire fences, a reminder of a militarized post-9/11 United States (Pope 2006, 11). Nolan frames unease with pervasive domestic surveillance when the echo of a gunshot linked with the execution of a corrupt police officer bleeds over a shot of Batman standing behind a bank of monitors. The sonic bridge creates an implicit connection between corrupt law enforcement activity and Batman's intelligence gathering, dependent on surveying the city's denizens without their knowledge. The superhero seems oblivious to such concerns. Referring to the monitors around him and speaking directly to the camera, he asks, "Beautiful, isn't it?"

His question and apparent awe at such technological vision illuminate the dualistic position the film takes—its revulsion is intermingled with wonder. Through the hero's break of the fourth wall, the film underlines its intentions. It forms an aesthetic of power where state control might lead to beauty for the beholder, while the watched, often economically or socially marginalized, become nothing more than color in an expansive portrait of urban life that only the wealthy superhero and the spectator have the privilege to see. Nolan considers the post-9/11 state's changed relationship with its citizenry, drawing a comparison between the untraceable Joker's terrorism and the subsequent scenario where citizens themselves are perceived as threats.

Through mirrored sonic cues, the film blurs the line between the superhero's and supervillain's practices. However, by emulating the God-like vision of drones via kinetic imagery, *The Dark Knight* illustrates the allure of a mechanical eye that represents the culmination of what Paul Virilio describes as warfare's marrying of camera with weaponry.

This helps explain the normalization of policies that privilege limitless executive power that impinges upon the rights of citizens.

Jeremy Bentham, in *Panopticon Letters*, wrote that for the family of the jailer charged with overseeing the panopticon, the sight of the prisoners "will supply in their instance the place of that great and constant fund of entertainment to the sedentary and vacant in towns—the looking out of the window. The scene, though a confined, would be a very various, and therefore, perhaps, not altogether an unamusing one" (Bentham 1995, 45). *The Dark Knight* suggests the fraught attraction of such entertainment, of a world where citizens are like prisoners, vulnerable to the surveyor's sight. Through vicarious visual access to the surveillance apparatus within the film, Nolan acknowledges the intriguing fractured subject position it fosters in the viewer, alienating because the objectified individual might see himself as a target, but also exhilarating in that a superior vantage point offers a taste of unchecked power.

Focusing upon an economically privileged protagonist, *The Dark Knight* provides perspective on the elite class's underexplored fascination with mass surveillance. The theme of class conflict becomes narratively central later, in *The Dark Knight Rises*, a film tinged with the concerns of the Occupy Movement and thus attuned to the absurdity of a hero whose superpower derives from his status as a member of the elite, the one percent. As Selina Kyle (Anne Hathaway), also known as Catwoman, reminds Wayne at a high-society ball, "There's a storm coming, Mister Wayne. You and your friends better batten down the hatches, because when it hits, you're all gonna wonder how you ever thought you could live so large and leave so little for the rest of us." *The Dark Knight* addresses its concerns about Wayne's economic status more obliquely, through jokes and brief but pointed visual compositions. The end result is a more valorizing rendition of the hero that helps to capture the magnetism of such a lofty position for those in the audience who want to be Batman, whom Wayne derisively refers to as "Copycats." State surveillance, the film ultimately suggests, reflects a class hierarchy wherein the elite see those below them as either naive buffoons, like a masked citizen wearing a comically ill-fitting costume who challenges Batman's right to perform extralegal activity, or potential terrorists who, like the Joker, seem to be everywhere and nowhere.

In an essay on global surveillance, David Murakami Wood reflects upon a gap in surveillance studies: "We need to understand more about the processes of by which surveillance is . . . embraced . . . by an emerging ruling class for their own perceived safety. We know relatively little about the technocratic or elite views of surveillance and the processes by which they come to understand it as normal and desirable for themselves, let alone the rationalities of its imposition on others" (Murakami Wood 2013, 324). Spectacles such as *The Dark Knight*, whose hyperwealthy protagonist enacts an artistic kind of control, might offer insight into such normalization. This form of surveillance is so all-encompassing, so capable of mapping the individual precisely in an urban panorama, that it takes on an aesthetic majesty. Batman's stated appreciation for his tableau of Gotham City created through the medium of surveillance represents not an incidental glimpse into a superhero's tastes but a worldview of the powerful wherein the lower classes are aestheticized, worth contemplation only when they signify the ruling class's hold. The sequence is discomfiting, for it suggests that genre forms encourage viewers to see themselves through this prism of the ruling class, whereby they might come to see their own subjugation as "beautiful."[11]

Nolan's characterization of Bruce Wayne as a wealthy surveyor builds on previous iterations of the character in both film and comics. The Wayne (Michael Keaton) of Tim Burton's 1989 *Batman* is also immediately linked to surveillance. In a hall of fantastic armor in Wayne Manor, where two reporters mill about, the film cuts to a security camera behind two-way glass, thus visualizing such equipment as a sort of armor for Wayne. Then a shot of Wayne in front of his monitors—from its initial zoom in upon a blurry screen to its opening up of the billionaire dwarfed by his many monitors—pays direct homage to Fritz Lang's 1960 *The Thousand Eyes of Dr. Mabuse*, about a mysterious villain who watches over a hotel from the Nazi era. The allusion taints the intention of the superhero's gaze. In Mark Waid and Alex Ross's 1996 *Kingdom Come* comic, an older Wayne sits in his Batcave, examining seemingly omniscient security footage of Gotham City and remotely commanding robotic iterations of Batman to stop criminals caught in his sights. Panels feature high-angle imagery where mechanical vigilantes encircle suspects. Progressively, the view grows more distant so that the criminals appear small and trapped under the spotlights of the machines. The spectral observer of the scene notes, "Batman has his city under control" (Waid and Ross 1997, 48) Bruce Wayne has aged into an Orwellian, even Mabuse-like figure whose control is interlinked with fear, and the city he supposedly protects is now subjected to the wealthy hero's all-seeing eye.

The unsavory, paranoid aspect of the superhero comes to the fore in Nolan's film. Indeed, *The Dark Knight* further emphasizes that Bruce

Wayne obtains his perch to clandestinely survey those beneath him through his wealth. In the scene where the billionaire first appears without his costume, his butler Alfred moves through his master's expansive penthouse with breakfast, only to realize that his charge is below ground. As Alfred drives to find him, the film cuts to an establishing shot of the hideout's front, an innocuous construction site. In the foreground, signs labeled with the Wayne Enterprises logo state "Private property. No trespassing." Unlike the richly decorated penthouse, Wayne's hideout remains bare, with the exception of a series of monitors that screen footage of the hero's former lover and his romantic rival. The cut-in on the monitors first shows crime scene footage of one of the Joker's bank robberies, followed by images of the lover, Rachel Dawes, and his competitor for her affections, the district attorney Harvey Dent. As they walk on the street, Wayne uses his peeping camera to zoom in rapidly on the woman, belying his defense that he uses surveillance merely for professional concerns. Wayne's penetrating gaze, the film makes clear, is fraught with personal desire. The butler quizzically states, "I trust you don't have me followed on my day off." Wayne, in the process of putting on a suit, quips back, "If you ever took one, I might." The scene suggests a grain of truth in his joke. By presenting privilege as synonymous with both privacy and unencumbered sight, the film lays the groundwork for Batman's later delight in a technologically enhanced view of Gotham City's citizens.

While it reiterates the genre trope of post-9/11 superheroes interlinked with the military-industrial complex, *The Dark Knight* more directly visualizes intelligence practices and policy shifts that privileged technological surveillance both internationally and domestically.[12] Most controversially, in 2005, *The New York Times* reported on a secret program of warrantless wiretapping that permitted the NSA to freely choose targets within the United States without any oversight from the Justice Department or the Bush administration (Risen and Lichtblau, 2005). Justice department lawyer John Yoo wrote a classified legal opinion shortly after the 9/11 attacks, claiming that the state could employ "electronic surveillance techniques and equipment that are more powerful and sophisticated than those available to law enforcement agencies in order to intercept telephonic communications and observe the movement of persons but without obtaining warrants for such uses" (qtd. in ibid.). Batman's sonar technology, which depends on private phones in order to function, winks at the clandestine Bush-era operation, framing its presentation in the film as a spectacular meditation upon the ethical stakes of the administration's policies.[13]

Although the Joker offers justification for such invasive action, the film underlines that this type of extralegal surveillance may push the state and its defender, Batman, toward its own brand of terrorism. When Batman stands atop a tower, adopting an iconic pose from the comic book, the film's soundtrack uses a sonic cue to link his listening with the actions of the Joker. The superhero cycles through different frequencies, capturing snippets of conversations, before listening in on the Joker's 911 call. The diegetic sounds of the dialogues are interwoven with the score featuring a leitmotif associated with the villain: overwhelming white noise. Through this parallel, the film indicates that the tactics of Batman morph into those of the Joker, since each depends on subjugating the citizenry.

This formal grappling reaches its apex when Batman employs his fantastic technology to gain a complete view of the city to track down the Joker. The set piece is visually marked by its shifting POV imagery as the camera luxuriates in the potency of technically empowered sight. Whereas the camera looked down on Batman when he listened in on citizens' phone conversations earlier in the film, it now adopts Batman's vantage point, described in the film as the "omni" view. To mark this shift, when he tells his employee Lucius Fox (Morgan Freeman), manning the monitors, "I need picture," glass lenses fall over Batman's eyes. His eyes appear to glow white, mirroring for the first time in the character's cinematic history the iconic rendition of the white, pupil-less eyes in the comic books. Omniscience through technological means is thus correlated with comic-book fantasy. The film, at this very moment of penetrating vision, highlights that a reality of present-day executive practice—be it domestic surveillance or drone warfare—belongs to the domain of the four-color superhero.[14]

For Paul Virilio, technology such as the drones that hover over the Middle East stands as the culmination of the progressive "fusion" between the weapons of war and cinema (Virilio 1989, 104, 111). Nolan's rendition of that merge is made deliberately exhilarating. Accentuating Batman's point about the urban panorama's beauty, the blue palette of both the monitors and the perspective through Batman's eyes is striking, a rare streak of color in the hero's often grey surroundings. When the equipment's sight, made to look like a gunsight in an explicit link to drone warfare, falls upon its target, the Joker, the screens flash red. On the bank of security monitors, the images of Gotham City resemble an abstract swarm of colors, made much more legible when the "omni" view takes up the frame. The kinetic, colorful, and fluctuating legibility of the staging encourages relishing the shift from watched-upon to watcher.[15]

Nolan does not promote a complete shirking of the more critical mode but continues to cultivate an ambivalent relationship to this kind of sight.

Even in this scene of supreme exaltation of technology, there exists a crucial moment of breakdown that promotes doubt about such intoxicating tools of control. Virilio speaks of "technological vertigo," which takes hold when technology provides so much information as to overwhelm and paralyze the soldier so that he can longer distinguish what really lies before him and what is projected onscreen (1989, 106). The confusion suffered by military forces in a time when the omniscience of cinema and the war machine's violent power are interlinked resonates with Batman's own plight when his surveillance technology stalls after a few strikes from the Joker. We return to the perspective of the "omni" camera, which was once defined by absolute clarity. Now it spins about and flickers briefly; then the feed cuts out. Fox's monitors shut off as well; then the camera cuts to a wide shot of Batman standing in place, evoking a feeling of paralysis. An eerie pause disrupts the action. The superhero cannot even see the Joker, whose visage takes up the frame of the glitchy omni view; nor can he defend against his next blow.

Such disorientation brims with implications. It serves as a caution regarding the military's overreliance on such technology against its enemies. In the *New York Times* article revealing the existence of the NSA's domestic surveillance program, an official noted that although he raised concerns about its legality, "people just looked the other way because they didn't want to know what was going on" (qtd. in Risen 2005). *The Dark Knight* infuses echoes of this scandal into its narrative, offering viewers a glimpse of the breakdown in protection of their liberties and their vulnerability to the state's machinations. Transforming the viewer into a favored subject of an all-seeing superhero, Nolan's film simultaneously offers a glimpse of privilege and denotes the audience's subjugated condition.

Seeing Spectacular State Violence Anew: The Shadow of Hurricane Katrina in *The Dark Knight Rises*

In 2012's *The Dark Knight Rises*, Gotham City is being contained by a masked terrorist, Bane. His threat to blow up the city with a nuclear WMD coerces the state to help keep Gotham citizens imprisoned. A U.S. soldier flatly tells one of Bane's subordinates, "You don't have enough men to stop 12 million people from leaving this island." With a smile, the terrorist replies, "No. No, we don't. But you do." They have their tête-à-tête on a bridge. It is also on a bridge where what look like Black bodies will later be hanged, which will be broadcast on the news. That both the military's negotiation and the lynching take place in a similar setting obliquely lays blame for the eventual deaths, rendered so spectacular, upon the American state. The film harnesses this shocking imagery to mediate institutional indifference toward the city and its populace. On a macro level, the state colludes with a terrorist, sustaining his hold over the city. This narrative framework exposes an impotent government whose own interests, at least to those on the ground, seem influenced by those of an aggressor.[16] That a bridge as a site of grotesque racialized violence is seen through the eyes of the news camera seems to affirm Sedgwick's assertion that state violence is not invisible but hypervisible and inherently spectacular. The film works to, paraphrasing Sedgwick, reframe the aperture on and challenge our relationship with such brutality.

Doane admits in a postscript to her essay that news coverage of the 9/11 attacks "blurred the already fragile opposition between catastrophe and crisis . . . transforming a political act into something with the proportions of a monumental natural disaster (or a grandiose battle between abstractly defined good and evil), at the expense of any more nuanced attempt at historical explication" (Doane 2005, 262). As seen on television, the disaster of 9/11 was taken out of any broader historical context. In the final film of Nolan's Batman trilogy, referring to the threat of terrorism and popular uprising, Catwoman describes it as an oncoming storm. *The Dark Knight Rises* brings together a host of post-9/11 catastrophes and crises, acting as a multidirectional reflection on these events. This comparative view shows how such spectacle might serve to re-inject nuance and provide historical perspective, grounding our understanding of the present state of emergency, its myriad costs, and how it might be manipulated by those in power. Inviting multiple perspectives on this political storm, from those of the state and the terrorist perpetrator to that of the racialized victim, the superhero film presents a fluid subject position. *The Dark Knight Rises*, more than earlier examples of the superhero genre, shows that perpetrator and victim exist on the same spectrum and bleed into each other. As it investigates the processes by which state violence comes to be spectacularized, the film exposes that our sympathies are similarly conflicted.

The film grapples with the politics surrounding the inherent spectacle of its hero, just as the comic book presents the superhero as valuable theater for the state. The film's various slippages between hero and villain are paralleled by the slippages within the film's allegory—Gotham City

stands for both a terrorism-stricken New York City following 9/11 and
New Orleans after Hurricane Katrina. Considering the film's Katrina-in-
spired iconography against various studies concerning the disaster, we see
that *The Dark Knight Rises* visualizes a collision of discourses that some
media scholars and sociologists argue were revealed by the hurricane.
With its shifts in points of view which include that of a terrorized Black
man and a state policeman who sees the city as a forbidding war zone,
the film depicts what has been called a new "biopolitics of disposability."
Its hero is repulsed by and resistant to such realities portrayed in the
news, demonstrating the limits of traditional media outlets in creating an
accessible forum to critically engage with such spectacular state violence.
These genre films cultivate a fraught imagination, at different moments
embracing state violence and bucking against it.

Through its direct citation of Miller's *The Dark Knight Returns*, the
film contemplates the relationship between such superhero myths and the
state that embraces their normalizing potential. The broader contours
of the plot seem indebted to Miller's work. The film considers Batman's
return to Gotham City after an eight-year absence to fight Bane. Although
Batman is now a criminal in the eyes of much of the establishment, he
has grown into a legend for the citizens. The presentation of Batman's
mystique, with children speaking about him in awe, reflects on the sway
of such a mythic vision of power. When Batman returns in the film, an
older policeman smiles and tells his rookie partner, "Oh, boy, you are in
for a show tonight, kid." Lifting this exchange with only some adjustment
from Miller's media-saturated opus, the film frames the superhero as a
spectacular "show"—lawless and intoxicating, able to turn excessive force
into fodder for collective fantasy.

Typical of the Nolan films, however, the work also emphasizes the
multivalence of genre symbols, suggesting that superheroic icons can
magnify the state's failures as easily as they draw focus upon its perceived
successes. Read politically, the film reveals the scope of Nolan's spectacular
lament about post-9/11 America and reflection on Hurricane Katrina and
the Bush administration's unwillingness to rescue the disenfranchised Black
population of New Orleans.[17] In a context where the catastrophes of the
post-9/11 world run together, the film suggests that Bush's handling of
Katrina was less a testament to the state's resilience against disaster than
to its corrosive disinterest, even suspicion toward marginalized populations.
The spectacular "show" offered by the superhero is framed in a manner
too volatile to be entirely co-opted by the state. When the state finally
fully embraces the superhero in the final moments, the film gestures to

the Joker to call attention to both the terrorizing power and the critical potential of such genre myths.

Via formal echoes with the previous films in the trilogy, Nolan positions his concern with symbolic fluidity, with the broken borders between hero and villain, perpetrator and victim.[18] The opening sequence, where Bane crashes a CIA plane and escapes with one of its informants, ends with a shot that mirrors one of Batman in *The Dark Knight*. Bane is lifted into an airplane with his informant, just as Batman was lifted in the earlier film with the Chinese man he sought to interrogate. The visual mirroring offers a framework to consider Batman, and in turn the state, as a terrorizing force.[19]

Yet, the film also visually links the weakened hero with the subjects of institutional violence. After Wayne has been brutalized by Bane and taken to a CIA black site–like foreign prison, the film presents an image of his bare feet against those of his captors' leather military boots. He has been transformed from the wealthy jailer of the first two films into a penniless prisoner. Batman is thus both aggressor and aggrieved, able to perceive state actors as perpetrators and to glimpse forgotten victims of such violence. His very amorphousness embodies the larger geopolitical pastiche of the film where, amid anxieties about war, terrorism, and disaster, Gotham City becomes an analogue to both post-9/11 New York City and post-Katrina New Orleans. Nolan's marriage of contemporary fears echoes the language of reporters about Katrina—the specter of terrorism that haunted New York emerged in the coverage of the Louisiana storm.

The mass media discourse on the hurricane is detailed in a sociological study of media coverage after 9/11, *Selling Fear,* by Brigitte L. Nacos, Yaeli Bloch-Elkon, and Robert Y. Shapiro. They document that journalistic accounts of the Bush administration's failures during the disaster often made references to terrorism: "[T]he bungled government response to Hurricane Katrina . . . laid bare the soft underbelly of America's disaster preparedness. It took this show-stopping natural disaster for critics inside and outside the news media to take up the state of terrorism preparedness . . . since terrorists—unlike hurricanes—hit without warning" (Nacos et al. 2011, 26). Katrina's affecting images of disaster were well suited for the visual medium of TV, thereby keeping the attentions of the fourth estate fixed on the ramifications of an unprepared government (ibid., 169). The spectacle of desperation propelled critical inquiry within the journalistic media. That spectacle might provoke engagement suggests the critical potential of a genre such as the superhero film built upon representations of "show-stopping" disaster. *The Dark Knight Rises* explores how such stories might invite more sustained critical engagement in its presentation of an urban purgatory, an American city abandoned by the state that resembles the Big Easy after Katrina.

During its most legible parallel to New Orleans, the film demonstrates how spectacle might push the viewer to perceive the desperation of victims of such a disaster. When Bane arrives, his major act of terrorism centers on a football stadium. The disaster exposes the limits of the government's own compassion for the city. Its centrality within the film recalls the media's focus on the New Orleans Superdome after the hurricane. Paralleling the racial makeup of the refugees in the stadium, Nolan's staging of the scene contains a marked racialized dimension. The attack is preceded by a rendition of "The Star-Spangled Banner." Bane takes the position of critic, framing the aesthetic qualities of the violent scene, when he listens to the song and comments, "That's a lovely, lovely voice." As the boy sings, the camera pans over the players, most of whom are Black. Black bodies are thus shown to be dispensable as well as the objects of spectacle, even entertainment. Bane appears to confirm this reading before he hits the detonator, as he states, "Let the games begin." Among the white multitude watching in the stands, the terrorist destroys only the mayor's skybox, gesturing to the radical and abrupt abdication of executive support for the cataclysm's victims. Nolan crosscuts between the stadium and scenes showing the Gotham police trapped underground by a series of well-placed bombs. A shot from above the field shows it progressively becoming a crater. The camera goes on to present one player who reaches safety in the end zone. He is the sole individual on the field to survive, his touchdown a mark of his exceptional status in Bane's game. The player turns around in the center of the frame to look upon the devastation. The camera for a moment shares the vantage point of this Black man, sharing his solitude as he looks at the desolation about him.

Yet among these apparently alternative viewpoints, state actors view the city and its inhabitants as part of a hostile war zone. Race scholar David Theo Goldberg's salient assessment of Katrina helps draw out yet another geopolitical linkage: "post Katrina New Orleans, in short, is simply Iraq come home" (Goldberg 2009, 89). He positions various cases of state-sanctioned private security forces killing Black people for looting as examples of the violence of the front line merging with the home front. Goldberg's proposed synthesis can be seen repeatedly in the imagery following Bane's attacks on the stadium, including Batman's camouflaged Batmobile patrolling Gotham streets, culminating when one of Batman's allies, Detective John Blake (Joseph Gordon-Levitt), confronts state police who block a bridge out of the city. Knowing that one of Bane's nuclear devices is about to detonate, Blake attempts to reason with the federal agents, begging them to let the impoverished and minority orphans under his care escape. Goldberg notes that during Katrina, "in the name of securing the city, New Orleans was quickly turned into an armed military camp"; the scene of the superhero film shows an American city turned into a prison for the same reasons (ibid., 89). Blake's approach provokes fire from the blockade before they blow up the bridge. This action sparks a brief series of shots of citizens cowering in fear. Blake then yells, "You sons of bitches! You're killing us!" Over the last line, the film cuts to a point-of-view shot from a state policeman's perspective, illustrating his distance from those caught in the city. The shot accentuates the degree to which Gotham has become militarized, as the border on the citizens' side is lined with barbed-wire fences and metal barriers. Thus the film lends the viewer a schema to see ordinary citizens as potential menaces, as enemies that must be restricted.[20] In some ways, the film achieves a more destabilizing effect here than when it shares the perspective of the terrorized Black subject on the football field, whose death resembles a normalized spectacle. In contrast, the film presents in this sequence the state's perpetrating perspective, pushing viewers to adopt the vantage point of a white police officer charged with killing racialized youth.

The film presents more gruesome imagery that brings together wartime violence and racial terror lynchings in the South. Bane catches Special Forces officers and proceeds to smother their Black leader. He then issues a stark directive: "Hang them where the world can see." The film presents images of the bodies hanging from a Gotham bridge, broadcast on television. Through the faraway framing of the news cameras, the film nullifies the military status of the soldiers, capturing them as black silhouettes. Imbuing this image of violence against Blacks in an American city with the tinge of a Near Eastern conflict, the shot is presented on an Al Jazeera–like news station, featuring Arabic letters at the bottom of the screen. Although Goldberg decries that in New Orleans "few seemed to notice that for domestic purposes America was mimicking tactics of militarization honed in the desert war," the superhero film, with the wide net that the genre permits, brings the correlation between Iraq and the southern American city fully into view (Goldberg 2009, 89).

Bane's punishment of Bruce Wayne, an *A Clockwork Orange*–like arrangement where the latter is imprisoned and forced to watch news of the city being destroyed, grows untenable when he sees what appears

to be the hanging Black bodies on screen (Fig. 4.1). He breaks the
television, pointing to a social reality that the superhero—not only the
character, but the genre itself—cannot face. This torture by Bane fits
with the larger characterization of Batman's villains in pre-9/11 editions
of the superhero film series: all have an urge to co-opt and twist popular media modes so that they represent the unrepresentable. In Tim
Burton's *Batman*, the Joker (Jack Nicholson) glances at the photographer
Vicky Vale's (Kim Basinger) portfolio. He flips through its various fashion photos with complete disinterest, calling each image "crap." When
he arrives at war photography of a dead body, he perks up and offers
his aesthetic critique to the artist and to the camera, "Ah! Now that's
good work! The skulls . . . the bodies . . . you give it all such a glow! I
don't know if it's art, but I like it!" The moment is eerie, showing the
sociopathic aesthetic of the villain. The way Joker directly addresses the
camera foreshadows the scene in Nolan's 2008 film where the camera
twists to his level, suggesting that the audience share his view, finding
the artistic rendering of suffering enjoyable. Supervillains offer a reality
the superhero can never acknowledge. Batman might find the surveillance
of a city beautiful, but he cannot look directly at spectacular images that
might make pleasurable the suffering of the marginalized.

Figure 4.1. Black bodies hanging in an abandoned American city, moments before
Batman shatters the screen in distress. This is one social reality even a superhero
cannot face. *The Dark Knight Rises.*

Such iconic images of racialized violence unveil a "biopolitics of disposability," briefly seen, some theorists have argued, within the state of emergency of New Orleans. Henry A. Giroux's essay "Reading Hurricane Katrina: Race, Class, and the Biopolitics of Disposability" argues that the event exposed that the minority population is not within "the sphere of human concern" for the state (Giroux 2006, 175). Giroux describes "a new kind of politics, one in which entire populations are now considered disposable, unnecessary burdens on state coffers, and consigned to fend for themselves" (ibid., 174) and argues that the footage of death projected out of New Orleans offered a view into this new politics. Linking such visuals with photographs of the murdered Black teenager Emmett Till, Giroux writes, "cadavers have a way of insinuating themselves on consciousness, demanding answers to questions that aren't often asked" regarding the state's terrorizing of the Black subject (ibid., 174).

Giroux finds that such politics oppose critical engagement, fostering an "abiding powerlessness [that] atrophies the public imagination and leads to political paralysis" (Giroux 2006, 190). *The Dark Knight Rises* also raises doubt about whether genre spectacle can function as a new imagination that exposes and counters the processes by which power holders spectacularize state violence. In one of the film's final scenes, the city leaders monumentalize the vigilante Batman in the form of a statue at City Hall, without reference to the state or Batman's previous antagonism toward its citizens. All the public needs to know is that Gotham has been saved.

The framing of the Batman statue forms a smiley face, recalling the terrorist Joker who sought in *The Dark Knight* to bring pandemonium to the city and expose the immorality of its institutions, where the rule of law is nothing but, in his words, "a bad joke" (Fig. 4.2). Furthermore, the monument is hidden under a purple veil, the same color as the villain's suit. The image of the smiley face is placed against a mid-shot of the disillusioned Commissioner Jim Gordon (Gary Oldman), who sits in the audience. Juxtaposing the more figurative shot from above the statue against the close-up of the commissioner suggests his critical eye toward political theater. The state has come to lionize an extralegal force without reckoning with or admitting its own failures. Nolan's closing film of his post-9/11 opus calls attention to how enduring images of power can be validating in executive discourse and potentially critical in mythic cinematic form. These symbols of spectacle have the potential to obscure the terrorizing force of state violence, whose victims can be forgotten and whose perpetrators, like the Joker himself, so easily slip in and out of view.

Figure 4.2. The Joker's smiley face emerges when the state embraces a vigilante. The supervillain's ultimate victory comes when the rule of law is indeed shown to be a joke. *The Dark Knight Rises.*

Nolan also gestures to the productive counternarrative. The film ends not with the broken Gordon, but with his protégé Blake, who has left law enforcement, claiming its "structures [were] becoming shackles." From afar, the retired Wayne pushes the young man to find the Batcave under his manor, which has become a home for the very troubled youths whom Blake defended against the state police. In *Batman Begins*, this cave is narratively defined as a site of resistance against the state and its institutionalized racism, as Alfred explains that a former Wayne family patriarch used it as a stop in the Underground Railroad. One reading on race and Batman offered by comic historian Regalado argues that Batman represented an attempt by white creators to co-opt the perceived strength of a threatening Black Other (Regalado, 124). Nolan changes Batman from a reactionary figure evoking fear of the urban Black man to a progressive one representing Black power. The site has additional metaphoric resonance, as it previously housed the bats that Wayne formerly feared. Through his journey to redeem himself, Wayne has learned the importance of fear. Nolan thus transforms a key theme of the series. In *Batman Begins*, "the power of fear" is articulated as a tool that allows the powerful to act with impunity. In *The Dark Knight Rises*, fear is reconstituted into a motivating force for the powerless that might promote critical agency. As Wayne escapes Bane's prison only when he recognizes the need to be afraid, so might viewers escape a desiccated, hermetically sealed public imagination for a moment, obliquely perceiving such fears projected within a mythic framework. The film's final wide shot of Blake in the cave, his back to the camera, renders him an everyman figure, a staging of Wayne's earlier assertion: "The idea was to be a symbol. Batman could be anybody. That was the point." The director shows that such spectacle has strength because of its fluidity, moving between oppression and resistance and bringing together multiple violent frames. Our perspective on spectacular state violence, *The Dark Knight Rises* demonstrates, can productively be reframed when both victimizer and victim remain in the shot.

Conclusion

In his memoirs, Donald Rumsfeld touts an unusual gift he presented to the president of Syria, Hafez al-Assad, in 1984: a satellite image of Damascus that included his presidential palace. Rumsfeld notes, "I gave Assad the photograph less to acknowledge his hospitality than to remind him that we were watching from above" (Rumsfeld 2012, 25). His anecdote establishes the superheroic, almost divine vision of power that the United States hoped to project. In an essay on the seductiveness of drones, on the machines' apparent "precise and imperative" nature, legal scholar Mary Ellen O'Connell argues that a similar attitude manifested in the policy of targeted killing that came to define President Obama's approach to counterterrorism (2011, 25). This attitude is so pervasive in conceptualizations of American foreign policy that the moral cost of the technology has become entirely lost or even negligible in the eyes of the public. Policies privileging killing over capture may be intended to promote a mere performance of power rather than an effective military act. O'Connell provides a sharp lens to examine superhero films as texts that merely valorize American power and offer a way to normalize spectacular state violence.

Bruce Wayne, contemplating the need for an alter ego in *Batman Begins*, speaks to the enlightening power of the very mythic symbols that come to be critiqued by the series's end. He tells Alfred, "People need dramatic examples to shake them out of apathy, and I can't do that as Bruce Wayne. As a man, I'm flesh and blood, I can be ignored, I can be destroyed, but as a symbol. . . . As a symbol I can be incorruptible, I can be everlasting." Only in the realm of such dramatic symbols, the film argues, can a public's apathy be shaken. Reframing the aperture on state violence, as these ambivalent tales highlight, does not entirely transform our vision, but it brings the pain of the victim in from the margins. Working through Walter Benjamin's assessment that "storytelling has an amplitude that information lacks," Doane finds that unlike information within the nonallegorical evening news, which only exists in the moment, "[m]eaning in storytelling has time to linger, to be subject to unraveling" (Doane 2005, 254). These often-bombastic films have an amplitude, a heightened register, that begins to unravel a politics spurred on by catastrophe.

The scene in *Superman Returns* when the superhero does not engage directly in the conflict but merely watches it on television is perhaps a tacit critique of this controversial war. Like a critical spectator, Superman engages with the imagery of state violence and the suffering it causes. To empathize with or at least to contemplate the victims on the screen, unmediated by a genre filter, is thus rendered a superheroic act. In their unresolved moments, challenging set assumptions, these superhero films might foster courage in viewers to perceive their collusion with perpetrating forces and test their capacity for empathy.

"9/11 Transformed the Whole Planet, Not Just America!"

The War on Terror's Shadow across Global Law and Cinema

Blood on the Red Carpet

DURING ONE OF MY CHILDHOOD visits to my mother's native village, Les Rousses, in the French Alps, my uncle proposed a French-language exercise. To get me out of my shell, he encouraged me to interact with storekeepers by myself as he watched from the sidelines, an ever-present cigarette hanging from his lips. Over the summer, I had grown more confident with my French and felt that perhaps I could truly pass as a local. My childish delusion was revealed the day I decided to buy flowers for my grandmother as a parting gift. I went into the local flower shop and said to the owner: "S'il vous plaît, est-ce que tu . . ." "Please, can you . . ." Inadvertently, I had switched between the formal "vous" and informal "tu." As I hit the second pronoun in my clipped language, the middle-aged woman's face lost its benign smile and contorted with anger. In a piqued voice she asked, "What did you just say to me?"

I became confused, as her reaction broke completely from the standard role-play that my uncle would perform with me. The florist's anger was completely unexpected. My uncle jumped into the shop,

coming between us to yell, "Il est Américain!" "He's American!" Only
later did I realize that with my olive skin, my accented French, and my
pronoun slip, I came off as an Arab boy, and a disrespectful Arab boy at
that. Strangely, my Americanness, which I felt so distant from growing
up in Montana, was being used to defend me, to occlude my Arabness.

My perceived identity and its intersections have been similarly
estranging during my yearly treks to the Cannes Film Festival, where
I seek out new films to study. Walking along the sunny Riviera, I feel
the same kind of stares I experienced in my grandparents' village of Les
Rousses. In Montana, the land of the cowboy, violence was only obliquely
threatened, whispered by a rogue schoolteacher or errant bully. But it
was here, in the sublimity of sunshine, tuxedos, and palm trees, that I
was once violently attacked while approaching the red carpet. The festival both exemplifies my privilege as a moviegoer and at times attests
to my powerlessness as a disabled product of French colonialism. Never
am I more aware of my cross-cultural identity as the son of a French
mother of Spanish heritage and a Tunisian father than when I wear my
Cannes accreditation badge and wander through the city's streets. At the
festival, which has featured some of the international films I discuss in
this chapter—films that redefine and repurpose the Hollywood genres
that this book has been concerned with thus far—I encounter myself in
a state of sensuous pleasure and psychic malaise.

Before my first visit to Cannes in 2009, I imagined a cinematic
heaven, a place where the world's finest movies were premiered, cele-
brated, and discussed. Certain aspects of that fantasy proved true. There
is a delicious decadence in walking out of a morning screening to look
down upon the shimmering Mediterranean at high noon. It is as though
a collective decision has been made to shirk the finest scenery nature
has to offer in favor of the scenery projected on the silver screen. However, Cannes is ultimately not a place to celebrate movies. Its renowned
competition for the prestigious Palme d'Or, where a selection of films
is judged by a panel of filmmakers and sometimes mercilessly criticized
by attending journalists, plays out against and within the Marché du
Film, where art and genre films from around the world are bought and
traded. Searching for films to research and exhibit at the universities
where I have studied and worked, I have had rare opportunities to watch
films in relative peace during the market screenings. However, my fellow market attendees are often agitated, glancing at their phones and
running out of the auditorium mid-screening. The press can frequently
be found discussing evocative movies with evaluative banalities. Standing

in line, I have heard that certain movies were "too long," "powerful," or "a sure contender for the Palme d'Or." It was later explained to me by one journalist that reporters are careful not to share any idiosyncratic thoughts on the featured films for fear of being scooped. Ideas on movies at Cannes, like the movies themselves, are commodities to be protected.

The intensity of a five-to-seven-movies-per-day schedule means that there is a marathon element to my festival-going—a test of my body. Each evening, I plan the next day's schedule—one that has me dashing from cinema to cinema over several kilometers. I need to navigate stairs, crowds, and suspicious security guards who will sometimes force me to take a long way around the building, turning a five-minute jaunt to cross a bridge into a twenty-five-minute jog. As the festival wears on, my ever-present limp can grow more pronounced as my muscles grow sore. I take the pain, of course, as the prospect of finding a new cinematic gem transcends those momentary afflictions. Only after more than a half-decade of regular attendance was I informed that there was a disability service for attendees. The revelation caused me to flash back to the needless hours standing in line in the sun, shifting my weight to my left side while I fantasized about a plush theater chair. This place was not made for people like me. The feeling of Otherness grew most pronounced when I was attacked by a Frenchman while waiting to walk on the red carpet.

The Theater Claude Debussy is a focal point of the Palais des Festival, directly below a giant awning that features the festival's logo. Seating more than a thousand people, the Debussy always has a long line that stretches into the faraway marina area. In 2012, during the last day of the festival, I was on my way to catching a personal record–breaking fifty-four films in ten days. I only needed to watch two more films. A light rain began to fall on the line for Michael Vinterberg's 2012 *The Hunt*, and I pulled out my umbrella. A scuffle broke out in front of me. Although the crowd dispersed, I stood my ground, oblivious to how the stage was being set. The white attacker locked eyes with me. I did not move or even look away. After all, that would involve losing my place in line! My unwillingness to move had nothing to do with courage. That day, I realized I have much in common with the New Zealand kiwi bird—not (only) a short and round stature but also a lack of fight-or-flight instinct. I simply could not imagine violence befalling me since, like the kiwi, I believed I had no predators.

The stranger silently walked up to me and punched me right in the face. The blow pushed the skin of my inner cheek into my teeth, cutting it up. As I fell, blood spilled from my mouth, a touch darker than the nearby red carpet. Unable to see clearly, since my glasses had been knocked off my head, I instinctively and shamefully yelled for the police. The suspicion I have toward such authorities in my academic research appeared to immediately dissipate in my panic. I really believed the state to be my protector. To my surprise, the police immediately apprehended the man. They had been at the scene the whole time and had chosen to simply watch the incident.

It hurt to walk because I had fallen on my right side and was incapable of catching myself, so I took a taxi to the police station. The police left me in a waiting room together with my attacker, who glared at me like a glassy-eyed hero from a Stanley Kubrick movie. When I was called in for my deposition, my "state as protector" illusion faded away as the French authorities seemed indifferent to my pain. I was repeatedly asked: Why did not I defend myself? Why, one officer wondered, did I not use my umbrella as a weapon? Their gently accusatory language implied that it was *I* who had behaved inhumanly. While I dictated what had occurred, the officer translated my halting statement into flawless French. Without prompting, the officer marked my identity as Maghrebian. Notably, this point goes unmarked in my U.S., French, and even my Tunisian passports, which all list my birthplace as Montana. Unlike in Les Rousses years before, my American identity had little influence on how I was perceived. The police would do the same years later when I reported my partner's phone stolen. For the French police, I was not a mixed-race French Arab or American—my Arabness was all-defining. Fareed Ismail Ben-Youssef: Maghrebian. The officer informed me that I would likely not get any remuneration from my assailant. Still, I pressed charges. I desired justice.

With the paperwork complete, I limped back into line for the next film at the Palais. At least, I thought, I can match my previous record of fifty-three films! Other festival goers recognized me as "that man who was punched," and some expressed shock that, in my bloody and bruised state, I wanted to watch another movie. I tried to ignore the implication from their concerned commentary that I might have been dissociating from the recent trauma. To take my mind off the sensation that my presence was causing around me, I called my sister, a lawyer, for advice about the incident.

She advised me not to pursue legal recourse against the man who had assaulted me but against the festival itself for their failure to provide security. While I did not share the thought aloud, I could not imagine moving forward with such charges. What if a court case meant that I would not be accredited as a festival attendee the next year? The day of disquieting revelations about myself included a view of how beholden I was to a French institution that left me in danger. I could not confront a systemic failure for fear of being exiled from the metropole's center. Even as I was aware of myself as a postcolonial subject in France, I clung to the center for fear of losing access to precious cultural capital. Such cowardly thinking made me wonder if I was hurting myself, leaving myself ever more marginalized, for my love of movies.

Gleaning the self-defeating edge in my response to the attack, I went into the cinema at the back of the Palais for Matteo Garrone's 2012 comedy *Reality*. As I watched the film, my mind continually replayed snippets of the attack:

> Angry eyes.
> The punch.
> My blood.
> My terror.

I wondered if I would be hurt again before the night was out and if my attacker was still wandering the streets. When my attention would flicker back to the film, I discovered an eerie echo to my own condition. Like the hero who is willing to lose a sense of himself for the prospect of fame on reality TV, I shared a potentially corrosive love for entertainment. We were both willing to leave our bodies behind, our real pains, for the glamour of the screen. *Reality* made me question what reality I subscribed to when I made my yearly pilgrimage to the festival. Still, for all the emotional repression that may have been signaled by my return to the theater that night, the film also helped me contemplate the violence that I had just met. Such a film was both an escape and an unflattering mirror.

The echoes between myself and the films of the competition would continue to shake me when I finally watched Vinterberg's *The Hunt* months later. The film that my attacker (not to mention the disinterested French police) deprived me of watching features a final scene that captures how I would come to view Cannes after the attack. Lucas (Mads Mikkelsen), a teacher falsely accused of child abuse, has been exonerated. However, a gunshot during a hunt with friends leaves him huddling on the ground. Lucas looks up and sees his assailant obscured by the late afternoon sunlight radiating behind him. When left alone, Lucas reckons with how his past may condemn him to permanent insecurity. It may be a testament to how hermetically sealed my existence had been that I saw Lucas's near-death experience as an analogue for my reaction to a random act of violence. But in the sparkling land of movies and rich food, I felt similarly menaced.

Judith Herman builds off the work of psychiatrist Mardi Horowitz when describing that, in order to heal, the traumatized need to develop a "new mental 'schema'" over their pain (Herman 1992, 41). International films such as *Reality* and *The Hunt*, so implicated in the day's violence, offered me the lens to create such new mental schemas on myself, providing a vocabulary to express my sometimes destructive desire and lingering fears. Several of the films featured in this conclusion show mixed-race subjects who find something in Hollywood genre cinema that allows them a sense of command in spaces where they would otherwise feel marginalized and alone. In the global cinema that can be found at Cannes and its market, I find my fractured self directly represented. It is the healing force of such revelatory representations that keeps me coming back to the alienating festival and its red carpet even when I know that I may always be haunted and may never truly belong.

The Necessity for a Global Vision on Post-9/11 Hollywood Genre Film

Cristi Puiu's *Sieranevada* (2016) takes place in a setting seemingly divorced from the present geopolitical moment—a cramped Bucharest apartment where a family prepares for dinner. The film's title, which recalls the American West, suggests a setting within an American framework and offers unexpected interconnectivities across space and time. The wandering and voyeuristic camera rarely comes to rest, moving through a home often overtaken by an expressionistic shadow that recalls the despairing genre of film noir. One person, however, always attracts the camera's attention: the youngest son, Sebi (Marin Grigore). A conspiracy theorist and ardent media consumer, he uses his iPad to teach his family about the connections among the 9/11 Truth movement, Fukushima, and the *Charlie Hebdo* terrorist attack. Faced with incredulous looks and mockery for his comparisons of seemingly disparate traumas, he eventually proclaims, "9/11 transformed the whole planet, not just America!" This conspiracy theorist's fevered declaration from a European vantage point recalls the Joker's own declaration about the global reach of the American superhero and the ways American policies and narratives stretch across the world. When we take seriously the stakes behind Sebi's assessment, we can explore how recent translations of Hollywood cinematic forms illustrate genre's corrosive and empowering sway over the identities and imaginaries of minority populations around the world in a time of global insecurity. Through a dynamic mode of genre scholarship that crosses borders and moves between international art and popular cinema, we bring into focus the expansive legal frameworks that define our post-9/11 world.

Shortly after 9/11, the United States spearheaded the creation of global security law. The attacks set the stage for an immediate transformation of international law led by an American executive dedicated to globalizing its War on Terror. The Bush administration harnessed the power it held as a member of the UN Security Council to pass UNSC Resolution 1373, which legal scholar Kim Lane Scheppele calls "the boldest resolution [the UN Security Council] had ever passed," emphasizing the unprecedented requirement for UN member states to align their domestic laws with its mandate (Scheppele 2013, 253). Its poorly defined key terms, such as *terrorism*, mired UN partners in the dangerous muddle of meaning that was emblematic of so much post-9/11 law, where human rights were supplanted by concerns for increased security (ibid., 253, 258). Given its binding nature, all member states fall under the parameters set by 1373.

Just as American policy has shaped international law since 9/11, so too has the shadow of America's global War on Terror fallen upon international cinematic works. Considering a range of films that either inhabit or comment upon genre types, I uncover echoes of the American productions examined in this book, haunted texts both compelled and repulsed by the exhilarating modes of Hollywood spectacle. These international films contain key disorienting moments that underline how film can both articulate regional concerns and reflect on the ways foreign governments have responded to America's wars.

Having wandered among Hollywood films such as *Sicario*, *Zodiac*, and *The Dark Knight*, this post-9/11 genre study concludes in a way that may seem surprising: with films that would be more at home at the Cannes Film Festival than in a multiplex. With the exception of Wu Jing's 2017 *Wolf Warrior 2*, a big-budget Chinese spectacle that incorporates elements of the American superhero and war film, these productions are often pitched at a much smaller scale than many of the films discussed thus far. These international films comment on a post-9/11 world as they embed Hollywood genres into their themes and visual style.

For their part, Hollywood films across every featured genre in this study have encouraged viewers to consider the nation on a transnational scale. For instance, *Logan*'s narrative centers on border crossing from

Mexico to Canada, situating the United States as not only imbricated within the broader continent but potentially secondary to the other powers. *The Counselor*'s viral marketing presents the coordinates to the center of Iraq within drone footage of Texas, while the film itself climaxes with a beheading on the streets of London's financial district. To comprehend present-day border violence and the regimes of capital and war that sustain it, *The Counselor* suggests that a global vision is a necessity. Moving between an American metropolis and Hong Kong, *The Dark Knight* reminds viewers not only of the reach of American extralegal power but also that such power violently antagonizes populations abroad. Post-9/11 Hollywood films invite us to view the United States from an international perspective and the nation's cinema from a similar global vantage point.

Turning to the global in my analysis is a first step within an emergent dialogue, a challenge to scholars of global cinema that aims to situate local cinematic texts examining state responses to terrorist threats within transnational frameworks. Such work might bring what Paul Giles describes as a "critical transnationalism" to contemporary genre studies (Giles 2003, 65). Giles finds that to "reinscribe classic American literature in a transnational framework is to elucidate ways in which it necessarily enters into negotiation with questions of global power" (ibid., 72). Reinscribing American genre cinema into this larger framework similarly highlights the ways filmmakers cannily negotiate and question a geopolitical terrain shaped by American visions of power. In moments of enigmatic and compelling ambiguity, examples of genre-tinged international cinema show how such visions might also be appropriated by those rendered Other and relatively voiceless within post-9/11 political discourse and law, to express and potentially transcend their marginalized condition.

Alba Sotorra's *Game Over*: Tracking the Shadow of the War on Terror

Alba Sotorra's 2015 documentary *Game Over* visualizes the shadow of America's War on Terror across an international pop cultural and geopolitical landscape. A pop culture–obsessed Catalan youth, Djalal, follows his war fantasies to the real-life war in Afghanistan. On his military tour, which he scrupulously films, the viewer is forced to watch both the tension and the tragedy as this soldier of Iranian descent is killing Near Eastern enemies. The documentary thus metaphorically posits that Djalal may be the target of his own sniper rifle. Such tension also motivates a key scene within Nassim Amaouche's unique 2009 banlieue western, *Adieu Gary*, discussed below. Both films bring to mind Franz Fanon's articulation of the ways that the popular culture of the metropole teaches the colonial subject to destroy himself. Post-deployment, and before cutting to a shot of Djalal's plastic guns, with which he obsessively plays video games, the camera lingers on the U.S. flag hanging in his bedroom. The montage visualizes the forces of soft power, where entertainment primes and numbs a subject to the state's war. The shot reinforces the implications of Djalal's comment from earlier in the film that identifies the right to own guns as a central part of the beloved "American way of life."

Game Over strives to show that visions of power promise a release for a youth who "feels trapped." They offer an apparently liberating path, a sense of agency, gestured to within the video games he plays. When Djalal fires at a target on the battlefield using a sniper rifle, the film articulates how genre myths may lead toward a vexed adoption of the perpetrating position. Throughout the film, Djalal is shown playing video games; even in his barracks on the front line, his avatar fires at all who appear onscreen. To underline the raised stakes of his first real kill, unmediated by the distancing frame of the video game, the film frames Djalal at home with his uncle watching the footage of the killing on their television. As his uncle laments that nothing came of his nephew going to war, they both watch as soldier Djalal adjusts his gun in such a way that it appears to be pointed directly at Djalal who sits in his bedroom (Fig. 5.1). Director Sotorra thus frames the potential victimhood of the victimizer—through

Figure 5.1. A veteran watches the footage of his first kill. His confrontation with his past perpetration means aiming his own rifle at himself. *Game Over.*

such violence, one may gain the means to destroy himself. Unlike in the video game footage, defined by its kinetic camera and explosive score, here the camera is fixed on the subject aiming his gun. Silence predominates. The reality of war has a stillness that separates it from the bombastic visions presented within Djalal's first-person shooter video games. Once Djalal does fire the live shot that hits an enemy, Sotorra cuts to black, as though the viewer cannot comprehend the experience of enacting this kind of violence. The screen remains dark, but Djalal's reaction, his long exhale, can be heard. He seems thrust outside the film's form, matching the psychic limbo in which he finds himself. His pop dreams leave him detached, even as he realizes their dominating power.

Watching some of the footage, Djalal's uncle calls him a mercenary fighting another man's war. However, by including footage filmed by Djalal of his more humanitarian work with Afghani children, Sotorra complicates a vision of the hero as a simple gun for hire. Capturing himself as both killer and aid worker, Djalal emerges as a lucid filmmaker and a self-aware chronicler of his position on a spectrum between perpetrator and victim. In war, *Game Over* suggests, Djalal reckons with the fraught possibility of the dual subject position as a consumer of projected visions of power and a willing arm of the state's war machine.

Kiyoshi Kurosawa's 2008 *Tokyo Sonata*, depicting an argument about a son's ambitions to join the U.S. army as well as his mother's nightmare sequence where the youth returns from Iraq, also rests on a fulcrum between the power of violent force and the impotence of geopolitical subjugation. The teenage protagonist, Takashi (Yū Koyanagi), like Djalal, searches for a kind of meaning but in the process risks deadening himself. In the epilogue, the film complicates the nightmare vision by revealing a subject whose Manichean framework has been challenged by war, much as *Game Over*'s hero ultimately gives his prized guns away and moves beyond his militaristic fantasies.

Sotorra's documentary ultimately shows the toll taken when the rest of the world is forced to play America's wartime game, and how individual subjects might challenge the rules set by the superpower. It is a valuable map by which we might stop at key points in contemporary global cinema to understand how filmmakers employ genre modes to lament and resist this game that all nations are now legally bound to play. The following genre-infused films contain moments when the specter of 9/11 emerges through the mass media: in *Adieu Gary*, video games testify to a French Arab youth's own increasingly subordinated condition following the post-9/11 moment, when to be Arab is to be abject; in

Felix van Groeningen's 2012 *The Broken Circle Breakdown*, the television highlights the insidious sway of the attacks over the lives of Belgian citizens, reflecting the perception that the needs of America trump those of the smaller European power. Televisions in *Tokyo Sonata* often detail the United States' war in Iraq, expressing an older generation's amnesia about U.S. dominance over Japan as well as a younger generation's desire to assume greater autonomy.

These texts go beyond merely expressing national weakness to offer a cogent argument about how a genre aesthetic might empower viewers to see and thus grapple with social or political realities. Just as Djalal, the consummate consumer of genre stories, seems able to capture the ambiguities of his own position as an enforcer of state will, these films explore the kind of lucidity, the moments of clarity, offered by violent genre myths. While all three gesture to how genre myths might permit viewers to transcend the myopia of the public discourse, in its epilogue *Tokyo Sonata* contains the most extended appreciation of aesthetics' power to awaken the viewer. We end with an examination of Wu Jing's enormously popular *Wolf Warrior 2* and consider a Rambo-like "Chinese superhero" facing the phantom of ISIS with a jingoistic confidence that is ultimately indicated to be theatrical bluster. These films explore the potential for genre myths to not only obfuscate the realities of state violence but also open an alternate relationship with those realities through their necessary collusion.

Nassim Amaouche's *Adieu Gary*: Adopting a Destructive Gaze on the Self

The French Arab protagonists of Nassim Amaouche's banlieue western *Adieu Gary* negotiate mass media envisionings of the "terrorist" in ways that highlight the added psychological pressures that post-9/11 laws placed upon Arab and racially mixed populations.[1] The film refashions the western aesthetic and its iconic heroes in a post-9/11 context to signify not strength but weakness. During dream sequences, the figure of Gary Cooper rides his horse down the city streets. The iconic sheriff's quiet demeanor and superior vantage point make him appear less a role model for the downtrodden than a policeman who surveys them. The film is infatuated by and alienated from such visions of western heroism. It thus provokes reflection on a phrase in James Baldwin's 1965 essay "The American Dream and the American Negro":

In the case of the American Negro, from the moment you
are born every stick and stone, every face, is white. Since you
have not yet seen a mirror, you suppose you are, too. It comes
as a great shock around the age of 5, 6, or 7 to discover that
the flag to which you have pledged allegiance, along with
everybody else, has not pledged allegiance to you. *It comes
as a great shock to see Gary Cooper killing off the Indians, and
although you are rooting for Gary Cooper, that the Indians are you.*
(Baldwin 1965; emphasis mine)

Adieu Gary represents the shock of the discursively and legally marginalized
realizing that in the post-9/11 moment they have become the enemies
of their heroes from popular culture.

In its appropriation of the ghost town convention, the film is a
unique example of the transnational western that depicts the disrupted
lives of banlieue youth, articulating the psychological disempowerment
of an ethnic group framed in legal terms as a potentially violent threat.
Adieu Gary centers on members of a French Arab family, each struggling
with their marginalized position in France. An ex-convict, Samir (Yas-
mine Belmadi), dreams of escape from his hometown and has a poster
of a Native American warrior on his wall—a visual link that suggests
the enemy status of Arab populations. His younger brother, Icham
(Mhamed Arezki), dreams of a return to North Africa. These young men
must wear ratlike uniforms complete with large ears at the supermarket
where they work. The costuming illustrates that the white citizens of the
metropole see these mixed individuals through a dehumanizing gaze—as
vermin. Even in their escapist pursuits, neither has opportunities to see
himself as a hero. In an emblematic scene involving video games, *Adieu
Gary* shows how Western pop cultural products create an unsustainable
subject position for the marginalized, in which, as in Sotorra's work,
feelings of power are generated through the destruction of demonized
representations of the self.

In *Black Skin, White Masks*, Frantz Fanon elucidated upon the impact
of European pop culture in "Tarzan stories, the sagas of twelve-year-old
explorers, the adventures of Mickey Mouse, and all those 'comic books;"
(Fanon 1968, 146). Fanon argues that these works carry a perverse dimension in which the racially marginalized subjects existing on the periphery of empire are placed in an untenable situation psychologically and
linguistically. *Adieu Gary* brings a parallel phenomenon into a post-9/11
context by showing the banlieue inhabitants playing video games and

relishing the killing of Arab terrorists. While this pop cultural annihilation distances the racially mixed individual from his Near Eastern roots, it is presented with a sense of exhilaration, playing out the process Fanon describes in a more ambivalent, visually compelling way.

Besides Gary Cooper, a military video game, what looks to be an edition from the series *SOCOM: U.S. Navy SEALs*, is the primary pop cultural object of the film's attention, filling the screen entirely. The privileged position of the video game underlines that the American soldier may be the contemporary equivalent to Cooper's sheriff. Allowing the viewer to play as American soldier or Arab terrorist, the game is a mediation of the wars that stemmed from the War on Terror. *SOCOM* seems ferociously alive as its camera weaves and bobs with the action, entirely unlike the slow-moving, steady camera of the main film. The players, Icham and the disabled drug dealer Abdel, seem emboldened and energized. The terrorist enemy is a pixelated and distant mass wearing a white turban. Once he falls into the players' crosshairs, he is flung back dead onto the desert floor. Cutting away from the virtual world, the film shows the two players sitting rigid and unblinking. As they take the perspective of American soldiers, they concentrate on the virtual environment with far more attention than on their own material one. Without a second thought, these sons of immigrants bandy about slurs, calling the fighters interchangeably terrorists and Arabs.

The scene of gleeful abandon in the digitized battlefield recalls Fanon's articulation of collective catharsis as experienced by the former colonial subject. The framework of the video game allows players of Arab descent to "subjectively adopt . . . a white man's attitude" (Fanon 1968, 147). A video game, then, permits the player to take on the white gaze at its most racist and violent, through the reticule of a rifle aiming to kill the blurred and aggressive vision of the Other.

Icham expresses the sheer pleasure of such an act when he brags about his video game exploits at the dinner table. Is his enjoyable adoption of the dominant colonial perspective, in Fanon's terms, an act "permeated with sadism" (Fanon 1968, 147)? On one level, Icham derives joy from shooting a representation of himself; however, the film encourages us to wonder what strength this vision of power offers the marginalized subject otherwise trapped in an economic, social, and psychic limbo. Icham's family points out that he is destroying Arabs onscreen; Icham's nonchalance about this fact suggests that this facet of the game is not what compels him. He sits at the head of the table and in the frame's center during his reminiscences about the video game; the film suggests paradoxically

that the transporting game "centers" him. The peripheral figure, armed
with a digital rifle, might for an instant be brought out of the margins
in his own mind. *Adieu Gary* shows that such visions might not simply
lead to a destruction of the self but also might allow for a simultaneous
and rare reassertion of the self, though it might be unsustainable and
necessitate the adoption of a destructive gaze.

Felix van Groeningen's *The Broken Circle Breakdown*: Inspiration and Disillusionment with Contested Genre Forms

Whereas Icham briefly inserts himself into the position of the U.S. soldier,
the protagonists of the Belgian melodrama *The Broken Circle Breakdown*
more fully inhabit the genre. The film shifts between references to the
western and the superhero, showcasing how these modes might inspire
and also function as sites for the performance of disillusionment with a
dominating post-9/11 American state.[2] The plot focuses on a couple of
bluegrass singers who struggle with the cancer diagnosis and eventual
death of their daughter—their changing relationship to American ideals
mirrored by their changing relationship with its myths. The mise-en-scène
is saturated with elements of Americana. An early wide shot features the
protagonist Didier's (Johan Heldenbergh) pickup truck cutting across a
field. Another shot shows a group of horses running alongside the vehicle. Markers of Belgium are obscured. Such imagery, combined with the
film's bluegrass score, transforms their world into a European Appalachia
crossed with the cowboy West.

Citing the Jew's guitar and the African's banjo, Didier frames
bluegrass as an art of power and pain, universally compelling for its
hopeful aspect as well as its ability to lament. Upon meeting Didier for
the first time and seeing that he sleeps in a trailer, his love, Elise (Veerle
Baetens), jokes, "You're a real cowboy after all." *Broken Circle* suggests
through Didier's discourse that the "real" cowboy is not necessarily tied
geographically to the American West but employs the genre's codified
ideals as a personal platform of expression. Van Groeningen articulates
the allure of genre for non-American filmmakers by foregrounding genre's
transnational origins. It stands as a site where regional identities might be
expressed through tropes that are synonymous with an imagined America.

Didier shows a canny understanding of how genre and folk forms
offer a vehicle through which to reckon with difficult realities. The min-

ers from across the globe whose music he admires, when working in the mountains, "to combat the hunger and the misery, they started singing songs about their dreams of a promised land, often about their fear of dying, their hope for a better life in the hereafter and their sorrow, their hard life." With Maybelle, their daughter, obsessed by the superheroine Mega Mindy, both the parents and the child's doctor use language infused with superhero tropes. Her doctor tells her to return for a checkup so that "we can see if Captain Chemo won the fight." Much like the miners Didier describes, adults employ the tropes of myth to render the grim reality of sickness more hopeful.

After suggesting the genre form's illuminating possibility, *Broken Circle* goes on to present a disillusionment about such myths, whose cultural sway seems linked with a unilateral post-9/11 American executive that also mobilizes such forms. 9/11 is first mentioned in the film when the parents play with their infant daughter. Although they remain oblivious to the breaking news of the World Trade Center attacks, the camera draws closer to the television (Fig. 5.2). The words of George W. Bush citing scripture are overlaid on the spectacular scene of destruction. By excerpting the biblical reference, "even I walk through the valley of the shadow of death," the film highlights the religious foundation of Bush's wartime rhetoric and thus transforms the attacks into a mythic cataclysm that merits righteous retribution. The camera then cuts to a shot where the television is central in the frame, featuring the American president speaking of the state's intention to defend freedom. A cactus sits next

Figure 5.2. The 9/11 attacks draw the film camera's attention, panning past the Belgian family playing together in the scene. Unbeknownst to them, America's trauma encroaches upon and directs their lives. *The Broken Circle Breakdown.*

to the TV, a reminder that the president often spoke of himself as a western sheriff. Genre in *Broken Circle* is presented as a tool for the powerless miners and for a powerful state. In this exceptional interlude, the camera engages in a dialogue with the contemporary moment, its catalyzing trauma, and the state leader who imposes his rhetoric upon it. The ominous presentation, marked by darkness and a low thrum in the soundtrack, denotes the perceived shadow of America upon individuals and their world.

Yet through the character arc of Elise, who in her grief takes on the moniker Alabama Monroe, the film underlines the transformative potential of myths. During her first conversation with Didier, he states: "I've been crazy about America all my life. . . . No matter where you're from, when you get there you can start all over again. It's a country of dreamers." This malleability of self becomes a vital means for Elise to confront her grief and avoid a stasis of mourning. She adopts the name of the Southern state and the last name of the founder of bluegrass, Bill Monroe, to create a new, more resistant identity that coexists with an expansive faith incorporating icons from Christianity and Hinduism. As we previously saw in the final scene of *Logan*, genre serves as a secular faith.

Ultimately, when Alabama commits suicide, the film's final image—a cut-in on the tattoo of her name—suggests the transcendent possibility offered by genre myth. Didier and his bandmates play bluegrass as his wife dies in the hospital. The scene begins in somber silence as Didier asks her, "Will you say hello to Maybelle for me if you see her?" Their music starts as the life-support machines are turned off, lacing her death with a joyous rhythm. As her vitals drop, the tune builds speed, as if the fleeting percussion of her heartbeat is replaced by the lasting song of bluegrass. The camera then cuts to her tattoo, which shows the name Alabama Monroe; the star on the right represents her lost child. Early on, Didier told his daughter about how a star's light extends forever into the universe, so it never goes out. By appropriating this analogy within the Alabama Monroe tattoo, Elise-as-Alabama figures herself as an undying star. With its earlier presentation of George W. Bush quoting Bible verse as he makes references to the shadow of death and resisting life-saving research on moral grounds, the film highlighted a post-9/11 public discourse driven by violence and division. Alabama's death embodies such deadening discourse while also offering a kind of fraught resistance. For those who can face her death and accept her new western identity, death might affirm life, and the solidarity it offers might open, rather than close, vital connections to others.

Kiyoshi Kurosawa's *Tokyo Sonata*:
Seeing America's Wars as a Noir Nightmare

Whereas the heroes of *Adieu Gary* and *The Broken Circle Breakdown* are indirectly affected by America's wars and unilateral approach to international law, the protagonist of Kiyoshi Kurosawa's *Tokyo Sonata* is a Japanese youth, Takashi, who joins America's conflict in Iraq. Takashi's argument with his parents about this and a nightmare sequence from the mother's perspective employ noir staging to depict a home space invaded by American political forces.

The film dramatizes a subservience that political commentators and theorists have pinpointed as a key aspect of then–prime minister Junichiro Koizumi's support of America's wartime ventures. His unquestioned support for U.S. policy, many critics found, pushed Japan's Security Defense Force into war. As explained by East Asian historian Gavin McCormack, the prime minister's "desire to prove 'trustworthiness' outweighed constitution, law, and morality" (McCormack 2004). McCormack explores how Japan's reliance on the United States for protection from North Korea mired the state within the Iraq conflict and cut against Japan's constitutional imperative of pacifism. Few have fully addressed the humanitarian cost of these recent transformations. This paucity of discussion around human consequences of wartime policies is key to understanding the critical force of *Tokyo Sonata*'s nightmare sequence, detailing a soldier coming home. The noir aesthetic counters such myopia, drawing attention to the often unremarked-upon costs of Japan's engagement in war and being pushed into the role of the perpetrator.[3]

Using expressionist technique, whereby an inner mood is visualized through shadow and light, the director infuses the Japanese home with darkness at the very moment when Takashi expresses his desire to go to Iraq and asks his father to sign his deployment paperwork. This sparks an argument about Japan's place in the world. When the father claims that the wider world's concerns are irrelevant, the son barks back, "That's why Japan's so hopeless. . . . It's the American military that protects Japan." As their argument escalates, he walks from the warm dining area into the coldly lit living room. He sits beside the television, which broadcasts news about America's war throughout the film, its blank screen creating negative space in the frame that positions the broadcasted Middle Eastern conflict as a rupture in the family home. The desperate mother brings both father and son back to the doorway between the dining room and the living room. When Takashi asks his father, "What am I supposed to do?" a train speeds by, creating a punctuation of light across the speech-less father's face. It is as though the war acts as an electric force that shocks the youth into reckless action and the father into passivity. The rumble of the train when the discontented son storms off speaks to the emotional tumult that the war sparks in the lives of ordinary Japanese.

The opening image of the nightmare depicting Takashi's home-coming establishes a dream logic by which the son's expressions of guilt are met by his mother's incomprehension. He walks in wearing military fatigues, the words US ARMY embroidered on his jacket, falls on the steps, and announces, "I'm so tired." To this, the mother expresses polite concern. A wide shot upon the front entrance of the home films their reunion at a remove, accentuating the emotional disconnection. The blue light evokes the deathly pallor of the argument between the father and son about his decision to join the army; there is no visual warmth in this scene. The dark wood paneling creates a fractured composition, so that the home appears to be broken up by bars, transformed into a site of entrapment. Kurosawa cuts away from the wide shot when Takashi declares, "I have killed many people." Then the film cuts to a close-up shot, emulating the gaze of the mother, who now sees her shell-shocked son with more frightening clarity. Following his admission of guilt, the scene shifts to the mother cutting vegetables in a brightly lit kitchen. It initially seems as though the violence of war has no effect on her normal existence; however, she then turns, compelled into the darkness of the dining room where her son sits. She moves into the shadow and wakes up screaming right just when her hand comes to rest upon Takashi's shoul-der. The nightmare, culminating in a kind of interrupted contact, signals the despair caused by the fracture, the crack between generations—one ignoring the violence that underpins the U.S.-Japan relationship while the other is deadened by it.

Myopia regarding contemporary Japan's costly interest in becoming a global power becomes most evident when Takashi's parents take their younger son, Kenji, to the hospital shortly before the mother's nightmare. As in every film discussed in this chapter, the television takes up the entire screen. The mirrored aspect ratio between the film frame and the television creates a formal parallel that highlights just how completely the Iraq War pervades the production and haunts its protagonists. A news-man announces the new policy whereby Japanese citizens can participate in the U.S. Army's deployment in the Middle East, before cutting to a series of interviews with affected youth. A man of Takashi's age says, "I support it. We have a lot of trade with America, so if America has a problem that means Japan's directly affected." During his testimony, the film cuts to a wide shot showing the parents looking on in silence. The use of shifting focus in the scene visualizes their willful distance from this geopolitical reality. The television and the parents are never in focus at the same time. When they go to face forward, looking away from the television, the television goes out of focus but remains centered between them. Another individual protests the policy on constitutional grounds. Blurred, the last speaker vocalizes their repressed thoughts when he admits, "I couldn't believe that our government let them join [the American military]." During the father's aforementioned argument with Takashi, the television appeared like a black hole in the frame. Here, in the harsh light of the hospital waiting room, we peer into the kind of psychic abyss it heralds, where the loss of a son to an American war personifies the nation losing its principles.

Genre as the "Claire de Lune" in Post-9/11 Public Discourse

Using a noir mode where shadows and blank screens express anxieties, *Tokyo Sonata* demonstrates genre's ability to make unspoken truths more fully legible and even overwhelming by expressing them through recognizable tropes that take over a film's form. The film also suggests the emancipatory potential of the violent myths alluded to in the previously cited films that play with Hollywood genre convention. *Game Over*'s protagonist insists on the necessity of the experience of war, speaking to how service may liberate a trapped youth. *The Broken Circle Breakdown* frames genre as a contested tool for artists to lament and for states to self-mythologize. *Adieu Gary* finds that genre visions of power accentuate the weakness of the marginalized while allowing a rare feeling of agency that may be impossible to sustain.

For its part, *Tokyo Sonata*'s epilogue contains word from Takashi that suggests how facing state violence head on, even participating in such actions, might free the consciousness. His letter to his mother features two stamps with the image of a bald eagle and his name signed in Latin characters, revealing his now hybridized mentality somewhere between the two powers. However, he does not emerge a deadened perpetrator; instead, he gleans the humanity in the stated enemy of both nations. He tells his mother, "I've learned that America isn't the only one that's right. That is why I have decided to stay in this country a while longer, so I can understand them better. I've come to the conclusion that the best path for me is to fight alongside the people of this country, in order to find true happiness." Through violence, Takashi experiences a push away from set prejudices and out of the U.S.–dominated framework by which Japan appears governed. The divine, saving violence that Macer in *Sicario* heralds seems visualized in this narrative about a soldier who goes off to war.

During its last scene, *Tokyo Sonata* offers an affecting reassertion of the aesthetic as a means to challenge and to inspire. The younger son, Kenji, performs an extended rendition of Claude Debussy's "Claire de Lune." Kurosawa presents the boy's entire performance, the very piano music that the father had previously banned Kenji from playing in an effort to make a principled (if unexplained) stance as the family's patriarch. The director presents aesthetic majesty within a space of brightness, antithetical to the nightmare sequence spawned by the older generation's refusal to reckon with state violence. The first stanza of the 1869 Paul Verlaine poem "Clair de Lune," which inspired Debussy's composition, offers insight into the critical work of the film:

> Your soul is a select landscape
> Where charming masqueraders and bergamaskers go
> Playing the lute and dancing and almost
> Sad beneath their fanciful disguises.

Kenji's flawless performance suggests that art may transport viewers to encounter sad realities that linger beneath the surface. His parents have previously turned away from scenes about war, only facing their fears in noir-tinged nightmares. Now they are fully attentive, even transfixed by their son's song. Culminating the film with such a performance, Kurosawa constructs a metaphor for genre cinema as a platform to confront taboos and to ease into discomfiting situations, so that we might confront our weaknesses: even they can be made beautiful.

Unlike the often somber films detailed so far, Wu Jing's recent *Wolf Warrior 2* alludes to fighting the War on Terror with vigor and boldness that reflect China asserting itself as the global hegemon (winked toward when the Chinese flag is presented at the same level as the United Nations flag during the film's final moments). However, the closing credits present a range of outtakes from the production that create skepticism about such virile nationalism—the highly sensationalistic, even propagandistic text invites us into a discomfiting world where China's militaristic strength is but a mirage, pure theater when competing against states such as the United States or nonstate (terrorist) actors that seek to disrupt the nation's monopoly on violence.

Wolf Warrior 2 centers on the adventures of the Special Forces soldier Leng Feng (Wu Jing), whom scholar Yiping Cai describes as "a freshly baked Chinese 'superhero'" (Cai 2019). The seemingly indestructible killing machine clads himself in the Chinese flag in one key sequence, becoming one with the nation's emblem. He thus brings to mind Captain America or the catchphrase of Superman, said to fight for "truth, justice, and the American way." The Chinese way of Leng Feng is emblemized by the film's militaristic invocation of the One Belt, One Road initiative, showing this Chinese superhero saving Africa from not only itself but also other powers that seek to transform it into a sphere of influence. However, in its final moments, the film moves to face Islamic terrorism in its global form. Critics such as Kim Lane Scheppele have noted that China has invoked UNSC Resolution 1373 to put more pressure on its local Muslim communities under the guise of terrorism prevention (Scheppelle 2013, "From a War").

After saving Chinese citizens from danger during an African civil war and defeating the cruel and amoral American mercenary known as "Big Daddy," Leng Feng seeks the solitary comfort of the mountains. During the closing credits, however, he is called back into action when his supposedly dead fiancée surfaces in a hostage video made by terrorists. The credits show a barren, snowy landscape, unpopulated and seemingly cut off from the political morass that defined the film's African battlefields. However, war (linked to the War on Terror) enters the setting through video footage on a cell phone, echoing the disruptive iPad of *Sieranevada* that projects violent acts of terrorism into a seemingly apolitical space. The device's screen and the hostage video take up much of the film frame. The imagery, recalling beheading videos that have circulated online, is initially presented in silence (Fig. 5.3), as though the specter of Islamic terrorism robs both the film and its hero of a voice. A strum of the guitar sounds when the hostage looks at the camera. The Wolf Warrior, clad in a fur that seems to transform him into a superheroic man-animal hybrid, then looks up from the phone's screen with an unblinking gaze of determination. Zooming out, the film speeds up to signal the propulsive energy of a hero responding to the distant terrorist threat. Cutting to black before showing the logo *Wolf Warrior 3* makes clear that the Wolf Warrior will now set his sights on the Middle East, the battleground of the United States for nearly two decades.

Immediately following the tundra sequence, swelling with an up-tempo score befitting the explosive imagery, the film presents an

Figure 5.3. A terrorist hostage video overtakes the frame, signaling China's own entrance into the War on Terror. *Wolf Warrior 2.*

outtakes reel that does some profound and critically destabilizing work (Fig. 5.4). Leng Feng, shown to be so indestructible in the earlier film, now (as actor-director Wu Jing) hits his head, bangs his elbow, and even runs in fear from the non-Chinese enemies! This behind-the-scenes look, common in Hong Kong action cinema, has a strangely disruptive effect in a brazenly nationalistic and seemingly earnest war film starring a super soldier. It frames a Chinese state operating with similar theatrical bluster. The film's proposed dream of China supplanting the United States to

Figure 5.4. In outtakes over the end credits, the "Chinese superhero" runs away from the foreign enemy. The nationalistic action film exposes the position of China as the commanding force in the War on Terror as nothing but theatrical bluster. *Wolf Warrior 2.*

engage in the War on Terror and take on a non-nation-state force such as ISIS is shown to be just that—a cinematic fantasy that can barely last for the duration of the film's running time. The outtakes sequence suggests that the War on Terror's visions of militaristic strength can be exposed as smoke and mirrors.

Thinking transnationally about post-9/11 genre cinema allows us to glimpse the shadow of the War on Terror upon the world. Although these few films all expressly discuss 9/11 and the ensuing wars, I hope that my own readings of works such as *Sin City* and *Zodiac* will inspire scholars to consider films more removed from the contemporary moment. If deployed critically with a conscious understanding of how their established tropes might express ambivalence, these visions of power can permit moments of resistance, and beautiful ambiguity might productively shift conceptual borders during a worldwide state of emergency.

In a time where the borders between nations have become ever more troubled and developments in global security law have transformed the geopolitical landscape into a claustrophobic noir city dictated by the whims of the United States, the boundaries between genres have shifted. Recent border westerns seem tinged with noir paranoia. The disparate noirs featured—near-parody and true crime—touch on the burden of superheroic vigilantes. The superhero film finds itself in a noir universe, where the fragility in power might be confronted. Breakdowns in the genre form, mixing tropes of the western, noir, and superhero, crack through these productions concerned with tracking the effects of the global War on Terror upon the local pop imagination. Just as the set conventions of genre permit filmmakers to negotiate and engage with the public discourse, so too might such parameters allow film scholars to pinpoint and work through breakdowns in the set borders between genre modes and even between Hollywood and global cinema. The comparative framework I propose thus becomes a key means of situating genre within a world where the American state and its corresponding visions of power begin to break free of jurisdictional boundaries—those established in the law or within genre storytelling.

The final scene of *Sieranevada* saliently frames the possibility of such a critical transnational approach to genre that invokes the logic of global security law. Sebi's family sits down to finally eat their much-delayed dinner. The family first decries the United States' unilateral wartime policy in Iraq, with one referencing Madeleine Albright's infamous correlation that the death of five hundred thousand children is worth it to end Saddam's life. They then express disillusionment with present-day Romania and even posit the state as a criminal entity. Police sirens quietly sound in the background as the family touches upon corruption on a national and global scale, suggesting that Sebi's conspiratorial, comparative framework contains a disruptive and threatening force. The film ends not in despair but in laughter directed at the film's prophet of conspiracy, showing that such a conspiracy theorist's worldview, embracing the multidirectional and lingering on interconnectivity and unseen links, might render existential fear moot. It draws out a sense of underlying logic in a world beyond a subject's control, or at least sparks a pacifying glimpse of a core absurdity. At the dinner table of a Bucharest apartment, we see the kind of transnational thinking—at once paranoid and liberated—that reflects both the disempowerment and the power that genre forms offer subjects feeling ever more marginalized and afraid within "a planet transformed by 9/11."

Notes

Introduction. Hollywood at Ground Zero

1. The 9/11 Memorial Museum (formally known as the National September 11 Memorial & Museum) is located at the World Trade Center site in New York City. It was opened to the public on May 21, 2014. Quotation from the documentary *Facing Crisis: A Changed World* verified using a transcript generously provided by the museum.

Chapter 1. "It was like a movie!"

1. Political scientist Brigitte L. Nacos catalogues the perception of the attacks as media spectacle in her research. She identifies "mass-mediated terrorism" as one where "media considerations [are central] in the calculus of political violence that is committed by nonstate actors against civilians" ("Terrorism as Breaking News: Attack on America," *Political Science Quarterly* 118, no. 1 [Spring 2003]: 23). I take seriously the possibility that media considerations shape and influence not only nonstate actors like terrorists but also state actors.

2. Here, and in this broader study, I adopt the definition of terrorist offered by political theorist Eqbal Ahmad, as any party who uses "coercive violence, violence that is used illegally, extra-constitutionally, to coerce" (Ahmad 1998). Ahmad's definition notably allows for both private actors and states to fall under the umbrella of terrorism. The Joker who seeks to undermine the established order through spectacular, nonsanctioned violence and coerce the citizenry into revolt is keenly aware of how the state (and its vigilante proxies, such as Batman) deploy similar coercive tactics that push, if not fully disregard, the boundaries of law.

3. The film reveals that such liberatory, populist language is but a lie to control the citizenry as Bane's cabal works to secretly destroy the city.

4. For many key players of the Bush administration, including Dick Cheney and Donald Rumsfeld, realism, where state interests matter above all stated ideals,

contained a moral component, becoming what neoconservative thinker Charles Krauthammer describes as "democratic realism." See Krauthammer's 2004 speech, "Democratic Realism—An American Foreign Policy for a Unipolar World." I will consider the contradictions in the efforts to create policies shaped by this uncompromising moral philosophy when these aforementioned executive actors also sought to create a legal framework supporting a "unitary executive," a presidency unencumbered by any obligations to either other branches of government or the tenets of international human rights law. See Mary L. Dudziak, "A Sword and a Shield: The Uses of Law in the Bush Administration," in *The Presidency of George W. Bush*, 39–58.

5. Cited in Slocum's review of the field, Stephen Prince's *Firestorm: American Film in the Age of Terrorism* speaks to a broader tendency to disregard the value of more oblique mediations of the present moment offered within genre cinema. As discussed in the introduction, Prince writes that the failures of literal-minded productions "suggest[s] that viewers are rejecting the role that popular cinema might claim in bearing witness to atrocity" (Prince 2009, 305). His study ends with an undercutting of genres with what he views as "impregnable" story formulas that fail to react to changes in the political landscape (ibid., 308). Hollywood remains in its past genre dreams, espousing answers disengaged from the moral dilemmas that define the post-9/11 moment. The success of blockbusters such as *The Dark Knight* would seem to show how atrocity can be witnessed within popular cinema while maintaining a strong sense of moral ambiguity fitting for a time marked by terrorism and global war. While Prince represents an extreme in his stance against the relevance of genre modes, his reservations point to the continued need for scholars to pay attention to and draw out the complex sociopolitical critiques from these popular forms of storytelling.

6. Ngai mobilizes the term *illegal alien* concurrently with *undocumented person*, showing how state and legal discourses can seem to mark a person as outlaw and contain a dehumanizing dimension even within studies ostensibly designed to critique such practices.

Chapter 2. On the Frontier between Hate and Empathy

1. In her essay "Hollywood Border Cinema: Westerns with a Vengeance," Camilla Fojas productively identifies central themes of the border western: "Many of the films that take place on or near the borderlands express 'American' anxieties, messianic prophecies, and fears about porous boundaries and the integration of the hemisphere through political intervention, economic globalization, and the transnational migration of people and goods" (Fojas 2011, 98). This chapter considers how these various anxieties and fears present in such films are inflected by the War on Terror.

2. The 2018 sequel to *Sicario*, Stefano Sollima's *Sicario: Day of the Soldado*, renders much more explicit many of the links between the U.S.-Mexico border space and the Middle East. The sequel begins with Middle Eastern terrorists

crossing the border, an act that permits U.S. military intelligence forces to operate with complete impunity. Featuring scenes of all-out war in broad daylight, *Sicario: Day of the Soldado* potently illustrates how, on a discursive level at least, the boundaries between the southern border and the front lines have continued to move since the first film's release.

3. In *Border Walls: Security and the War on Terror in the United States, India, and Israel*, Reece Jones performs comparative work between the border policies of the United States and Israel as well as the discourses of fear that undergird them. Jones cites the 9/11 attacks and the Second Intifada as providing the necessary political and public will to embark on large-scale border wall and border security projects, which were framed against "an enemy-other in the global war on terror . . . an evil that has no place in the modern world" (Jones 2012, 6–7). Perhaps *Sicario*'s citation of a historical ancient Jerusalem is meant not only to push viewers to perform transnational comparative work but also to encourage an appreciation for the state's mobilizing of the archetype of a premodern enemy. Does the state also configure the Mexican as an enemy-Other that stands outside of time, a radical threat to the project of modernity?

4. Prats's conception of the western as a form that vacillates trepidatiously between remembering and forgetting the nation's genocidal past helpfully frames the utility for such a type of storytelling in depriving the present of any contextualizing or implicating detail. For instance, what history is forgotten when Osama bin Laden is compared to a wanted bandit by George W. Bush? The creation of the mythic past of the West, a setting defined by its never fully settled nature, paradoxically resembles a forgetting of the present, a gap in a culture's vision. Nostalgia for a generic past, a moment that never was, breeds a myopia that can be harnessed by the state for narrativizing its actions.

5. Lee Mitchell posits that a key part of the reconstitution of masculinity that he finds to be central to the western is the literal destruction of the male body: it must "be beaten, distorted, and pressed out of shape so that it can paradoxically become what it already is" (Mitchell 1996, 160). The process of physical recuperation parallels an emotional growth so that the hero becomes a man in both body and soul (ibid., 176). This manner of identity formation resonates not with the figure that the film denotes as the quintessential cowboy, Melquiades, but with his killer, Mike. The rattlesnake poison leaves his body as the venom toward the Mexican leaves his mind; hence, through the healing of Mike, the film plays with genre conventions so that the patrolman becomes not a "man" but a human capable of compassion.

6. All readings in this chapter are based on the extended cut of the film released on February 11, 2014. Portions of the reading of *The Counselor* appeared in my research article "Where Our Hungers Trump Morality: The Border in Ridley Scott and Cormac McCarthy's *The Counselor*," *Southwestern American Literature* 42, no. 2 (2017): 7–27.

7. The film suggests the importance of its comic tone when, after a drug trafficker explains the never-ending circulation of a body across the border done by cartels to irritate him, he quips, "They think it's a fucking joke, they think

it's funny. In this business, you got to have a sense of humor, you know?" Payan repeatedly employs the term *absurd* to describe the conflation of discourses that occur around the border as well as the ignorance of political actors about the interrelation of the Mexican and American economies as well as each country's national security (Payan 2006, 17, 20, 74, 140). How, *The Counselor* encourages us to ask, can the absurd be consciously deployed to heighten moral ambiguity even as it exposes the bizarre assumptions that underpin contemporary political discourse?

8. *The Counselor* draws a more direct parallel between drug dealers and financiers earlier in the film. In a scene where traffickers unload cocaine from a septic truck, a financier in a blazer and a trafficker in mechanic's overalls discuss the loopholes in international trading. Capping their discussion, the trafficker laughingly remarks, "Shit, you know, of all the people, you and I should know if electronic money earns an extra day of interest when it crosses an international date line." Although these words link the two men and the enterprises they represent, the financier's final request points to their shared depravity. He asks whether he can see the body that was hidden in one of the truck's oil drums as a punishment for offending the drug cartels. At this morbid curiosity, even the trafficker is surprised. The actors operate with the same perpetrating mentality, the very same disinterest in the human costs of their activities.

9. Although cartels have been known to employ spectacular acts of violence to frighten local populations, even posting videos of killings on YouTube, writings about the drug economy have noted that violence is a core feature of day-to-day business operations (Martin 2013, 44). Part of the horror of *The Counselor* is in how it demonstrates that horrible acts of violence, including the filmed murder of Laura, testify not to the presence of a malevolent evil but to the routine costs of doing business.

10. The crumpled-up Mexican newspaper in the shot might also refer to the failure of traditional media sources in Mexico to effectively cover the War on Drugs out of fear of repercussions from local cartels. In "Drug Wars, Social Networks, and the Right to Information: Informal Media as Freedom of Press in Northern Mexico," Guadalupe Correa-Cabrera and José Nava explore this self-censorship as well as the power of informal media within Mexico to sidestep such strictures. Informal media, such as blogs, have a degree of anonymity that allows them to frame the causes of violence and, the authors argue, provoke authorities to change their policies accordingly (Correa-Cabrera and Nava 2013, 17–18). The scene described here is of interest in part because it frames genre as an informal medium operating with the same freedoms, hence permitting it to work outside of the more limited rhetorical realm of the mainstream news outlets. Such liberty allows the film to boldly state its broad critique, which extends from an ineffective mass media framing the border in mythic terms that fails to account for the cross-bordered cultures of consumption to a potentially hypocritical viewer enmeshed within an economy of desire.

11. Andreas's translations of Calderón's language about his War on Drugs shows that the president positioned his endeavor in the same Manichean terms as Bush did his War on Terror in 2001. Calderón stated: "It will be an all-out war, because the possibility of coexisting with drug trafficking organizations is no longer viable. There's no turning back. It's us or them" (qtd. in Andreas 2001, 150).

12. The actions of Calderón's administration were heavily criticized by organizations such as Human Rights Watch (HRW), which concluded: "Mexico's military and police have committed widespread human rights violations in efforts to combat organized crime, virtually none of which are being adequately investigated" ("Mexico: Widespread Rights Abuses"). In a 2011 report, *Neither Rights Nor Security: Killings, Torture, and Disappearances in Mexico's "War on Drugs,"* HRW found that Mexican police exist within a culture of impunity, kidnapping, torturing, and killing those with no relation to the drug trade. Describing the "dangerous rhetoric" of the Calderón administration, HRW reported that his government often presented falsified statistics to "cast the victims as criminals" (*Human Rights Watch* 2011, 10). The forced disappearances in particular served to create a stark sense of powerlessness for the victim's loved ones. As the wife of a disappeared man described, "We don't know even know what to do anymore. We know who did this and we can't do anything" (ibid., 13). Such reports frame Calderón's drug policy as a war between a callous and increasingly militarized police force and the ordinary citizens of the border regions.

Chapter 3. Femmes Fatales as Torturers and Lost Detectives in a Fragile City

1. In keeping with the theme of waking up to trauma's impact and the role such films can play, Scott Frank's 2014 noir *A Walk Among the Tombstones* visualizes a culture asleep before the attacks. Unlike *25th Hour*, the film draws attention not downward to the wreckage of the World Trade Center but upward to the sky above New York. Set in the city in 1999, *A Walk Among the Tombstones* presents its villain reading the *New York Daily News* over breakfast. The paper features the headline "Y2K worries" over a photo of an ascending plane, and a subtitle refers to a possible "travel nightmare" that the bug might cause. A wide shot positions his newspaper in the frame's center, signaling Y2K's central place in the culture's mind. He tells his partner, "People are afraid of all the wrong things." As he speaks, the sound of a plane engine grows in the soundtrack, before a cut to an establishing shot of the Hudson River with a plane descending into the city. By deploying the iconography of the 9/11 attacks, the film emphasizes what should be a true source of fear while gesturing to the failure of imagination that the 9/11 Commission concluded was a crucial cause of the intelligence community's inability to prevent the attacks (National Commission 2004, 339–47). The pointedly anachronistic scene transforms a noir killer into a soothsayer who points out the

naïveté of a pre-9/11 United States. In genres such as noir, murderers are often those who invite the audience to see what they wish to ignore.

2. Hardt and Negri provide a historical context in their work *Multitude*. Following the end of the Cold War in 1989, the United States found itself the world's only superpower, becoming the dominant force over all nation-states, at least militarily. American military power became more centralized, and with that shift came an added emphasis on bodiless and bloodless war (Hardt and Negri 2004, 42). The post-1989 Revolution in Military Affairs, or RMA, sought to "make war practically risk-free for US soldiers, protecting them from the threats of any adversary" (ibid.). Antithetical to this system was the suicide bomber, fully realized in the popular consciousness in the wake of 9/11. With evocative and almost sensationalistic language, the scholars highlight the uniqueness of this enemy, calling him "the dark opposite, the gory doppelgänger of the safe bodiless soldier" (ibid., 45).

3. In an essay titled "*Kiss Me Deadly*: Evidence of a Style," Alain Silver encapsulates this critical assessment, writing that the film "typifies the frenetic post-Bomb LA with all its malignant undercurrents" and bristles with an "underlying sense of nuclear peril" (Silver 1996, 209). Silver argues that the film represents a culmination of classic film noir's fascination with total obliteration.

4. Essays in the influential anthology *Women in Film Noir* testify to how the femme fatale has long been seen as a complex figure in feminist discourse who, at times, functions to expose male weakness even though her very formation suggests the preponderance of a masculinist discourse within popular cinema. Film scholar Janey Place begins her essay "Women in Film Noir" by admitting that classic film noir "is a male fantasy" (Place 1998, 47). And yet, Place finds that the genre offers a rare vision of empowered femininity in Hollywood cinema of the period. Such tensions have always been a part of the essence of the femme fatale, who has been perceived as a response to a supposed domestic shift on the home front after World War II. The femme fatale has been read as representing newly independent women whom veterans encountered upon their return from war. Hierarchies were shaken and, in this historical reading of the genre, it is understood to capture what Silvia Harvey describes as an "erosion of expectations" following the war, where the very liberty of women at home brought into relief postwar male disempowerment (qtd. in Bould 2005, 65).

5. The film begins and ends with the classic variant of the femme fatale on the verge of being assassinated by a contract killer. After the killer embraces her and declares his love, his gun fires. The screen briefly explodes in white, a visual trope that the film employs with slight variation at every moment of connection between men and women. This visual stutter recalls a sexual climax through its initial linking of the man's metaphoric orgasm and the femme fatale's death; however, it also suggests the impossibility of any profound union and highlights that they exist in separate, opposing spheres. As discussed in the chapter's introduction, such breakdowns in the diegesis feature prominently within post-9/11

noir, functioning as a meta-commentary on how the attacks both challenged and reaffirmed the role of the genre in mediating their historical moment.

6. In the original *Sin City* comic series, Miller acknowledges and briefly grapples with the misogynistic edge of such noir imagery. A vignette from the tale "That Yellow Bastard" includes a self-professed art photographer, whose work has won "all kinds of awards," asking permission to photograph a stripper heroine (Miller 1996, 14). In his initial appearance in the background, the art photographer stands in the same visual plane as the story's villain, the titular Yellow Bastard, which suggests that Miller is aware that he skirts very problematic territory: luxuriating in the objectified feminine form under the guise of pulp art (ibid., 10). Such imagery risks undercutting the series' complex imagining of female empowerment by turning these autonomous subjects into purely objects to be gazed upon and ogled.

7. For further elaboration of Marcus's view on the insidious aspects of the discourse on rape and ways it can be undermined, see "Fighting Bodies, Fighting Words: A Theory and Politics of Rape Prevention," in *Feminists Theorize the Political*, 385–403.

8. Contemplating the significance of the Lynch narrative as it relates to establishing a deeply gendered view of the Iraq War, gender scholars Lindsay Feitz and Joane Nagel focus on moments that reveal the icon of Lynch to be a starlet in the big-budget production that was the Iraq War, including the testimony of an Iraqi doctor present at her rescue that "there were no [Iraqi] soldiers in the hospital . . . it was like a Hollywood film . . . they made a show for the American attack on the hospital (resembling) action movies like those of Sylvester Stallone" (qtd. in Feitz and Nagel 2008, 207). His statement reveals Lynch's rescue to be a choreographed finale to showcase a weakened femininity.

9. In the essay "*Klute* 1: A Contemporary Film Noir and Feminist Criticism," Christine Gledhill ponders whether a woman's discourse manifests within film noir and offers a summary of the key thematic and aesthetic features of the genre, many of which *Sin City* reworks. The presentation of Nancy in the saloon from Hartigan's point of view mirrors Gledhill's assessment that the noir woman "is filmed for her sexuality. Introductory shots, which catch the hero's gaze, frequently place her at an angle above the onlooker" (Gledhill 1998, 32). The very superior visual position of the noir woman suggests the power that her sexuality has over the male protagonist. Ayako Saito's essay "Occupation and Memory: The Representation of Woman's Body in Postwar Japanese Cinema," detailing several iconic films that thematize the lives of female erotic dancers in postwar Japanese cinema, provides a salient framework to consider the ambivalent space that the stripper Nancy occupies, both sexually empowered and objectified by the onlookers. Saito argues that the body of the stripper, an entertainment figure brought to Japan with American occupying forces, captured "the contradictions of defeat and occupation" and reflected Japan's emasculated men and newly liberated women (Saito 2014, 330). She finds that "the sheer cinematic presence

and power of the lively dynamic bodies . . . subverts the potential objectification of their bodies" (ibid., 339).

10. In "Wonder Woman and the Reinvention of the Feminine Ideal," Kelli Stanley articulates the mythic roots of the heroine, alluding to her subversive edge as well as her inextricable connection with the very sort of sadomasochistic power practiced by Gail and her real-world equivalent, Lynndie England. Created in 1940 by William Moulton Marston, the superheroine who tied her male enemies in the Lasso of Truth embodied his beliefs that "women are inherently superior to, and should dominate, men" (Stanley 2005, 146). Marston fervently believed that to free themselves from the bonds of male patriarchy, women had to uncover their inner dominatrix. According to comic book lore, Wonder Woman came to the United States from a mythical paradise island inhabited exclusively by divine Amazonian women. Stanley argues that in antiquity, Amazonians functioned as the symbol of the Other, whose very presence in popular culture buttressed the established order (ibid., 145). Aspects of this subordination exist in the traditional costume of the heroine, who problematically teetered between master and slave, bound by her lasso as often as she bound others.

11. Stanley finds that the metal bracelets create the fantasy of a reconquest, a tangible reminder that this supreme vision of feminine power can be cowed (2005, 163).

12. Revealing the intention of this rendering, in *The Dark Knight Returns*, Frank Miller draws metal bracelets on a prostitute dressed up as Wonder Woman who had been savagely beaten (Miller 1986, 135). This drawing indicates that he is keenly aware of the significance of switching the composition of the bracelets as a mark of the liberated and dangerous quality of these women.

13. In the essay "Theses on the Questions of War: History, Media, Terror," anthropologist Rosalind C. Morris links the discourse of British colonization with the U.S. war in Afghanistan by arguing that they were underpinned by the same mission, where "white men sav[e] brown women from brown men" (2002, 162). Women were the fulcrum upon which colonial violence operated, the wounding of their bodies emblematic of the colony's broader supplication to the metropole. Morris finds that the war in Afghanistan was validated and propelled by a narrative of emancipation centered upon Afghani women "tearing off of veils" (ibid.). Both colonization and the twenty-first-century conflict spectacularized the woman's body, transforming it into a show that articulated either the depths of colonial subjugation or the heights of freedom permitted by the U.S. military.

14. Commenting on the covert use of fake menstrual blood by female soldiers to psychically break prisoners at Guantanamo Bay, a revelation that was leaked to the press, Oliver argues that the bodily fluid "has become a top-secret interrogation technique"(Oliver 2008, 4). The blood may threaten the male subject because it "provokes fears of women's procreative powers" or "conjures the maternal body as an uncanny border and ultimate threat to individual autonomy" (ibid.). In the shot of Gail, the film's explicit call for "women's blood"

is juxtaposed against a framing that emphasizes her armed dominatrix uniform. Oliver's reading, working from Sigmund Freud's assessment of the *unheimlich* or uncanny, also provides a view of the metaphoric features of the vignette's climactic scene where the invading male forces are destroyed within an Old Town alley.

15. The subversive weight of this connotation can best be understood by a brief reflection on the critical response to *300*'s portrayal of the brave Greeks fighting against the foreign hordes. Upon the film's release in 2007, critics found that the hyper-exaggerated work reflected the jingoistic rhetoric that defined the Iraq War and underpinned broader conceptions of the U.S. relationship with the Middle East. Conservative commentator Bill Walsh, writing for *The Weekly Standard*, considers the myth to be vital to Western national identity, as the liberated Spartans' "sacrifice helped preserve the notions and institutions which blossomed into the glorious civilization eventually built on Greek foundations" (Walsh 2007). Critics such as Walsh labeled *300* the quintessential cinematic representation of Bush's war in the Middle East, which rendered glorious the president's ideals that championed the spread of democracy. Although the critical establishment read *300* far too simply, much as it did *Sin City*, Walsh's allegorical assessment is useful for clarifying the symbolic force of linking the women with the Spartans and the men with the Persian enemy forces.

16. Michael Mann's 2008 *Public Enemies* tracks the genesis of this mindset in its portrayal of the FBI's manhunt for bank robber John Dillinger, emphasizing the cinema's crucial role in mythologizing Bureau Chief Hoover (Billy Crudup) and his agents as intrepid heroes who chase down their targets in the shadows. The film portrays Hoover as obsessed with sculpting his media image. One scene cuts from the FBI chief delivering a speech to his image on the big screen, reinforcing that the G-Man ideal was created in the movies. Hoover moves in front of the press's cameras to induct a new generation of "junior G-Men." The film next frames a group of children wearing crisp suits, then transitions into a black-and-white aesthetic that evokes the look of newsreel stock, using the color shift to transition into the cinema, where Dillinger and his gang plan their next heist. The youths present in the scene metaphorically underscore the indoctrinating effect such early public relations campaigns had upon the psyches of future FBI agents.

17. For a brief overview of Nixon's adoration of Hollywood, consult chapter 1 of Francis Wheen's history of the seventies: *Strange Days Indeed: The Golden Age of Paranoia*, 20–39.

18. In the director's cut of *Zodiac*, the sequence that follows the movie theater scene is the aforementioned extended sonic montage that illustrates the passage of four years, with sound cues from both popular music and current events. Through the use of a blank screen, the film positions the contemporary political universe as an overwhelming cacophony, implicitly situating the mass art of cinema as the vehicle that brings coherence both to broad political transformations and, in

presenting President Ford's declaration of his absolute pardon of Richard Nixon, to the executive's elision of the legal landscape.

Chapter 4. Soaring above the Law

1. The post-9/11 superhero films feature the superheroes of the two largest American publishers: DC Comics and Marvel Comics. Although both tell stories about popular heroes, a key aesthetic distinction between the two modes stems from their comic book roots—DC stories are typically set in an allegorized America, while Marvel tales take place in a more recognizable United States. For example, DC has the gothic Gotham City whereas Marvel has New York City. DC films, presenting the mythic exploits of icons such as Batman and Superman, tend to be more outwardly skeptical of institutions of power, the military, and law enforcement, as though the added allegorical distance permits more ambiguity and ambivalence.

2. In his study of Obama's foreign policy team, *The Obamians*, journalist James Mann notes, "[w]hile the Obama administration rejected the Bush administration's rhetoric about a 'global war on terror,' the change seems to be mostly a decision not to put those words together anymore while still preserving the concepts and using each of the words separately" (Mann 2012, 109). Mann's conclusion was echoed by former vice president Dick Cheney: "I think he has learned that what we did was far more appropriate than he ever gave us credit for while he was a candidate" (qtd. in ibid., 115).

3. Comic book sales were extremely high during the war. Not only was an estimated 84 percent of youths aged between twelve and seventeen reading these comic books each week, soldiers also devoured them, as they represented more than 28 percent of all books shipped overseas (O'Rourke 2007, 114).

4. Other superhero films have more directly staged meetings between the different eras encompassed by superhero stories—from the moral clarity espoused by characters during World War II to the moral opacity of today's War on Terror. In Marvel's 2014 *Captain America: Winter Soldier*, the titular hero (Chris Evans) goes to meet his love from the forties, Peggy Carter (Hayley Atwell), in hospice. While the World War II veteran Captain America has been perfectly preserved, having literally been frozen in time, his love is now decrepit. Carter sees the stridently principled hero through her dementia's haze, suggesting that only delusion gives any sense to his presence in a seemingly unprincipled world. Through this scene, the film articulates the absurdity of such an ideal-driven hero in our current geopolitical climate.

5. Besides offering a useful reading of the film's terrorist plot as a spectacular reenactment of the 9/11 attacks, film critic Michael Marano offers a new historicist account that links the creation of the League of Shadows and its head Ra's Al Ghul in the pages of the Batman comic books to the terrorist activity of the early seventies (Marano 2008, 81). As a figure, Ra's "bring[s] the kinds of conflict

fomented by Black September and Baader-Meinhof into the familial conflict of ancient Greek and early modern tragedy" (ibid., 79). This paternal relationship to terrorism, central to post-Vietnam iterations of the character, shows that the terror that Batman inspires in his enemies can be fruitfully perceived through the prism of political critique, as a kind of terrorism. See Marano's "Ra's al Ghul: Father Figure as Terrorist" in *Batman Unauthorized: Vigilantes, Jokers, and Heroes in Gotham City,* ed. Dennis O'Neil and Leah Wilson (Dallas, TX: BenBalla Books, 2008), 69–84.

6. Regarding this particular aesthetic feature, Christopher Nolan notes, "We spent a lot of time determining exactly how much of Batman to show, how much of his fighting to show. I had always looked to a representation of Batman that would be more from the criminal's point of view, so that you would see less of him. You would see him as more frightening . . . almost more animal-like" (*Shaping Mind and Body* 2005).

7. Christopher Nolan's own articulation of the formal logic behind the combat scenes underscores the intended critical dimensions of the superhero film: "I want to take [the fighting] back to a grubbier place, a place where you feel the punches a bit more, and you're actually a bit more concerned about the violence onscreen. There has been a lot of very, well, I think excessive use of wire-work and martial arts and everything to the point where violence loses its threat . . . and you become a bit comfortable watching it in that way" (*Shaping Mind and Body* 2005).

8. Testifying before Congress in 2002, the head of the CIA Counterterrorist Center, Cofer Black, emphasized the shift in thinking within the executive branch: "This is a very classified area, but I have to say that all you need to know: There was a before-9/11, and there was an after-9/11. After 9/11, the gloves come off" (Priest and Gellman 2002).

9. Following the 9/11 attacks, Congress passed the USA PATRIOT Act, which codified many practices related to surveillance that had previously been sanctioned by the judiciary, particularly a loosening of the standards needed to obtain court warrants (Scheppele 2004, 1034). Critics of the PATRIOT Act have lamented how, by expanding the definition of "terrorism" to cover domestic activity, the law gives excessive power to the state to arrest anyone they care to define as political dissidents. "Terrorists" might effectively be anyone, whether or not they harbor violent intentions toward the United States and its people. This lack of definition also applies to the term *enemy combatant,* which Bush used in his executive memos establishing the rules for the "War on Terror." Loose definitions of enemies permitted the administration to sidestep legal precedent and indefinitely detain whoever fell into these broad categories. How the Joker in this film, and villains throughout the trilogy, easily adopt civilian clothes is not just a demonstration of the omnipresence of terrorism; rather, given that the trilogy is largely from the paranoid perspective of the wealthy Bruce Wayne, it suggests a new legal reality where the spectator, just an ordinary face in the crowd, is suspect.

10. This moment in the interrogation room is the most explicit parallel made between Wayne/Batman and the Joker. Their physicality and mannerisms

are linked throughout the film. For instance, at a party, Wayne clandestinely tosses out his champagne, while the Joker does the same, albeit far more publicly, when he takes a champagne from a glass. Just as Batman speaks in a growl when wearing his mask, so too does the usually lilting villain when he commands a copycat Batman to "Look at me!" These conflations perhaps push the viewer to look more closely at the philosophical parallels between the two beings who seem, at first, to be opposed.

11. Indeed, the shift in the spectator's point of view between jailed and jailer, between marginalized and central, suggests the nuanced intersectional work that the superhero film accomplishes. Intersectionality, a branch of identity studies focused on the fluid cross-sections that form a subjectivity, offers, in the words of film scholars Vivian M. May and Beth A. Ferri, "a more fruitful exploration of the paradoxes of subjection and agency while also allowing further appreciation of the productive and liberatory possibilities of multiplicity, porosity, and ambiguity" (May and Ferri 2002, 146). Through *The Dark Knight*, the viewer transcends intersections, to move from disempowerment to empowerment—able to see the invisible intersections obscured in the worldview of the powerful, and to question the threat of a hyper-intersectional figure such as the Joker in a system designed to categorize and compartmentalize subjects. At the same time, the film offers insight into how an amorphous identity might not be simply a tool against the established order but a tool for it as well.

12. The USA PATRIOT Act loosened the standards applied to obtain court warrants and also expanded whom could be targeted for surveillance from identified foreign agents to those loosely involved with any international terrorism investigation (Scheppele 2004, 1031, 1037). Along with the PATRIOT Act, in 2002, Attorney General John Ashcroft issued guidelines that lowered the threshold required to use intrusive surveillance technology (ibid., 1040).

13. Those charged with law enforcement in the film have a relatively laissez-faire attitude toward legal checks on their power. When the sympathetic DA Harvey Dent gives Batman's chief ally, Lieutenant James Gordon, warrants of search and seizure on several banks without knowing the reasons for the request, Gordon notes, "In this town, the fewer people know something, the safer the operation." These men act without any sense of accountability, merely going through the motions of obtaining the proper authorization. How different are they, then, from the vigilante Batman? How different are they from an executive liberated by the PATRIOT Act, John Ashcroft's far-reaching guidelines, and the NSA's surveillance program?

14. A member of a design team for iRobot, a drone producer with links to the military, stated, "We were all influenced by science fiction" (qtd in Singer 2009, 164). In response, a colleague replied, "But now we are finding that our stuff is getting more advanced than science fiction" (ibid.). Recalling the footage of a target taken from a Predator Drone, Pakistan's Interior Minister A. Rehman Malik exclaimed, "It was a perfect picture. We used to see James Bond movies where he talked into his shoe or his watch. We thought it was a fairy tale. But

this was fact!" (Mayer). These various testimonies show that drone designers mine generic fiction for inspiration and actors on the battlefield conceptualize their impact through a lens shaped by genre icons. See P. W. Singer, *Wired for War: Revolution and Conflict in the 21st Century* (New York: Penguin, 2009), and Jane Mayer's in-depth essay on the CIA drone program, "The Predator War," *The New Yorker*, October 26, 2009.

15. In their survey of the ethical and legal concerns of drone warfare, "The Laws of Man Over Vehicles Unmanned," legal scholars Brendan Gogarty and Meredith C. Hagger caution that the superheroic aura of drones contrasts with a decidedly fallible reality: "Drones have largely arisen from the annals of science fiction, and the potential for their mystique to overwhelm the filters of criminal justice is equally strong as it has been in other technological revolutions. Despite their mystique, drones feeds' are not completely reliable" (Gogarty and Hagger 2008, 131). Nolan both shows the overwhelming force of such technology and finds ways to expose the underlying risks of such inherent fascination.

16. Due to the national government's passivity, in the view of the skeptical Detective John Blake, "Gotham lives under a warlord like some failed state." The film also presents more micro level rhetorical expressions of the state's dehumanizing view of the city and its inhabitants. A Special Forces soldier, whose National Emergency Relief uniform links him to institutions such as the Federal Emergency Management Agency (FEMA), refers to the Gotham police whom Bane has trapped underground as "men who haven't seen daylight in three months." Blake shouts back, "*Police officers* who haven't seen daylight in three months." Their present condition of struggle strips the Gotham police of their socially constructed identities. The pessimism the heroes of the film have toward the government is further made clear by Commissioner Gordon's cynical reaction to the American president's declaration, "People of Gotham, we have not abandoned you." Asked to explain the meaning behind that statement, Gordon answers, "It means we're on our own." Through such touches, Nolan correlates Gotham to New Orleans and frames the state in *The Dark Knight Rises* as analogous to an ineffectual Bush administration.

The state's reluctance to proactively intervene in Gotham City mediates the Bush administration's condition of supreme and costly inaction in the wake of Hurricane Katrina. Legal scholar Sean McGrane explains in "Katrina, Federalism, and Military Law Enforcement: A New Exception to the Posse Comitatus Act" that the federal government chose not to lead the situation on the ground and give its soldiers the right to perform law enforcement actions due to fears that they would impose on Louisiana's right to state sovereignty. The situation in New Orleans, primarily in regard to looting, approached anarchy (a scenario restaged in the chaotic city scenes of *The Dark Knight Rises*), making it impossible for the city and Louisiana to guarantee the rights of its inhabitants. McGrane suggests that the administration's decision was motivated by concerns surrounding its image. Paul McHale, then-assistant secretary of defense for homeland security, framed the dilemma: "Could we have physically moved combat forces into an American city, without the governor's consent, for purposes of using those forces . . . for law enforcement duties? Yes. . . . Would you have wanted that on your conscience?" (McGrane 2010, 1329). McGrane reveals an executive paralyzed by how representations of its power might be broadcasted, an anxiety that ultimately cost innocent lives. In the sequence where the president states his supposed solidarity with the people of Gotham City, the film shows him simply going through the motions of support.

17. When speaking about the film's concerns, Nolan foregrounds an interest in the tensions between a multitude and a privileged few. He describes the film as "as a historical epic with all kinds of great storytelling taking place during the French Revolution. There's an attempt to visualise certain things in this film on this large scale that are genuinely troubling to the idea of an American city. Or, to put it another way: revolutions and the destabilising of society have happened everywhere in the world, so why not here?" (qtd. in Vejvoda 2012). His words attest to a wider historical concern, encouraging spectators to consider the film through the shadow of states of emergency such as Katrina, which challenged the possibility of cohesion within an American city.

18. In *The Dark Knight*, when Bruce Wayne dines with District Attorney Harvey Dent, their conversation touches on a host of relevant concerns: the symbolic role of Batman, the ethics of vigilantism, and the dangerous allure of a state of emergency. Dent speaks in admiring terms about the Roman tradition of suspending democracy during times of crisis and instilling an emergency dictatorship. When one of his conversation partners retorts that Julius Caesar refused to give up his power, Dent states, "You either die a hero, or you live long enough to see yourself become the villain."

Perhaps the most elegant expression of the amorphous line between oppressor and oppressed in *The Dark Knight Rises* occurs through an understated homage to Nagisa Ôshima's 1983 *Merry Christmas, Mr. Lawrence*, about a Japanese captain's love for a resistant prisoner of war whom he tortures. Batman is psychologically tortured by Bane, left in a foreign prison to watch the city fall into chaos. Linking the two films, actor Tom Conti plays a prison translator in both. The homage acts as a more subtextual expression of the amorous link between hero and villain that the Joker plays with in the previous film. Quoting Cameron Crowe's romantic comedy 1996 *Jerry Maguire*, the Joker tells Batman, "You complete me." Taking on the dream logic of Ôshima's POW film, the imprisoned Wayne dreams of his and Bane's mentor, Ra's Al Ghul. The terrorist leader tells him, "Now you understand that Gotham [and its decadence] is beyond saving and must be allowed to die!" On a subconscious level, Gotham's supposed protector may share some of the same loathing toward the city and its excesses as the terrorists he fights. His urge to control the city may stem not from altruistic concern, but from a more megalomaniacal, tyrannical place. Batman, to his horror, begins to see himself as a villain.

19. Slavoj Žižek takes an opposing approach, demonstrating what the conflations show of the villain's potential heroism. While noting that Bane

"stands for the mirror image of state terror, for a murderous fundamentalism that takes over and rules by fear," Žižek also posits him as a figure of revolutionary love within a philosophical tradition that extends from Christ to Che Guevara. Examining the character's stated affection for his leader, the daughter of Ra's Al Ghul, the theorist reads the villain's philosophy as more authentic, more human than Batman's. See Žižek's essay "The Politics of Batman," *The New Statesman*, August 23, 2012.

20. This sequence includes a close-up shot of the officer looking on in horror after he issues his command to destroy the bridge: the humanity lies within the victimizer as much as within the victim. Moreover, by remaining for a moment with the policeman trapped by his own orders, the film encourages us to appreciate the victimhood of the victimizer. Can genre push farther into more complex territory than many of the more polemical theorizations on the subject of New Orleans, destabilizing governing Manichean formulations?

Chapter 5. "9/11 Transformed the Whole Planet, Not Just America!"

1. Portions of the reading of *Adieu Gary* appeared in my research article: "Disrupted Genre, Disrupted Lives: Adieu Gary and the Post-9/11 Banlieue as Ghost Town," *Studia Filmoznawcze* (Film Studies), Special Issue on the Transnational Western, 38 (June 2017): 75–89.

2. In his survey of European involvement in the Iraq War, policy scholar Hartwig Hummel notes that Belgium did not participate directly in any aspect of the Iraq War. The vast majority of Belgian citizens opposed the war, with more than 84% finding the intervention to be unjustified. Belgium only "allowed movement of troops and materiel for the Iraq war from US bases in Germany to the Belgian port of Antwerp" (Hummel 2007, 9). Through the angry Didier, frustrated by U.S. post-9/11 action, *Broken Circle* voices the popular and official opposition to U.S. policy. Van Groeningen's staging of the 9/11 attacks, wherein the news of the event overtakes the camera's attention, suggests the powerlessness of the Belgian. However, *Broken Circle* also presents the distorting tendency to view the United States as a mythic, omnipotent entity. Unlike her husband, who goes on to blame the Bush administration's stance against stem cells for the death of his daughter, Elise does not perceive the United States as a monolith whose actions dictate their reality in Belgium.

3. In "Emotional Spaces and Places of Salaryman Anxiety in *Tokyo Sonata*," Romit Dasgupta proposes that the presentation of the father in a Guantánamo Bay–like jumpsuit at work against the narrative thread of the son volunteering for war acts as a "deliberate subtextual referencing of Japan's complex (and relatively impotent) position in its partnership with the US in the post–Cold War/ post-9/11 world—specifically the increased pressure for Japan to take a more active role in US-led global military efforts" including sending its Security Defense Force

to Iraq (Dasgupta 2011, 380). Dasgupta reads the nightmare scene solely as an expression of the nation's impotence; I read it as also a noir lament about Japan abandoning its constitutionally inscribed humanist principles.

Works Cited

Adieu Gary. 2009. Dir. Nassim Amaouche. Studio Canal, 2009. DVD.

Ahmad, Eqbal. 1998. "Genesis of international terrorism." *DAWN*, October 25. http://www.hartford-hwp.com/archives/27d/083.html.

Alexander, Jeffrey C. 2004. "Toward a Theory of Cultural Trauma." In *Cultural Trauma and Collective Identity*, edited by Jeffrey C. Alexander, et al., 1–30. Berkeley: University of California Press.

Altman, Rick. 2012. "A Semantic/Syntactic Approach to Film Genre." In *Film Genre Reader IV*, edited by Barry Keith Grant, 27–41. Austin: University of Texas Press.

Andreas, Peter. 2001. *Border Games: Policing the U.S.-Mexico Divide*. Ithaca: Cornell University Press.

Anker, Elizabeth. 2014. *Orgies of Feeling: Melodrama and the Politics of Freedom*. Durham: Duke University Press.

The Asphalt Jungle. 1950. Dir. John Huston. Criterion Collection, 2016. DVD

The Avengers. 2012. Dir. Joss Whedon. Walt Disney Studios Home Entertainment. 2014. DVD.

Back to the Future. 1985. Dir. Robert Zemeckis. Universal Pictures Home Entertainment, 2015. DVD.

Baldwin, James. 1965. "The American Dream and the American Negro." *The New York Times*, March 7. https://www.nytimes.com/books/98/03/29/specials/baldwin-dream.html.

Baron, Zach. 2012. "Summermetrics: Spider-Man Again?" *Grantland*, July 3. http://www.grantland.com/story/_/id/8125889/andrew-garfield-emma-stone-amazing-spider-man.

Batman. 1966. "The Joker Goes to School." Season 1, Episode 15. Dir. Murray Golden. ABC, 2020. Amazon streaming edition.

Batman. 1966. "The Joker is Wild." Season 1, Episode 5. Dir. Don Weis. ABC, 2020. Amazon streaming edition.

Batman. 1989. Dir. Tim Burton. Warner Home Video, 1998. DVD.

Batman Begins. 2005. Dir. Christopher Nolan. Warner Home Video, 2005. DVD.

Batman v Superman: Dawn of Justice. 2016. Dir. Zack Snyder. Warner Home Video, 2017. iTunes copy.

Bazin, André. 1971. "The Western, or the American Film Par Excellence." In *What Is Cinema? Volume II*, edited and translated by Hugh Gray, 140–48. Berkeley: University of California Press.

Becker, Jo, and Scott Shane. 2012. 'Secret 'Kill List' Proves a Test of Obama's Principles and Will." *The New York Times*, May 29. https://www.nytimes.com/2012/05/29/world/obamas-leadership-in-war-on-al-qaeda.html.

Benjamin, Walter. 1986. "Critique of Violence." In *Reflections: Essays, Aphorisms, Autobiographical Writings*, edited by Peter Demetz, 277–300. New York: Schocken.

Bentham, Jeremy. 1995. *Jeremy Bentham: The Panopticon Writings*. Edited by Miran Bozovic. London: Verso.

Ben-Youssef, Fareed. 2017. "Disrupted Genre, Disrupted Lives: Adieu Gary and the Post-9/11 Banlieue as Ghost Town." *Studia Filmoznawcze* (Film Studies). Special Issue on the Transnational Western 38 (June): 75–89.

———. 2017. "Where Our Hungers Trump Morality: The Border in Ridley Scott and Cormac McCarthy's *The Counselor*." *Southwestern American Literature* 42, no. 2: 7–27.

Bergen, Peter L. 2012. *Manhunt: The Ten-Year Search for Bin Laden—from 9/11 to Abbottabad*. New York: Crown.

Bicker, Phil. 2012. "Pete Souza's Portrait of a Presidency." *Time.com*, October 8. http://lightbox.time.com/2012/10/08/pete-souza-portrait-of-a-presidency.

bin Laden, Osama. 2005. In *Messages to the World: The Statements of Osama Bin Laden*, edited by Bruce Lawrence. London: Verso.

Birdman or (The Unexpected Virtue of Ignorance). 2014. Dir. Alejandro González Iñárritu. Fox Searchlight, 2015. DVD.

Black Sunday. 1977. Dir. John Frankenheimer. Paramount, 2003. DVD.

Blade Runner 2049. 2017. Dir. Denis Villeneuve. Warner Brothers, 2018. DVD.

Bonitzer, Pascal. 1992. "Hitchcockian Suspense." In *Everything You Always Wanted to Know about Lacan (But Were Afraid to Ask Hitchcock)*, edited by Slavoj Žižek, 15–30. New York: Verso.

Boose, Lynda E. 1993. "Techno-Muscularity and the 'Boy Eternal': From the Quagmire to the Gulf." In *Gendering War Talk*, edited by Mariam G. Cooke and Angela Woolacott, 67–106. Princeton: Princeton University Press.

Bould, Mark. 2005. *Film Noir: From Berlin to Sin City*. New York: Wallflower Press.

Breznican, Anthony. 2012. "Eyewitness Accounts Paint Horrific Portrait of Shooting at 'The Dark Knight Rises' Screening." *EW.com*, July 20. https://ew.com/article/2012/07/20/theater-shooting-eyewitness-account.

The Broken Circle Breakdown. 2012. Dir. Felix van Groeningen. New Video Group, 2014. DVD.

Burch, James. 2008. "The Domestic Intelligence Gap: Progress Since 9/11?" *Homeland Security Affairs*. Proceedings of the 2008 Center for Homeland Defense and Security Annual Conference, April. https://www.hsaj.org/articles/129.

"Bush: Bin Laden 'Prime Suspect.'" 2001. CNN.com, September 17. http://www.cnn.com/2001/US/09/17/bush.powell.terrorism/.

Bybee, Jay, and Alberto Gonzales. 2005. "August 1, 2002 *Memo Re: Standards of Conduct for Interrogation*, AKA the Torture Memo." In *The Torture Debate in America*, ed. Karen J. Greenberg, 317–60. New York: Cambridge University Press.

Cai, Yiping. 2019. "New Superheroes Have Arrived: Made in China, for Domestic Consumption Only." In *Wolf Warrior II: The Rise of China and Gender/Sexual Politics*, edited by Petrus Liu and Lisa Rofel. The Ohio State University, April 10. u.osu.edu/mclc/online-series/liu-rofel/#F.

Captain America: The Winter Soldier. 2014. Dir. Joe Russo. Walt Disney Studios Home Entertainment, 2014. DVD.

Cascone, Sarah. 2020. "Police in the US Have Embraced the Punisher Skull as an Unofficial Logo. Now the Character's Creator Is Asking Artists of Color to Reclaim It." *artnet*, June 10. https://news.artnet.com/art-world/punisher-black-lives-matter-1883013.

Chancer, Lynn Sharon. 1993. "Prostitution, Feminist Theory, and Ambivalence: Notes from the Sociological Underground." *Social Text* 37, no. 37 (Winter): 143–71.

"CIA Reportedly Disbands Bin Laden Unit." 2006. *The Washington Post*, July 4. https://www.washingtonpost.com/wp-dyn/content/article/2006/07/04/AR2006070400375.html.

A Clockwork Orange. 1971. Dir. Stanley Kubrick, Warner Bros., 2007. DVD.

"Continued Support for U.S. Drone Strikes." 2013. Pew Research Center for the People and the Press, February 11. http://www.people-press.org/2013/02/11/continued-support-for-u-s-drone-strikes/1/.

Cook, David A. 1981. *A History of Narrative Film*. New York: Norton.

Corkin, Stanley. 2004. *Cowboys as Cold Warriors: The Western and U.S. History*. Philadelphia: Temple University Press.

Correa-Cabrera, Guadalupe, and José Nava. 2013. "Drug Wars, Social Networks, and the Right to Information: Informal Media as Freedom of Press in Northern Mexico." In *A War That Can't Be Won: Binational Perspectives on the War on Drugs*, edited by Tony Payan, Z. Anthony Kruszewski, and Kathleen A. Staudt, 95–118. Tucson: University of Arizona Press.

Couch, Aaron. 2017. "Bane Creators on Donald Trump's Inauguration Speech and Why They Voted for Him." *The Hollywood Reporter*, January 23. www.hollywoodreporter.com/heat-vision/bane-creators-donald-trumps-inauguration-speech-why-they-voted-him-967229.

The Counselor [unrated extended cut]. 2014. Dir. Ridley Scott. 20th Century Fox, 2014. Blu-Ray.

Danner, Mark. 2004. *Torture and Truth: America, Abu Ghraib, and the War on Terror*. New York: New York Review of Books.

The Dark Knight. 2008. Dir. Christopher Nolan. Warner Home Video, 2008. DVD.

The Dark Knight Rises. 2012. Dir. Christopher Nolan. Warner Home Video, 2012. DVD.

"The Dark Knight Trailer—Dominos Pizza—Exclusive." 2010. youtube.com, June 30. https://www.youtube.com/watch?v=-ZzWjifpn_A.

Dasgupta, Romit. 2011. "Emotional Spaces and Places of Salaryman Anxiety in *Tokyo Sonata*." *Japanese Studies* 31, no. 3 (December): 373–86.

The Departed. 2006. Dir. Martin Scorsese. Warner Home Video, 2007. Blu-Ray.

Desta, Yohana. 2019. "The Joker Didn't Inspire the Aurora Shooter, but the Rumor Won't Go Away." *Vanity Fair*, October 2. https://www.vanityfair.com/hollywood/2019/10/joker-aurora-shooting-rumor.

Dickos, Andrew. 2002. *Street with No Name: A History of the Classic American Film Noir*. Lexington: The University Press of Kentucky.

Dimendberg, Edward. 2004. *Film Noir and the Spaces of Modernity*. Cambridge: Harvard University Press.

Dirty Harry. 1971. Dir. Don Siegel. Warner Home Video, 2008. DVD.

Doane, Mary Anne. 2005. "Information, Crisis, Catastrophe." In *New Media, Old Media: A History and Theory Reader*, edited by Hui Kyong Chun and Wendy and Thomas Keenan, 251–64. London: Routledge.

"Donald Rumsfeld: What Did He Know?" 2004. *The Economist*, May 22. https://www.economist.com/united-states/2004/05/20/what-did-he-know.

Dudziak, Mary L. 2010. "A Sword and a Shield: The Uses of Law in the Bush Administration." In *The Presidency of George W. Bush: A First Historical Assessment*, edited by Julian Zelizer, 39–58. Princeton: Princeton University Press.

Ehrenreich, Barbara. 2004. "Feminism's Assumptions Upended." *Los Angeles Times*, May 16. articles.latimes.com/2004/may/16/opinion/op-ehrenreich16.

Engelhardt, Tom. 2007. *The End of Victory Culture: Cold War America and the Disillusioning of a Generation*. Amherst: University of Massachusetts Press.

Facing Crisis: A Changed World. 2014. Prod. Clifford Chanin. Northern Lights Productions. On permanent exhibition at the National Septembe 11 Memorial Museum & Museum.

Faludi, Susan. 2007. *The Terror Dream: Fear and Fantasy in Post-9/11 America*. New York: Metropolitan Books.

Fanon, Frantz. 1968. *Black Skin, White Masks*. Translated by Charles Lam Markmann. New York: Grove Weidenfeld.

Feitz, Lindsey, and Joane Nagel. 2008. "The Militarization of Gender and Sexuality in the Iraq War." In *Women in the Military and in Armed Conflict*, edited by Helena Carreiras and Gerhard Kümmel, 201–25. Netherlands: VS Verlag für Sozialwissenschaften.

Finn, Jennifer. 2014. "Chief Curator Jan Ramirez Reflects on Journey to 9/11 Memorial Museum." National September 11 Memorial & Museum 9/11 MEMORIAL, August. https://www.911memorial.org/connect/blog/chief-curator-jan-ramirez-reflects-journey-911-memorial-museum.

Fojas, Camilla. 2011. "Hollywood Border Cinema: Westerns with a Vengeance." *Journal of Popular Film and Television* 39, no. 2: 93–101.

Foucault, Michel. 1977. "Discipline and Punish, Panopticism." In *Discipline and Punish: The Birth of the Prison*, edited by Alan Sheridan, 195–228. New York: Vintage.

Fournier, Lauren. 2017. "Auto-Theory as an Emerging Mode of Feminist Practice Across Media." YorkSpace, May 15. https://yorkspace.library.yorku.ca/xmlui/handle/10315/33700.

Game Over. 2015. Dir. Alba Sotorra. Dir. of Photography Jimmy Gimferer. Dirk Manthey Film. Digital copy provided by the filmmaker.

"George Bush uses 'The Google.'" 2006. youtube.com, October 24. https://www.youtube.com/watch?v=90DKubFKwVo.

Giles, Paul. 2003. "Transnationalism and Classic American Literature." *PMLA* 118, no. 1 (January): 62–77.

Giroux, Henry A. 2006. "Reading Hurricane Katrina: Race, Class, and the Biopolitics of Disposability." *College Literature* 33, no. 3 (Summer): 171–96.

Gledhill, Christine. 1998. "*Klute* 1: A Contemporary Film Noir and Feminist Criticism." In *Women in Film Noir*, edited by E. Ann Kaplan, 20–34. London: British Film Institute.

Gogarty, Brendan, and Meredith C. Hagger. 2008. "The Laws of Man over Vehicles Unmanned: The Legal Response to Robotic Revolution on Sea, Land and Air." *Journal of Law, Information and Science* 19: 73–145.

Golash-Boza, Tanya Maria. 2012. *Immigration Nation: Raids, Detentions, and Deportations in Post-9/11 America.* Boulder, CO: Paradigm Publishers.

Gold, John R., and George Revill. 2003. "Exploring Landscapes of Fear: Marginality, Spectacle and Surveillance." *Capital and Class* 27, no. 2 (July): 27–50.

Goldberg, David Theo. 2009. *The Threat of Race: Reflections on Racial Neoliberalism.* Oxford: Wiley-Blackwell.

Goldberg, J. 2016. "The Obama Doctrine." *The Atlantic.* April. http://www.theatlantic.com/magazine/archive/2016/04/the-obama-doctrine/471525/.

Goldsmith, Jack. 2009. *The Terror Presidency: Law and Judgment inside the Bush Administration.* New York: Norton.

Goodman, Ellen. 2005. "The Downside of Equality." *The Boston Globe.* September 30. www.boston.com/news/globe/editorial_opinion/oped/articles/2005/09/30/the_downside_of_equality.

The Graduate. 1967. Dir. Mike Nichols. MGM, 1999. DVD.

Greenwood, Max. 2017. "Miller and Bannon Wrote Trump Inaugural Address: Report." *thehill.com*, January 21. https://thehill.com/homenews/administration/315464-bannon-miller-wrote-trumps-inauguration-address-report.

Hansen, Miriam. 1993. "Early Cinema, Late Cinema: Permutations of the Public Sphere." *Screen* 34, no. 3 (October): 197–210.

Hardt, Michael, and Antonio Negri. 2004. *Multitude: War and Democracy in the Age of Empire.* New York: Penguin.

Herman, Judith. 1992. *Trauma and Recovery: The Aftermath of Violence—from Domestic Abuse to Political Terror.* New York: Basic Books.

Holleran, Scott. 2005. "Wing Kid." Box Office Mojo, October 20. http://boxofficemojo.com/features/?id=1921&pagenum=2&p=.htm.

Human Rights Watch. 2011. *Neither Rights nor Security: Killings, Torture, and Disappearances in Mexico's "War on Drugs."* New York: Human Rights Watch.

Hummel, Hartwig. 2007. "A Survey of Involvement of 15 European States in the Iraq War 2003." *PAKS WORKING PAPER SERIES.* Düsseldorf: Parliamentary Control of Security Policy.

The Hunt. 2012. Dir. Thomas Vinterberg. Arrow, 2013. DVD.

Hutchings, Stephen, and Kenzie Burchell. 2018. "Media Genre, Disrupted Memory and the European Securitization Chronotope." In *Memory and Securitization in Contemporary Europe*, edited by V. Strukov and V. Apryshchenko, 155–85. London: Palgrave Macmillan.

I Died a Thousand Times. 1955. Dir. Stuart Heisler. Warner Bros., 2009. DVD.

"Imaginationland Episode I." *South Park*. Dir. Trey Parker. Comedy Central, 2007.

"Imaginationland Episode II." *South Park*. Dir. Trey Parker. Comedy Central, 2007.

"Imaginationland Episode III." *South Park*. Dir. Trey Parker. Comedy Central, 2007.

Iron Man. 2008. Dir. Jon Favreau. Paramount, 2008. DVD.

Jameson, Fredric. 1995. *The Geopolitical Aesthetic: Cinema and Space in the World System.* Bloomington: Indiana University Press.

Jerry Maguire. 1996. Dir. Cameron Crowe. Sony Pictures Home Entertainment, 1996. DVD.

Jolin, Dan. 2012. "The Making of Heath Ledger's Joker." *Empire*, August 7. https://www.empireonline.com/movies/features/heath-ledger-joker/.

Jones, Nate. 2016. "Revisiting *Zoolander*'s Weird History With 9/11." *Vulture*, February. https://www.vulture.com/2016/02/revisiting-zoolanders-weird-history-with-911.html.

Jones, Reece. 2012. *Border Walls: Security and the War on Terror in the United States, Israel, and India.* London: Zed.

Kahan, Dan M. 1997. "Ignorance of Law Is an Excuse: But Only for the Virtuous." *Michigan Law Review* 96, no. 1: 127–54.

Kampf, Lena, and Indra Sen. 2006. "History Does Not Repeat Itself, But Ignorance Does: Post-9/11 Treatment of Muslims and the Liberty-Security Dilemma." Humanity in Action. https://www.humanityinaction.org/knowledge_detail/history-does-not-repeat-itself-but-ignorance-does-post-9-11-treatment-of-muslims-and-the-liberty-security-dilemma.

Kane, Bob. 1940. *Batman #1.* New York: DC Comics.

Kaplan, E. Anne. 2005. *Trauma Culture: The Politics of Terror and Loss in Media and Literature.* Piscataway, NJ: Rutgers University Press.

King, John. 2001. "White House sees Hollywood Role in War on Terrorism." CNN.com, November 8. https://www.cnn.com/2001/US/11/08/rec.bush.hollywood/.

Kiss Me Deadly. 1955. Dir. Robert Aldrich. MGM, 2001. DVD.

Kracauer, Siegfried. 1995. "The Mass Ornament." In *The Mass Ornament: Weimar Essays*, edited by Thomas Y. Levin, 75–88. Cambridge: Harvard University Press.

Krauthammer, Charles. 2004. "Democratic Realism—An American Foreign Policy for a Unipolar World." Public speech, Washington, DC.

Krutnik, Frank. 1991. *In a Lonely Street: Film Noir, Genre, Masculinity*. New York: Routledge.

Legrand, Michel. 1968. "The Windmills of Your Mind." English lyrics by Alan Bergman and Marilyn Bergman. Performed by Noel Harrison. *The Thomas Crown Affair*. 1968. Dir. Norman Jewison. 20th Century Fox, 2006. DVD.

Logan. 2017. Dir. James Mangold. 20th Century Fox, 2017. Amazon streaming edition.

The Lord of the Rings: The Return of the King. 2003. Dir. Peter Jackson. New Line Cinema, 2004. DVD.

The Magnificent Seven. 1960. Dir. John Sturges. MGM Studios Inc., 2021. Amazon streaming edition.

Mann, James. 2012. *The Obamians: The Struggle inside the White House to Redefine American Power*. New York: Viking.

Marano, Michael. 2008. "Ra's al Ghul: Father Figure as Terrorist." In *Batman Unauthorized: Vigilantes, Jokers, and Heroes in Gotham City*, edited by Dennis O'Neil and Leah Wilson, 69–84. Dallas: BenBalla Books.

Marcus, Sharon. 1992. "Fighting Bodies, Fighting Words: A Theory and Politics of Rape Prevention." In *Feminists Theorize the Political*, edited by Judith Butler and Joan W. Scott, 385–403. New York: Routledge.

Martin, William C. 2013. "Cartels, Corruption, Carnage, and Cooperation." In *A War That Can't Be Won: Binational Perspectives on the War on Drugs*, edited by Tony Payan, Z. Anthony Kruszewski, and Kathleen A. Staudt, 33–64. Tucson: University of Arizona Press.

The Matrix. 1999. Dir. Lana Wachowski and Lily Wachowski. Warner Bros., 2021. Amazon streaming edition.

Mayer, Jane. 2009. "The Predator War." *The New Yorker*, October 26.

May, Vivian M., and Beth A. Ferri. 2002. "'I'm a Wheelchair Girl Now': Abjection, Intersectionality, and Subjectivity in Atom Egoyan's *The Sweet Hereafter*." *Women's Studies Quarterly* 30, no. 1 (Spring): 131–50.

McCarthy, Cormac. 1985. *Blood Meridian, Or the Evening Redness in the West*. New York: Random House.

McCormack, Gavan. 2004. "Koizumi's Japan in Bush's World: After 9/11." *The Asia-Pacific Journal: Japan Focus*, December 10. www.japanfocus.org/-gavan-mccormack/2111/article.html.

McCoy, Alfred W. 2006. *A Question of Torture*. New York: Metropolitan.

McGrane, Sean. 2010. "Katrina, Federalism, and Military Law Enforcement: A New Exception to the Posse Comitatus Act." *Michigan Law Review* 108, no. 7 (May): 1309–40.

Merry Christmas, Mr. Lawrence. 1983. Dir. Nagisa Ōshima. Criterion Collection, 2010. DVD.

"Mexico: Widespread Rights Abuses in 'War on Drugs' | Human Rights Watch." 2011. Human Rights Watch, November 11. https://www.hrw.org/news/2011/11/09/mexico-widespread-rights-abuses-war-drugs.

Middleton, Katherine, and Carlton David Craig. 2012. "A Systematic Literature Review of PTSD among Female Veterans from 1990 to 2010." *Social Work in Mental Health* 10, no. 3 (May): 233–52.

A Mighty Heart. 2007. Dir. Michael Winterbottom. Paramount Vantage, 2007. DVD.

Miller, Frank. 1986. *The Dark Knight Returns*. New York: DC Comics.

———. 1991. "Sin City: Episode 4." In *Dark Horse Presents #53*, edited by Randy Stradley, 2–9. Portland, OR: Dark Horse Comics.

———. 1994. *Sin City: The Big Fat Kill #2*. Portland, OR: Dark Horse Comics.

———. 1995. *Sin City: The Big Fat Kill #5*. Portland, OR: Dark Horse Comics.

———. 1996. *Sin City: That Yellow Bastard #5*. Portland, OR: Dark Horse Comics.

Mitchell, Lee Clark. 1996. *Westerns: Making the Man in Fiction and Film*. Chicago: University of Chicago Press.

Moench, Doug, and Tom Mandrake. 1986. *Batman #399*. New York: DC Comics.

Morag, Raya. 2020. *Perpetrator Cinema: Confronting Genocide in Cambodian Documentary*. New York: Columbia University Press.

Morris, Rosalind C. 2002. "Theses on the Questions of War: History, Media, Terror." *Social Text* 20, no. 3 (Fall): 149–75.

The Most Dangerous Game. 1932. Dir. Ernest B. Schoedsack and Irving Pichel. Criterion Collection, 2020. DVD.

Mueller, John, and Mark G. Stewart. 2012. "The Terrorism Delusion: America's Overwrought Response to September 11." *International Security*, 37 (Summer), no. 1: 81–110.

Murakami Wood, David. 2013. "What Is Global Surveillance? Towards a Relational Political Economy of the Global Surveillant Assemblage." *Geoforum*, 49 (October): 317–26.

Nacos, Brigitte L. 2003. Nacos, Brigitte Lebens, Yaeli Bloch-Elkon, and Robert Y. Shapiro. 2011. *Selling Fear: Counterterrorism, the Media, and Public Opinion*. Chicago: University of Chicago Press.

Nacos, Brigitte L. "Terrorism as Breaking News: Attack on America." 2003. *Political Science Quarterly*, 118, no. 1 (Spring): 23–52.

Naremore, James. 1995–96. "American Film Noir: The History of an Idea." *Film Quarterly* 49, no. 2 (Winter): 12–28.

———. 2008. *More than Night: Film Noir in its Contexts*. Berkeley: University of California Press.

National Commission on Terrorist Attacks upon the United States. 2004. *The 9/11 Commission Report: Final Report of the National Commission on Terrorist Attacks upon the United States*. Washington, DC: National Commission on Terrorist Attacks upon the United States.

Nel, Philip. 2010. "Obamafiction for Children: Imagining the Forty-Fourth U.S. President." *Children's Literature Association Quarterly* 35, no. 4 (Winter): 334–56.

Ngai, Mae M. 2004. *Impossible Subjects: Illegal Aliens and the Making of Modern America*. Princeton: Princeton University Press.

Noto, Phil. 2002. "Art." In *9-11: The World's Finest Comic Book Writers and Artists Tell Stories to Remember: 2*, edited by Paul Levitz, Eddie Berganza, Ivan Cohen, Will Dennis, Lysa Hawkins, Matt Idelson, Mike McAvennie, Tom Palmer Jr., Peter Tomasi, Stephen Wacker, Michael Wright, and Linda Fields, 173. New York: DC Comics.

Obama, Barack Hussein. 2020. "A President Looks Back on His Toughest Fight." *The New Yorker*, November 2. https://www.newyorker.com/magazine/2020/11/02/barack-obama-new-book-excerpt-promised-land-obamacare.

O'Connell, Mary Ellen. 2011. "Seductive Drones: Learning from a Decade of Lethal Operations." *Journal of Law, Information and Science* (August): 11–35. http://ssrn.com/abstract=1912635.

O'Connor, Rory. 2017. "Logan Berlin 2017 Review." *The Film Stage*, February 17. https://thefilmstage.com/reviews/berlin-review-logan-sees-hugh-jackman-lay-down-the-claws-with-remarkable-class.

Oliver, Kelly. 2008. "Women: The Secret Weapon of Modern Warfare?" *Hypatia* 23, no. 2 (April–June): 1–16.

O'Rourke, Dan. 2007. "The 'Transcreation' of a Mediated Myth: Spider-Man in India." In *The Amazing Transforming Superhero!: Essays on the Revision of Characters in Comic Books, Film and Television*, edited by Terrence Wandtke, 112–28. Jefferson, NC: McFarland.

Parkinson, John. 2014. "DHS Rebuffs Congressman's Claim ISIS Infiltrating Southern Border." ABC News Network, October 8. abcnews.go.com.

Payan, Tony. 2006. *The Three U.S.–Mexico Border Wars: Drugs, Immigration, and Homeland Security*. Westport, CT: Praeger Security International.

Pelvit, Leann. 2021. Letter to the author, January 20.

Perlmutter, Dawn. 2005. "Mujahideen Blood Rituals: The Religious and Forensic Symbolism of Al Qaeda Beheading." *Anthropoetics* 11, no. 2. http://anthropoetics.ucla.edu/ap1102/muja/.

Pin-Fat, Veronique, and Maria Stern. 2005. "The Scripting of Private Jessica Lynch: Biopolitics, Gender, and the 'Feminization' of the U.S. Military." *Alternatives* 30: 25–53.

Place, Janey. 1998. "Women in Film Noir." In *Women in Film Noir*, edited by E. Ann Kaplan, 47–68. London: British Film Institute.

Pope, Paul. 2007. *Batman: Year 100*. New York: DC Comics.

———. 2017. Interview by author, October 2.

Prats, Armando José. 2002. *Invisible Natives: Myth and Identity in the American Western*. Ithaca: Cornell University Press.

Prince, Stephen. 2009. *Firestorm: American Film in the Age of Terrorism*. New York: Columbia University Press.

Priest, Dana, and Barton Gellman. 2002. "U.S. Decries Abuse but Defends Interrogations." *The Washington Post*, December 26. https://www.washingtonpost.com/archive/politics/2002/12/26/us-decries-abuse-but-defends-interrogations/737a4096-2cf0-40b9-8a9f-7b22099d733d/.

Public Enemies. 2009. Dir. Michael Mann. Universal Studios Home Entertainment, 2009. DVD.

Pupavac, Vanessa. 2004. "War on the Couch: The Emotionology of the New International Security Paradigm." *European Journal of Social Theory* 7, no. 2 (May): 149–70.

Rabinowitz, Paula. 2002. *Black and White and Noir*. New York: Columbia University Press.

Rancière, Jacques. 2004. "Who Is the Subject of the Rights of Man?" *South Atlantic Quarterly* 103, no. 2/3 (Spring/Summer): 297–310.

Recchia, Edward. 1996. "Film Noir and the Western." *The Centennial Review* 40, no. 3: 601–14.

Reality. 2012. Dir. Matteo Garrone. Oscilloscope, 2021. Amazon streaming edition.

Redmond, Helen. 2013. "The Political Economy of Mexico's Drug War." *International Socialist Review*, July. http://isreview.org/issue/90/political-economy-mexicos-drug-war.

Rich, Ruby. 1995. "Dumb Lugs and Femmes Fatales." *Sight and Sound* 5, no. 11: 6–11.

The Rider. 2017. Dir. Chloé Zhao. Sony Pictures Classics, 2021. Amazon streaming edition.

Risen, James, and Eric Lichtblau. 2005. "Bush Lets U.S. Spy on Callers without Courts." *The New York Times*, December 16. https://www.nytimes.com/2005/12/16/politics/bush-lets-us-spy-on-callers-without-courts.html.

Taylor, Gary W., and Jane M. Ussher. 2001. "Making Sense of S&M: A Discourse Analytic Account." *Sexualities* 4, no. 3: 293–314.

Rogin, Michael Paul. 1988. *Ronald Reagan, the Movie and Other Episodes in Political Demonology*. Berkeley: University of California Press.

Rorty, Richard. 1993. "Human Rights, Rationality, and Sentimentality." In *On Human Rights: The Oxford Amnesty Lectures 1993*, edited by Stephen Shute and Susan Hurley, 111–34. New York: Basic Books.

Rosas, Gilberto. 2006. "The Managed Violences of the Borderlands: Treacherous Geographies, Policeability, and the Politics of Race." *Latino Studies* 4: 401–18.

Rothberg, Michael. 2009. *Multidirectional Memory: Remembering the Holocaust in the Age of Decolonization*. Stanford: Stanford University Press.

———. 2019. *The Implicated Subject*. Stanford: Stanford University Press.

Rules of Engagement. 2000. Dir. William Friedkin. Paramount, 2000. DVD.

Rumsfeld, Donald. 2012. *Known and Unknown: A Memoir*. New York: Sentinel Trade.

Saito, Ayako. 2014. "Occupation and Memory: The Representation of Woman's Body in Postwar Japanese Cinema." In *The Oxford Handbook of Japanese Cinema*, edited by Daisuke Miyao, 327–62. Oxford: Oxford University Press.

Sanyal, Debarati. 2006. *The Violence of Modernity: Baudelaire, Irony, and the Politics of Form*. Baltimore: Johns Hopkins University Press.

Saving Private Ryan. 1998. Dir. Steven Spielberg. Dreamworks Video, 1999. DVD.

Scheppele, Kim Lane. 2013. "The Empire of Security and the Security of Empire." *Temple International and Comparative Law Journal* 27: 241–78.

———. 2013. "From a War on Terrorism to Global Security Law." Institute for Advanced Study, Fall. https://www.ias.edu/ideas/2013/scheppele-terrorism.

———. 2004. "Law in a Time of Emergency: States of Exception and the Temptations of 9/11." *University of Pennsylvania Journal of Constitutional Law* 6: 1001–83.

Schmidt, Susan, and Vernon Loeb. 2003. "Lynch Kept Firing until She Ran Out of Ammo." *The Washington Post*, April 3. http://old.post-gazette.com/nation/20030403rescuenatp3.asp.

Schopp, Andrew. 2009. "Interrogating the Manipulation of Fear: *V for Vendetta*, *Batman Begins*, *Good Night, and Good Luck*, and America's 'War on Terror.'" In *War on Terror and American Popular Culture: September 11 and Beyond*, edited by Andrew Schopp and Matthew B. Hill, 259–86. Madison: Fairleigh Dickinson University Press.

Schneier, Bruce. 2009. "Beyond Security Theater." Schneier on Security, November. https://www.schneier.com/essays/archives/2009/11/beyond_security_thea. html.

"Securing America's Borders Fact Sheet: Border Security." 2002. White House, Office of the Press Secretary, January 25. https://georgewbush-whitehouse. archives.gov/news/releases/2002/01/20020125.html.

Sedgwick, Eve Kosofsky. 2003. *Touching Feeling: Affect, Pedagogy, Performativity*. Durham: Duke University Press.

Senk, Sarah. 2015. "The Glass Bowl of Memory: Plotting 1993 at the National 9/11 Memorial Museum." Post45, June. http://post45.org/2015/06/the-glass-bowl-of-memory-plotting-1993-at-the-national-911-memorial-museum/.

Shaping Mind and Body. 2005. DVD Extra. *Batman Begins*. 2005. Dir. Christopher Nolan. Warner Home Video, 2005. DVD.

Sicario. 2015. Dir. Denis Villeneuve. Lionsgate, 2015. Blu-Ray.

Sicario: Day of Soldado. 2018. Dir. Stefano Sollima. Columbia Pictures, 2018. Amazon streaming edition.

The Siege. 1998. Dir. Edward Zwick. 20th Century Fox, 1999. DVD.

Sieranevada. 2016. Dir. Cristi Puiu. Mandragora Movies, 2016. DVD.

Silver, Alain. 1996. "Kiss Me Deadly: Evidence of a Style." In *Film Noir Reader*, edited by Alain Silver and James Ursini, 209–36. Pompton Plains, NJ: Limelight Editions.

Sin City. 2005. Dir. Frank Miller and Robert Rodriguez. Dimension Films, 2005. DVD.

Singer, P. W. 2009. *Wired for War: Revolution and Conflict in the 21st Century*. New York: Penguin.

Slocum, David. 2011. "9/11 Film and Media Scholarship." *Cinema Journal* 51, no. 1 (Fall): 181–93.

Southland Tales. 2008. Dir. Richard Kelley. Sony Pictures, 2014. iTunes copy.

Spider-Man 2. 2004. Dir. Sam Raimi. Sony Pictures Home Entertainment, 2004. DVD.

"Spiderman-Trailer with World Trade Center." 2007. youtube.com. https://www. youtube.com/watch?v=bjtXUULtH4E.

The Spirit of America. 2001. Dir. Chuck Workman. Calliope Films, 2001.

Stanley, Kelli E. 2005. " 'Suffering Sappho!': Wonder Woman and the (Re)Invention of the Feminine Ideal." *Helios* 32, no. 2 (Fall): 143–71.

State v Ostrosky, 667 P. 2d 1184. 1983. Alaska Supreme Court.

Stolberg, Sheryl Gay. 2008. "New Significance for Bin Laden Hunt." *The New York Times*, September 12. http://www.nytimes.com/2008/09/12/us/politics /12web-stolberg.html?_r=1.

Superman Returns. 2006. Dir. Bryan Singer. Warner Home Video, 2006. DVD.

The Thomas Crown Affair. 1968. Dir. Norman Jewison. 20th Century Fox, 2006. DVD.

The Thousand Eyes of Dr. Mabuse. 1960. Dir. Fritz Lang. Image Entertainment, 2008. DVD.

The Three Burials of Melquiades Estrada. 2005. Dir. Tommy Lee Jones. Sony Pictures Home Entertainment, 2000. DVD.

300. 2007. Dir. Zack Snyder. Warner Home Video, 2007. DVD.

Tilo Jung. 2017. "Trump vs. Bane (Inauguration Speech)." youtube.com, January 20. https://www.youtube.com/watch?v=dI3MARgU0s8.

Tirman, John. 2006. "Immigration and Insecurity: Post-9/11 Fear in the United States." Social Science Research Council, July 28. borderbattles.ssrc.org.

Toffoletti, Kim, and Victoria Grace. 2010. "Terminal Indifference: The Hollywood War Film Post-September 11." *Film-Philosophy* 14, no. 2: 62–83.

Tokyo Sonata. 2008. Dir. Kiyoshi Kurosawa. E1 Entertainment, 2010. DVD.

The Trip to Spain. 2017. Dir. Michael Winterbottom. Shout Factory, 2017. DVD.

True Lies. 1994. Dir. James Cameron. 20th Century Fox, 1999. DVD.

Trump, Donald. 2015. "Here's Donald Trump's Presidential Announcement Speech." *Time*, June 16. time.com. https://time.com/3923128/donald-trump-announcement-speech/.

———. 2017. "The Inaugural Address." January 20. https://trumpwhitehouse. archives.gov/briefings-statements/the-inaugural-address/.

———. 2019. "Remarks by President Trump after Meeting with Congressional Leadership on Border Security." January 4. https://trumpwhitehouse.archives. gov/briefings-statements/remarks-president-trump-meeting-congressional-leadership-border-security/.

25th Hour. 2002. Dir. Spike Lee. Touchstone Pictures, 2003. DVD.

United 93. 2006. Dir. Paul Greengrass. Universal Pictures Home Entertainment, 2006. DVD.

"Urban Ed." *Ed, Edd n Eddy*. Dir. Danny Antonucci. Cartoon Network, 2000.

"US Elections: Barack Obama Jokes He Is Superman." 2008. *The Telegraph* (London), October 17. http://www.telegraph.co.uk/news/worldnews/barack obama/3213768/US-elections-Barack-Obama-jokes-he-is-Superman.html.

"US Remembers 9/11 Still Haunted by bin Laden." 2007. *The Sydney Morning Herald*, September 12. https://www.smh.com.au/world/us-remembers-911-still-haunted-by-bin-laden-20070911-yee.html.

Vejvoda, Jim. 2012. "Nolan: The Dark Knight Rises is a Revolutionary Epic." IGN Entertainment, Inc., June 5. https://www.ign.com/articles/2012/06/05/ nolan-the-dark-knight-rises-is-a-revolutionary-epic.

Ventura, Elbert. 2008. "Zodiac: File It Under: Serial Killer Flick/Brief on Behalf of a Just, Liberal Society." *Slate*, January 7. www.slate.com/articles/arts/ dvdextras/2008/01/zodiac.html.

Verlaine, Paul. 1869. "Clair de Lune." *Fêtes galantes* (1869). Trans. Chris Routledge. "Featured Poem: Clair de lune by Paul Verlaine." The Reader Organisation, March 30, 2009. https://www.thereader.org.uk/featured-poem-3/.

Vice. 2018. Dir. Adam McCay. 20th Century Fox, 2019. DVD.

Virilio, Paul. 1989. *War and Cinema: The Logistics of Perception*. Trans. Patrick Camiller. New York: Verso.

Waid, Mark, and Alex Ross. 1997. *Kingdom Come*. New York: DC Comics.

The Walk. 2015. Dir. Robert Zemeckis. Sony Pictures Home Entertainment, 2016. DVD.

A Walk Among the Tombstones. 2014. Dir. Scott Frank. Universal Pictures Home Entertainment, 2015.

Walker, Peter. 2016. "The Rock Movie Plot 'May Have Inspired MI6 Source's Iraqi Weapons Claim.'" *The Guardian*, July 6. *theguardian.com*.

Walsh, Bill. 2007. "True Thermopylaes." *The Weekly Standard*, March 15. https://www.washingtonexaminer.com/weekly-standard/true-thermopylaes.

Watt, Peter, and Roberto Zepeda. 2012. *Drug War Mexico: Politics, Neoliberalism and Violence in the New Narcoeconomy*. London: Zed Books. Kindle edition.

Weiner, Tim. 2013. *Enemies: A History of the FBI*. New York: Random House.

Wheen, Francis. 2010. *Strange Days Indeed: The 1970s, the Golden Days of Paranoia*. New York: Public Affairs.

Williams, Raymond. 1977. *Marxism and Literature*. New York: Oxford University Press.

Wolf Warrior 2. 2017. Dir. Wu Jing. Well Go Usa, 2017. DVD.

Wolff, Michael. 2016. "Ringside With Steve Bannon at Trump Tower as the President-Elect's Strategist Plots 'An Entirely New Political Movement' (Exclusive)." *hollywoodreporter.com*, November 18. https://www.hollywoodreporter.com/news/steve-bannon-trump-tower-interview-trumps-strategist-plots-new-political-movement-948747.

World Trade Center. 2006. Dir. Oliver Stone. Paramount, 2006. DVD.

The Wrong Man. 1956. Dir. Alfred Hitchcock. Warner Home Video, 2008. DVD,

X-Men. 2000. Dir. Bryan Singer. 20th Century Fox, 2020. Amazon streaming edition.

Yellow Submarine. 1968. Dir. George Dunning. Capitol, 2012. DVD.

Yen, Hope, and Colleen Long. 2018. "AP Fact Check: President Trump's Rhetoric and the Truth about Migrant Caravans." NewsHour Productions LLC, November 2. https://www.pbs.org/newshour/politics/ap-fact-check-president-trumps-rhetoric-and-the-truth-about-migrant-caravans.

Zegart, Amy B. 2007. *Spying Blind: The C.I.A, the FBI, and the Origins of 9/11*. Princeton: Princeton University Press.

Zhao, Chloé. 2018. Interview by author, January 30.

Žižek, Slavoj. 2012. "The Politics of Batman." *The New Statesman*, August 23.

Zodiac. 2007. Dir. David Fincher. Warner Brothers, 2008. DVD.

Zodiac: The Director's Cut. 2008. Dir. David Fincher. Warner Brothers, 2008. DVD.

"*Zodiac* Production Notes." 2007. Paramount Pictures Press Kit.

Index

221

CPSIA information can be obtained
at www.ICGtesting.com
Printed in the USA
BVHW031138291222
655240BV00008B/163

9 781438 489261